THE LAW OF ARREST, SEARCH AND SEIZURE

J. SHANE CREAMER, ESQ.

Director, Pennsylvania Crime Commission;
Formerly First Assistant United States Attorney
for the Eastern District of Pennsylvania;
Consultant to the National Crime Commission

W. B. SAUNDERS COMPANY

PHILADELPHIA, LONDON, TORONTO 1968

W. B. Saunders Company: West Washington Square
Philadelphia, Pa. 19105

12 Dyott Street
London W.C.1

1835 Yonge Street
Toronto 7, Ontario

The Law of Arrest, Search and Seizure

 Press of W. B. Saunders Company. Library of Congress catalog card number 68-57420.

To Mary-Ellen

Foreword

The business of policing a nation is only now emerging as a true profession. Any profession has trouble enough with the inner pangs of growth and maturation; the police are facing these problems in the midst of social revolutions that have been sweeping through America for the past thirty-five years. Caught in the turbulence of the times, the police are overwhelmed by seemingly insurmountable complexities and a multiplicity of conflicting roles.

We tell the policeman to be a soldier in the war on crime, a diplomat spreading peace and order among man, a social worker helping to mend the nation's injustices and a bridge between the world of the established and the world of the deprived. We tell the policeman to understand and make adjustments for the culture of the poor and the disadvantaged; but in many instances we pay him a salary that places him and his family in the economic ranks of the poor and we deny him the same rights of protest. He works nights one week, days the next. If tired and afraid, he is strictly accountable as a man who is not tired and afraid. If frustrated, he is not to react; if cursed, he is only to smile. He makes an arrest in two minutes and spends three hours typing his own offense reports. He is forced to spend hour upon hour in crowded, dirty, undignified courtrooms, waiting for the two-minute "trial" process. He is told to enforce the gambling laws and he watches the politicians collect contributions from the gamblers. He must arrest chronic alcoholics as criminals and carefully overlook the politically protected afterhours bars. A free cup of coffee is police corruption; the wining and dining of public officials by private contractors is acceptable practice.

Policemen, more than those in any other profession, know the hypocrisy and failures of the political process, the devastating gap between the ideals and the achievements of social justice. The policeman's office is the street. Armed with a nightstick, a revolver and perhaps canisters of disabling gas, he is sent into society's nights of despair and asked to make friends, prevent crime, keep the peace and apprehend all criminals. Man's weaknesses and society's injustices are the doorsteps of the policeman's beat. Somehow, he is to walk among them in strict adherence to the dignity and majesty of the law. The policeman must bring to his task what he cannot see elsewhere in society. This book was written to help him do that.

It is a tragedy of our times that the phrase "law and order" has become to many the antithesis of justice. If a constitution truly expresses the ideals and aspirations of a nation, the police should want to adhere to its mandates and the people should demand that adherence. For the policeman, there can be no civil disobedience to the Constitution as interpreted by the Supreme Court of the United States. Unfortunately, the complexities of the crime crisis are beclouded by the simplistic and inaccurate notion that recent Court decisions have handcuffed the police and caused increases in the crime rate. Many policemen who berate the Supreme Court have little knowledge of what the decisions actually hold and why such a holding was deemed necessary. Basic misconceptions about the use of police authority are vividly illustrated in the common police complaint that they must utilize Marquis of Queensbury rules against a criminal who gouges, bites, kicks, and scratches. Policemen have expressed to me with great emotion their firm belief that no innocent man ever objected to a short detention on the street for questioning or a car stop accompanied by a superficial search of the automobile. Indeed, some police officials believe that innocent citizens welcome these and other intrusions upon privacy as an indication that the police are doing their job in preventing and controlling crime. The "us vs. them" dichotomy in police thinking about the Supreme Court is reflected in the repeated lament that if only one more justice had been on "our side," this 5-4 decision or that 5-4 decision would have gone "our way." Belligerence towards the courts breeds a deep frustration and gives birth in alleys, streets, and houses to illegal control procedures and other short-cuts that never receive public and judicial review.

Mr. Creamer's book takes us along the path from police complaints to police compliance. As a former prosecutor and also a teacher of criminal law and procedure at the Philadelphia Police Academy, the author commands great respect in the police world and appreciates the needs therein. He has written a commonsense exposition of what the revolution in criminal procedure means to the practitioner. Any policeman who reads and studies these pages should become not only a more effective law enforcement officer but also a man who understands as never before the meaning of justice and the bases for our constitutional guarantees. Mr. Creamer explains the historical background of these guarantees and tells in readable form why they must be applied ever so strictly and ever so broadly in today's mass society. I would even venture to guess that after studying the contents of this volume, most policemen will understand, as Justice Cardozo did not, why the criminal must go free because the constable has blundered.

The chapters on arrest, search, and seizure in the first section of the book bring together the general knowledge that any policeman must have. The remainder of the book, with its individual descriptions and explanations of recent Supreme Court decisions, offers specific descriptions not only of the facts and holdings of the cases but also of their practical implications as the policeman does his job on the street. Prosecutors as well will obtain invaluable assistance from this section of the book.

It is a generally unrecognized fact that a policeman must know the dictates of criminal procedure better than the prosecutor and the judge. The policeman carries no law books and cannot retreat to the law library. There are no short recesses and continuances in the street. He must react immediately and instinctively in many situations. In these times, evidence is suppressed not because of police action deliberately undertaken to flout the Court's mandates. Lack of knowledge, carelessness, and a dearth of policy guidelines and supervision are more often the cause of improper actions. I hope that a book such as this will impress upon police administrators and upon district attorneys the need for carefully developed and fully implemented policy pronouncements in all areas of criminal procedure. Continuous training and guidance will improve the policeman's general attitude towards his work and help him understand and cope with the law's requirements. Inasmuch as most police action involves citizen contact that is not oriented towards prosecution, this training and guidance is the only truly effective source of constant, universal legality in police action. The exclusionary rule just cannot reach the millions of police-citizen encounters undertaken in the peacekeeping and crime-prevention roles of the police.

In 1931, the National Commission on Law Observance and Enforcement stated: "Respect for law, which is the fundamental prerequisite of law observance, hardly can be expected of people in general if the officers charged with enforcement of the law do not set the example of obedience to its precepts."

Knowledge is the first step towards such obedience. That is why this book is so important.

HENRY S. RUTH, JR.*

Philadelphia, Pa.

*Henry S. Ruth, Jr. is an Associate Professor of Law at the University of Pennsylvania Law School. He was formerly Deputy Director of the President's Crime Commission and Special Attorney for the Organized Crime and Racketeering Section of the United States Department of Justice.

Preface

> ...Officials of the criminal justice system itself must stop operating, as all too many do, by traditions or by rote. They must re-examine what they do. They must be honest about the system's shortcomings with the public and with themselves. They must be willing...to make advances.
>
> President's Crime Commission

For the past seven years, I have had the pleasure of working side by side with federal, state, and local law enforcement officers. During that time I have grown to respect the competence, resourcefulness, and enthusiasm of these dedicated officers.

In those same seven years, there has been a legal explosion detonated by the Supreme Court of the United States that has virtually turned law enforcement upside down and inside out. Confusion about the Supreme Court's decisions since 1960 has abounded.

The confusion I have seen led me to write this book. For seven years, I have spent a great deal of time both within and outside of courtrooms untangling the surface confusion created by these decisions. Working day in and day out attempting to solve the legal problems of the prosecution has provided—I hope—a practical insight into the major areas affected by the Supreme Court decisions.

Contrary to the false prophets who have flourished with the confusion, the recent Supreme Court decisions are not death blows to law enforcement. They do not handcuff police.

Contrary to popular belief, these decisions are not confusing. They are logical and almost perfectly symmetrical.

They protect individual rights without sacrificing public safety.

An officer who knows about these decisions will be a better officer—a professional officer. He will, in the long run, be a more skilled adversary against evil and a man who is better equipped to offer compassionate help to people who really need help.

Criminal justice in America desperately needs to advance to meet the complex problems of the 20th century. Law enforcement officers must lead that advance. "One man," as President Kennedy once said, "can make a difference and every man should try."

For law enforcement, the advance towards better justice must begin with greater knowledge of the law. This book is dedicated to assisting that advance.

I would like to thank Mrs. Robert Troxel for her help in the preparation of this book. In addition, three officers from the Police Department in Lower Merion Township, Pennsylvania, contributed to a thoughtful review of the book. They were: Major G. A. McLaughlin, superintendent of police; Captain P. J. Joyce; and Lieutenant H. J. Gross.

J. S. C.

Contents

INTRODUCTION

CONSTITUTIONAL LIMITATIONS ON POLICE POWERS

The United States Constitution and the Bill of Rights are every citizen's written guarantee that the force of government will not be harnessed against him arbitrarily. These two hallowed documents stand solidly as an effective barrier against the unfair, unjust use of governmental power.

The criminal law is the cutting edge of the law. It is in the area of criminal law that the impact of government becomes the most severe and the most devastating to the citizen. To assure that the criminal law is not used arbitrarily or for venal personal motives, our Bill of Rights tempers the impact of criminal enforcement by creating certain limitations on police powers in this country.

In the broad view, these constitutional limitations on police powers require law enforcement officers to have prior justification before swooping down on a citizen. In Nazi Germany the Gestapo operated under a system of no limitations or legal restraints and literally could seize any citizen at any time without cause. In our free society, the Constitution absolutely prevents this type of harrowing police tactic.

It is important for all professionally minded law enforcement officers to be intellectually honest with themselves by conceding that constitutional limitations on police in a free society are a necessity and not a luxury. We live in a time when an impulsive or unwarranted arrest or search can mark a citizen for the rest of his life. In our modern, complex society the police should strike out against the citizen only for cause. The Constitution is each citizen's assurance that the cutting edge of the law will not slash in his direction without prior justification.

From a practical point of view, it is essential for the law enforcement officer to have a feeling for and understanding of the constitutional limitations on police powers and the rules and procedures that have been developed concerning them. Without a knowledge in this area, a police officer today is straitjacketed by his ignorance. For if an officer does not know the laws of arrest and of search and seizure from a constitutional point of view, he certainly will be inhibited in the use of his ultimate powers of arrest and search.

There have been far too many instances in the past where hardened, dangerous criminals went free because of technical errors in law enforcement. The purpose of this Handbook is to assist the police officer in preventing such errors so that the criminal cannot escape.

THE CONSTITUTION

There are three concepts about the Constitution that are important from a law enforcement officer's point of view. The first characteristic of the Constitution that needs to be emphasized is the fact that it is the supreme law of the land. Under our system of law the Constitution is of paramount importance, and all other areas of law must yield in the event of conflict. The laws of contracts, real property, negligence, corporations, and even criminal law are emphatically subordinate to constitutional law in this country. One aspect of our judicial system underscores the supremacy or priority of our constitutional law. If someone alleges violations of his constitutional rights, he will get an immediate hearing in any state or federal courtroom that he enters. Contrast this with a possible delay of five or six years in obtaining a courtroom for a civil jury trial and one can see the top priority constitutional law attains in our jurisprudential system.

The second area to be highlighted about the Constitution is its intention to fragment or limit the total power and the total force of government. The basic underlying philosophy of our forefathers in drafting the Constitution was to divide the powers of government into three separate but equal branches of government—the executive, the legislative, and the judicial. By dividing government into three branches, our forefathers were attempting to assure that no one man or no one group could effectively take over the full panoply of governmental powers in this country. Each of the three branches of government was designed to act and actually does act as a check or balance on the power exercised by the other branches. A police officer, who is in the executive arm of government, reinforces this basic philosophy of the Constitution every time he goes to the courts for an arrest or search warrant since he is assuring that two branches of government, rather than one, determine the citizen's fate.

The third outstanding feature of the Constitution is its stability. While there have been more than eight thousand serious attempts to amend the Constitution since its enactment nearly two hundred years ago, only twenty-five proposals have become the law of the land. During the important years of growth and development of our nation, up until the present time, this aspect of stability of our supreme law has been an important factor in establishing government by rule of law.

THE BILL OF RIGHTS

Basically, the Bill of Rights restricts and regulates the powerful forces of government at the critical impact area between government and the citizen. The first ten amendments, which are basic assurances of individual freedom in this country, are, in effect, nothing more than the Ten Commandments of what the forces of government cannot do. These ten amendments are not merely hollow, empty promises because they are enforced fully by the courts.

THE FOURTH AMENDMENT

The right of the people to be secure in their persons, houses, papers, and effects, against unreasonable searches and seizures, shall not be violated, and no warrants shall issue, but upon probable cause, supported by oath or affirmation, and particularly describing the place to be searched, and the persons or things to be seized.

The Fourth Amendment was designed to protect each citizen's privacy. That right is the right to be free from the prying eyes and ears of government. It is the core of individual freedom.

Because the right to privacy is so highly valued in our free society, the Fourth Amendment places specific limitations or restrictions on certain police powers. Police powers are divided into two general classifications – police investigative powers and police arrest powers.

Police investigative powers include but are not limited to:
the power to *stop*
the power to *frisk* – for self protection only
the power to *question*
the power to *detain*
Police arrest powers are:
the power to use *force*
the power to *search*
the power to exercise *seizure* and *restraint*

Essentially, the Fourth Amendment demands that a police officer must not use his investigative powers indiscriminately. From a constitutional point of view, every action a police officer takes against a citizen must be justified by the facts. Police should investigate people appearing in a background of suspicious circumstances. The suspect may be stopped, and if the officer reasonably fears for his safety or suspects a crime of violence in the offing he may frisk, detain, and ask questions. Stopping, frisking, detaining, and questioning on the street or on the scene are all serious intrusions on the right to privacy, but the right to privacy must yield when police are drawn into a lawful threshold inquiry because of unusual or suspicious conduct.

Essentially, the Fourth Amendment dictates that a police officer can never use his arrest powers unless he is confronted with sufficient facts that would lead a reasonable person to believe that someone has committed a crime. A police officer's arrest powers are the ultimate weapons spanning government and society. Consequently, the Fourth Amendment requires a police officer to act only on facts sufficient to invoke his awesome arrest powers.

In summary, then, from a constitutional viewpoint, police may lawfully use their investigative powers only when there is a factual justification of suspicious circumstances. Only where there is probable cause or a combination of facts that generate a reasonable belief that the suspect committed a crime can the police use their powers to arrest.

THREE CONSTITUTIONAL STANDARDS. There are three critical Fourth Amendment concepts that are all important for police officers – whether they are local, state or federal law enforcement officers. "Unreasonableness," "Probable Cause," and "Particularity" are the names of the three magic formulas that will resolve a law enforcement officer's uncertainty about the Fourth Amendment.

The Fourth Amendment in its very language prohibits only "*unreasonable* searches and seizures" and not *all* searches and seizures. It is difficult to get an all-inclusive focus on what makes an arrest, search or seizure unreasonable. The basic guideline here is that the officer must be particularly careful not to exceed his lawful authority.

Under our system of law, a police officer is empowered by lawful authority to arrest for a past or present felony and a present misdemeanor. An officer's lawful authority to arrest then is clear and well-defined. So also is an officer's power to search – basically, he has none. It is most important that law enforcement officers realize that they have absolutely no lawful authority to make a search independently.

There are only three ways in which a police officer obtains lawful authority to make a search:

By the authority of a *search warrant*
Authority by virtue of a *lawful arrest*
By the authority of a waiver of *consent*

When a police officer does not have a search warrant and has not obtained consent, he must justify the search on the basis of a legal arrest. It is important to underscore the fact that searching by the police is unequivocally the using of an arrest power. A police officer is given the power to make a search when he makes a lawful arrest for the purpose of protecting himself and preventing the destruction of evidence.

Unreasonableness. "Unreasonableness" under the Fourth Amendment is determined in large measure by examining whether or not the officer exceeded the scope of his lawful authority. When an officer makes a search on his own, since he is using one of his awesome arrest powers, he must have sufficient facts that would justify an arrest *before* he initiates his search. Most "unreasonable" searches are ones in which officers did not have sufficient facts to justify the use of their arrest power.

Probable Cause. Of all the standards in constitutional and criminal law, probable cause is the most important from a legal point of view. The phrase "probable cause" appears in the Fourth Amendment itself, so it is indisputably recognized to have constitutional dimensions. The concept of probable cause is more than two thousand years old. It comes to us from both Roman law and the Common Law of England.

In 99 out of 100 cases the standard of probable cause determines whether or not a search warrant is valid. In 100 out of 100 cases, the standard of probable cause determines whether or not an arrest is lawful.

The phrase "probable cause" is generally defined as: *"Facts or apparent facts, viewed through the eyes of the experienced police officer, which would generate a reasonable belief that a crime has been committed."*

The essence of probable cause is *facts*. Suspicious facts, sinister facts, and guilt-laden facts in combination, when a criminal act has been committed, create probable cause. The probable cause formula is based not only on actual facts but also on probable facts. In other words, an officer can be wrong about the facts that he is acting on, but so long as he accepts them in good faith, they can be used to justify an arrest or a search.

In a courtroom, facts establishing probable cause are not barred by any of the technical rules of evidence. Prejudicial facts can and should be developed at probable cause hearings. Even more significantly there is no Hearsay Rule preventing the presentation of hearsay evidence at a suppression hearing.

Finally, it is important to emphasize that the Supreme Court has indicated that they will measure this probable cause standard in a commonsense and nontechnical manner. The Supreme Court has equally emphasized the fact that the burden of proof at the arrest and search level is merely "a reasonable belief that someone has committed a crime" and not the criminal trial burden of "guilt beyond a reasonable doubt."

Particularity. The concept of particularity applies generally to all searches and seizures but is especially important in the area of search warrants. The Fourth Amendment requires particularity as to the place to be searched and the person or things to be seized. The constitutional standard of particularity requires that search warrants be specific, not only concerning *who* or *what* is to be searched, but also about *what* is to be seized.

The particularity restriction of the Fourth Amendment, in effect, limits the scope of the place to be searched and the items that are to be searched for. As a safeguard to the citizen, it requires the officer to know what he is looking for and where he will find it before he begins his search. The particularity requirement is the most technical of the Fourth Amendment rules, yet it is the easiest for the officer to know and control.

This introduction focuses on the need for officers to know the three basic Fourth Amendment formulas by which arrests, searches and seizures are judged by the courts. In making an arrest or conducting a search, the guidelines of reasonableness, probable cause, and particularity must all be considered by the officer to insure that a criminal will not benefit from a technical mistake by the officer. Every time a criminal escapes on a technicality, justice is defeated.

THE FIFTH AMENDMENT

> *No person shall . . . be compelled in any criminal case to be a witness against himself, nor be deprived of life, liberty, or property, without due process of law.*

The purpose of every search and seizure is to find incriminating evidence against someone. The Fifth Amendment right against self-incrimination is therefore subtly but inexorably intertwined with the Fourth Amendment in the search and seizure area.

More than seventy years ago, the Supreme Court indicated that the Fifth Amendment casts its broad protective cloak over the Fourth Amendment to provide, in effect, a double mantle of constitutional protection for the citizen who becomes the object of governmental intrusion. This double-barreled constitutional protection of the Fourth and Fifth Amendments in combination is always present in the courtroom where suppression hearings are held. It is a subtle but significant factor for the officer to both know and appreciate, since it comprises – in large measure – the overriding attitude of the Court in judging delicate constitutional issues.

CONSTITUTIONAL STANDARDS AND THE POLICE OFFICER

Every day that a police officer straps on his gun he puts his life on the line. It is essential, then, that every officer have a thorough knowledge of how to protect himself and others with his revolver.

Equally important these days is the need for the officer to know and evaluate the legality of what he is doing and what he wants to do in enforcing the laws. If the officer wants to prevent a criminal from making a technical escape from justice, that officer must be thoroughly familiar with the Fourth Amendment constitutional standards of reasonableness, probable cause, and particularity. In reality he must be as familiar with these vital legal concepts as he is with his own gun.

CHAPTER I

PROBABLE CAUSE

The law enforcement officer who does not thoroughly understand the standard of probable cause is in the unenviable position of a man who doesn't know what he is doing. For in order to make a valid arrest, with or without a warrant, or to make a search, a police officer must have probable cause. In order to prepare arrest and search warrants the officer must know how to articulate probable cause. Equally important to the law enforcement officer, particularly at this time, is the fact that if he is sued civilly for false arrest or false imprisonment, the most important issue at trial is the probable cause upon which he acted. In a civil rights criminal prosecution against an officer, for instance, the critical issue at trial is the officer's probable cause. Obviously, a thorough knowledge and understanding of the standard of probable cause is essential for all law enforcement officers.

DEFINITION

Probable cause for an arrest is defined as a combination of facts or apparent facts, viewed through the eyes of an experienced police officer, which would lead a man of reasonable caution to believe that a crime is being or has been committed. Probable cause for the issuance of a search warrant is defined as facts or apparent facts viewed through the eyes of an experienced police officer which would lead a man of reasonable caution to believe that there is something connected with a violation of law on the premises to be searched. These definitions of probable cause are not new; they have always been the law in this country. Not only are these definitions an accurate statement of the federal law relating to probable cause, but they are also an accurate statement of the law of each of the 50 states. Probable cause is then truly a national uniform constitutional standard. It is the magic formula that provides most of the answers to legal questions under the Fourth Amendment.

SIGNIFICANCE

> *. . . And no warrants shall issue, but upon probable cause . . .*
>
> Excerpt from the Fourth Amendment to the Constitution of the United States.

These nine words have given the concept of probable cause its greatest power—its constitutional dimensions. This means, of course, that because the Constitution and the Bill of Rights are the most important laws in our nation, probable cause must be treated with the highest priority by our courts. Of all the sacred constitutional rights that a citizen enjoys in this country, none is more precious than this right under the Fourth Amendment. It gives the citizen protection in this area of the most critical impact of society on the individual—the impact of a police arrest or a police search.

The fact that the concept of probable cause has constitutional dimensions assures uniform interpretation in every court in the United States.

It is essential to realize that according to the philosophy of probable cause, the courts throughout our country have the primary responsibility of determining whether or not a person is to be arrested or a home is to be searched. This primary responsibility of the courts assures the citizen that his rights will not be violated by overzealous law enforcement officers. Of course, there are countless emergencies where the police officer must act and act immediately. In practical law enforcement, it is impossible to go to the courts for evaluation of the probable cause involved in every contemplated arrest. But it is important to remember that the ultimate decision as to proper grounds for arrest and search lies with the courts and not with the police. The police frequently must act on their own, but when they do, it is essential for the courts to scrutinize the facts and circumstances surrounding the arrest. There is no other way to protect the delicate balance of individual rights against police necessity.

ESSENTIAL CONCEPTS

PROBABLE, NOT ACTUAL, CAUSE. The stronger the combinations of facts and circumstances showing guilt, the stronger the probable cause to make an arrest. It is essential to realize that the term "probable" means exactly that. If the police officer, acting in an emergency, gathers facts or apparent facts in good faith, he will be judged on those facts regardless of whether or not they are actually true. So long as the officer accepts his facts in good faith, he may rely on them even if they subsequently turn out to be wrong.

CAUSE, NOT SUSPICION. The concept of probable cause unequivocally demands that an arrest or a search be made for *cause,* not for suspicion. A police officer may not arrest on a hunch, or on a guess, or on mere suspicion. A police officer may arrest only if he has a reasonable belief, based on the facts confronting him, that someone has committed a crime. Consequently, under the constitutional standard of probable cause, the dragnet arrest, the arrest for suspicion, the arrest for investigation, the arrest on an open charge, and the arrest for protective custody, are all illegal and unconstitutional. This standard of probable cause prevents the police officer from arresting now and finding the crime later.

FACTS VIEWED THROUGH THE EYES OF THE EXPERIENCED OFFICER. The courts evaluate the facts as viewed by the experienced officer rather than as they would be viewed by the average layman. Law enforcement, particularly in more recent times, has become more and more complex. One example is that the factual patterns of a gambling enterprise are virtually unknown to the average layman. The police, on the contrary, are sensitively attuned to the recurring patterns of a numbers operation. For this reason, facts constituting probable cause are reviewed by the courts as seen by the experienced officer. This allows the officer the necessary latitude to explain the full significance of certain material facts. It would be basically unfair and impractical to straitjacket the police officer by restricting him to view facts as a layman.

FACTS TAKEN IN GOOD FAITH. The standard of probable cause is a very versatile one. It is versatile in that virtually any kind of fact may be an element of showing someone's guilt. The only limitation at all, as far as facts are concerned, is that they must be facts taken in good faith. Any fact may be taken from any source so long as the law enforcement officer believes the fact to be true. If an officer knowingly attempts to use a false fact as part of his probable cause, any action that he takes will be unlawful. The purpose of gathering facts to establish probable cause is for the law enforcement officer, by facts, to establish a personal belief in guilt. If the officer knows his facts are not true, he is not only committing fraud but he is also placing himself in a position where he can be sued civilly or criminally for misconduct in office. Because the constitutional concept of probable cause is facts under oath, an officer who knowingly embraces falsehood is toying with perjury. The purpose of the oath is to assure that the facts are true. Consequently, the only limitation on a law enforcement officer in this area of probable cause is that he must gather only such facts as he personally believes are true. It is not material if at a later date the officer's judgment proves to be wrong. In other words, if an officer accepts a fact that he believes to be true but it subsequently develops that it is not true, the fact will be accepted by the court as part of the probable cause for an arrest, so long as the officer accepted the fact in good faith. Where the good faith of an officer is particularly critical is in the area of a civil or criminal suit for false arrest or for false imprisonment. Here the good faith of the officer and the reasonableness of the facts upon which he acted are the crucial determining factors of prosecutions.

FACTS THAT CONSTITUTE PROBABLE CAUSE. Any and all facts accepted in good faith by a law enforcement officer may constitute elements of probable cause. There is virtually no limitation on the type of fact that an officer may gather as probable cause to justify an arrest. An officer may receive information at a roll call, from an informant, from a citizen, or from a fellow-officer, and that information, regardless of where it came from, so long as it was accepted in good faith, may be considered as part of the probable cause for police action.

In the realm of probable cause, there is no restriction on the type of facts which may constitute probable cause, and also there is no restriction on the presentation of facts by the police officer. In other words, in the realm of probable cause, there are no rules of evidence. It is essential to realize, particularly, that the officer is not straitjacketed by the traditional rules of evidence in presenting his probable cause so that probable cause does not have to be made up of legally admissible factual evidence. It is difficult for the professional law enforcement officer who has schooled himself and who knows the rules of evidence to suddenly find an area in law where they are to be totally disregarded. But it is very important that the police officer not be inhibited at the probable cause inquiry by adhering to the strict rules of evidence.

The most difficult rule of evidence for the police to discard is the Hearsay Rule. "Hearsay," as used in the rules of evidence, means facts not within the personal knowledge of the witness testifying. It means, generally, facts that have been relayed from one person to another. The probable cause inquiry, or the suppression hearing, is held out of the presence of the jury and, therefore, the court is not concerned with the rules of evidence. The court is concerned with inquiring into the state of mind of the arresting officer to discover all the facts that he acted upon.

Facts are the essence of probable cause – particularly sinister, guilt-edged, or guilt-laden facts. The quality that makes probable cause persuasive is a combination of facts that leads to a reasonable belief of guilt. The law enforcement officer should be sensitive to the need for gathering these combinations of facts, because they can lay an invincible constitutional basis for an arrest or search.

BURDENS OF PROOF. The basic reason why none of the rules of evidence apply in the probable cause stage of a criminal proceeding is that the burden of proof is entirely different. There are three distinct burdens of proof required at the three distinct stages of criminal prosecutions, and it is important that these three different burdens of proof not be confused. The first stage of a criminal proceeding is the arrest for probable cause. The burden of proof at this probable cause stage is to establish *a reasonable ground for belief in guilt.* At the probable cause stage, courts do not place any emphasis on the admissibility of evidence. The second stage of a criminal proceeding is the preliminary arraignment or hearing before a judicial officer. This immediately follows the arrest and here the prosecution must make out a *prima facie* case in order to have the court hold the accused to answer the charge. This is the level where the rules of evidence first appear and the court must determine whether there are sufficient grounds to believe that an offense has been committed and that the accused person committed it. If a *prima facie* case (assuming all of the prosecution's evidence is true) is made out, the accused is held to answer to higher authority. The third stage of a criminal proceeding is the trial, where the burden of proof on the prosecution is to prove the defendant *guilty beyond a reasonable doubt.* Here the rules of evidence are enforced with the utmost vigilance and only evidence in admissible form may be presented to the jury.

AMBIGUOUS FACTS – CAUTION. An equivocal or ambiguous fact has frequently been relied upon by law enforcement officers to establish probable cause. The courts, however, have generally held that equivocal or ambiguous facts cannot of themselves create a reasonable belief of guilt. Consequently, facts that are not clothed in suspicion strong enough to imply criminality cannot separately establish probable cause. Only incriminating or guilt-laden facts are strong enough to satisfy the standard of probable cause. Equivocal, ambiguous, or neutral facts are dangerous to the law enforcement officer because he can be lulled into a false sense of security by them. There is a need for objectivity here. The police officer should evaluate his facts in two categories. First, those facts which demonstrate guilt, such as flight or furtive movements; and, second, the ambiguous facts which, of themselves, do not demonstrate guilt, such as a man unloading a car or a man tipping his hat. Overreliance on ambiguous non-guilt-producing facts can be hazardous.

HEARSAY INFORMATION. The ultimate weapon of law enforcement, particularly with regard to the probable cause concept, is hearsay information. Hearsay information is defined as a communication of facts from someone to the police officer in action. That someone can be an anonymous person, an informant, a citizen, a fellow police officer, a judge, or anyone. That someone can be a child or an adult, a saint or a sinner. That someone – no matter who he is – is commonly referred to in law as the "source" of the information. Of course, the Hearsay Rule does not bar the presentation of hearsay information at probable cause inquiries. All that is required is that the law enforcement officer accept whatever information is given to him in good faith.

One indestructible constitutional safeguard in the probable cause concept is that the facts setting forth probable cause must be under oath. That is, whoever takes the affidavit must swear – in good faith – that he believes all the facts are true. This constitutional safeguard applies in full strength to hearsay information, even though it comes from a different source than the law enforcement officer who is testifying at a suppression hearing or who is taking out warrants. This is the one great constitutional limitation on probable cause facts generally, and on relayed information specifically. Because the officer himself has no first-hand knowledge of facts relayed to him, courts insist on knowing as much as can possibly be revealed about the source of the information. If the source is a con man, or an unreliable person, or an anonymous person, courts are reluctant to place much reliance or value on the information. In contrast, if the source of the information is particularly strong, such as a reliable informant or another police officer, courts generally place more confidence in the relayed facts. This is just a matter of common sense. The stronger and more credible the source of the information, the more reliable that information generally is. So the person who gives the information is vital, for the court must evaluate the truth of the facts advanced by hearsay information. The difficult determination for the court is whether or not the hearsay facts are true. Speculation, rumor, or the chance of false facts is abhorred by the courts. Arrests or searches based solely on undisclosed informants' accusations have never been upheld by the courts. To allow such arrests or searches would be a death blow to the essential "facts under oath" constitutional requirement. The pursuit of any court inquiry is after truth. Although the hearsay barrier has been removed by the courts in the probable cause hearing, the court is still in quest of truth. Therefore, when hearsay information is used to contribute toward establishing probable cause, the source of the information is one vital measuring rod of the truth of the information. Since the officer who takes an affidavit or testifies at a suppression hearing cannot swear to the truth of the hearsay information from his own direct personal observations, the truth of the information is just as strong as its source.

In addition to identifying the source, there is another technique of demonstrating the truth of hearsay information that must be fully understood. This technique is called corroboration. The professional police officer should attempt in any way possible to corroborate hearsay information that is relayed to him from any source. "To corroborate" means to make more certain or to confirm. Each time information is corroborated by independent police investigation, the loud echo of truth resounds.

No one can dispute that in modern police work, hearsay information plays a dominant role. That is why an officer must know how the courts evaluate hearsay information in this most important probable cause area of criminal law. Once the law enforcement officer fully understands this commonsense approach by the courts to hearsay information, his arrest and search problems should be considerably lessened. Once the law enforcement officer fully realizes that the only realistic way to establish the truth of hearsay information at the probable cause level is by identifying the source and describing the police corroboration of the information, his uncertainty in this area should vanish. No professionally minded law enforcement officer can afford the luxury of ignorance here.

CHECKLIST OF PROBABLE CAUSE

With no intention to be all-inclusive, the following checklist presents guilt-laden facts which courts throughout the country have recognized as solid building blocks of probable cause:

1. Flight
2. Furtive movements
3. Hiding
4. Attempt to destroy evidence
5. Resistance to officers
6. Admissions or confessions
7. Evasive answers
8. Unreasonable explanations
9. Fingerprint identification
10. Hair follicle identifications
11. Handwriting comparisons
12. Fabric comparisons
13. Identification of suspects by witnesses
14. The Emergency Setting – crime zone
15. The Emergency Setting – automobile
16. Ballistics
17. Contraband or weapons in plain view
18. Criminal record
19. Hearsay Information – informant
20. Hearsay Information – fellow officer
21. Hearsay Information – general
22. Expert police opinion
23. Police corroboration
24. Unusual or suspicious conduct
25. Fact of crime or felony

CHAPTER II

INVESTIGATIVE TECHNIQUES

WHEN TO INVESTIGATE

Under the philosophy of the Bill of Rights and the Constitution, government – particularly law enforcement officers – must leave citizens alone unless there is some reason to investigate them. Investigations of citizens should be made only where there is substantial credible information to justify or necessitate a police inquiry.

Our government and our system of justice is built on the premise that the individual dignity of each citizen must be carefully protected. Courts will be swift to protect individual dignity against any and all unwarranted and unnecessary governmental invasions. Our citizens have, in effect, an absolute right to be free from the prying eye of government. Our citizens have a right not to be investigated. The general rule then is not to investigate unless some reliable raw facts are developed that justify governmental intrusions into a citizen's privacy.

CRIMINAL INVESTIGATION

Criminal investigation involves the gathering of facts for the purpose of protecting citizens and solving crimes. There is a wide variety of police techniques used in obtaining facts, but the primary purpose is to gather guilt-laden facts that establish both the fact that a crime has been committed and the identity of the person committing the crime.

The first cardinal rule of criminal investigation is that law enforcement officers must use *restraint* in pursuing facts. In today's world, the force of government is awesome, and the power of government in the criminal field must be invoked only with great restraint. The courts, in executing dictates of the Constitution and the Bill of Rights, guarantee to each citizen that the police will act fairly and justly when investigating the citizen.

The courts measure police conduct in the area of the Bill of Rights on the yardstick of "restraint." Overpowering responses by the police when confronted with minimal or ambiguous circumstances are discouraged by the courts. In contrast, the restrained escalation of police responses in direct proportion to justifiable facts is encouraged by the courts. At every step of an investigation the police should operate with such restraint as would indicate to the courts that the officers were fully aware of the individual dignity and right to privacy of every citizen. Each action taken by police in a criminal investigation—no matter how seemingly insignificant on the surface—has the impact of shock waves bombarding someone's individual privacy. Consequently, courts have to sharpen their focus to observe in minute detail the action of the police at each stage of the criminal investigation.

The second cardinal rule for law enforcement officers is that criminal investigation can be accomplished only by lawful means. The purpose of criminal investigation is not to capture and destroy the enemy—it is to see that justice is done. The primary function of criminal investigation is to prevent crime and to protect our citizens by seeing the guilty punished. It is equally important to see that the innocent do not suffer.

Criminal investigators, under our system of law, are critical ministers of justice and should be more interested in seeing that justice is done than in compiling criminal statistics. It is essential for law enforcement officers to know that the unconditional "war on crime" does not entitle the police to use unlawful methods in any of their battles.

Consequently, in criminal investigation, officers should be fair and just and use only lawful techniques, and should scrupulously avoid misstating or not disclosing essential facts that would establish innocence.

THE FOUR "I'S"

Inspection

Area
Specific

Information

From police
From citizens
From informants
From anonymous sources

Interrogation

In custody
Field
General inquiry

Investigation

- Investigative powers
  - Stop
  - Frisk
  - Question
  - Detain
- Binoculars and cameras
- Undercover agents

Electronic eavesdropping
- Penn Register
- Wiretapping
- Trespass radio transmitting bug
- Walking bug

Mail cover
Lie detector test
Blood test
Hair samples
Line-up
Use of informants
Information or evidence from private citizens
Police entry
Car stops
Road blocks
Police arrest powers
Alcohol tests

INSPECTIONS

INSPECTIONS ARE NOT AN INVESTIGATIVE TECHNIQUE. Routine inspections of home or commercial establishments for health and safety reasons may be made by inspectors, without warrants, when no one challenges the inspection. Inspections made for the general welfare are considered by the courts to be limited, necessary invasions of privacy and since they are not performed by law enforcement officers, the inspections can generally be made without warrants. The purpose of an inspection is to check health and safety hazards and not to look for incriminating evidence.

In the event that someone contests an inspection of his home or apartment by health or safety inspectors, then, according to the Supreme Court of the United States, the authorities must obtain a warrant to make the inspection. This applies to both residences and commercial buildings. The purpose of requiring a warrant when an inspection is contested is to have an independent, neutral judicial officer evaluate the need for the inspection.

Law enforcement officers should avoid any clandestine arrangements with health inspectors to get them to look for incriminating evidence. The powers of a health and safety inspector are to promote the general welfare and do not include the power to search indiscriminately for incriminating evidence. Any sinister arrangements between a law enforcement officer and a health or safety inspector is unlawful and will result in the suppression of evidence.

On the other hand, if an inspector, in making a lawful health inspection of a building, sees, as an example, contraband, he can and should report seeing the contraband to the police. Then the police should act—but only with a search warrant based on the information supplied by the health inspector. Inspections are generally of two varieties—either area or widespread inspections, or specific inspections of particular properties. The rule that no warrant is necessary except in the event of a contested inspection applies both to "area" and "specific" inspections.

INFORMATION

The one ingredient that permeates the whole field of criminal investigation is information. At almost every step or at every level of a criminal investigation critical hearsay information is received by the police and becomes woven into the main fabric of the investigation.

Information frequently is the life's blood of an investigation, and it is important for law enforcement officers to enlarge their knowledge concerning the technique of using and developing hearsay information in criminal investigations.

Police officers need to understand the judicial view of this vital investigative weapon. The courts give full faith and credit to hearsay information at the investigative level, but they are duty-bound to carefully review hearsay information—particularly where it is being used as part of the justification for an arrest or a search. The court's responsibility is to evaluate the hearsay information for *reliability*. If in the court's opinion the hearsay information supporting an arrest or search is reliable, credible, and believable, then the court must accept hearsay information at full value. In contrast, if the court is skeptical about the reliability of the information it must be rejected.

COURT TESTS FOR RELIABILITY

The Supreme Court of the United States has clearly defined two judicial tests for judging the reliability of hearsay information at the investigative-arrest-search level.

The first judicial test is the *source* of the information. This is a good commonsense rule that dictates that the content of hearsay information becomes stronger and more reliable depending upon the strength of the source of the information. Information from police, public officials, citizens, or reliable informants commands respect. However, information from informants whose reliability is unknown, from some known criminals, or from anonymous callers is considered to be much weaker.

To the court and the police, then, the source of incriminating information in an investigation is extremely important. Both the courts and the police should be interested in acting only upon reliable information. The credibility and reliability of hearsay information increases in direct proportion to the strength of the source of the hearsay information. Police – at the investigative state of criminal proceedings – should be constantly evaluating the source of the incriminating information against the reliability standards that the courts follow.

There is a second test used by the courts to evaluate the reliability or credibility of information at the arrest-search level. This second test is the *corroboration* test. Basically, the corroboration test is made by comparing the specific allegations of the hearsay information with the events that occur after the information is received. As an example, in the leading case of *Draper v. United States*, 358 U.S. 307 (1959), a federal narcotics officer received information from a confidential informant who had been reliable in the past that a light complexioned Negro of a certain size and weight, wearing a tan raincoat and a hat, would get off a train in Chicago carrying a black satchel that concealed a large supply of narcotics. The narcotics officer went to the railroad station in Chicago and observed a man fitting the exact description. The man was dressed in the manner in which the informant said he would be and was carrying a black satchel. All of these facts, which occurred after the confidential informant gave the narcotics officer the incriminating information against Draper, corroborated the informant's information. Corroboration of information by later events strengthens the reliability or credibility of the information. The Supreme Court, in the Draper case, held that the informant's information was substantially corroborated by the subsequent events—that is, by Draper's getting off the train in Chicago, his matching the description given by the informant, and his carrying of the black satchel—which was found to have contained narcotics after Draper was arrested by the agent. The Supreme Court held that the arrest of Draper was lawful and that the search of the bag for narcotics was incident to Draper's arrest, and the narcotics were not suppressed.

At every step of an investigation the professional police officer should make a conscious effort to corroborate any hearsay information that is channeled into the mainstream of his investigation. The more resourceful an officer is in corroborating hearsay information, the less of a problem with the credibility gap. It is absolutely essential that when the source of the information is weak—such as an anonymous call—the corroboration of the information by the police must be particularly strong. The courts are obliged to accept only hearsay information that is reliable.

The usual after-effect of unreliable hearsay information is the suppression of evidence. The Constitution demands that probable cause consist of a combination of *reliable* facts that generate a reasonable belief that someone has committed a crime. The *source* test and the *corroboration* test applied by the courts guarantee the reliability of facts—particularly hearsay facts—at the arrest-search level. This assures each citizen protection against unreliable accusations from shadowy sources. Such rules are essential for the protection of liberty in a free society.

CONFIDENTIAL INFORMANTS

The use of the term "confidential informant" to describe the source of incriminating hearsay information at the arrest-search level is not a magic wand that can be used by the police to strengthen the credibility of the hearsay information. In reality, the mere phrase "confidential informant" has, in the abstract, about the same strength of credibility as an anonymous source. In other words, the magic phrase "confidential informant" does nothing in itself to bolster the source value of the incriminating information.

Therefore, the phrase "confidential informant" used by the police to describe the source of hearsay information at the arrest-search level does not by itself establish the credibility of the information. For the credibility factor to rise, it is necessary that the courts know more about the confidential informant. As a practical matter there are all kinds of confidential informants. Some are extremely reliable, some are fairly reliable, and others are not reliable at all.

The cardinal rule concerning confidential informants at the arrest-search level is that the officer should describe the confidential informant as fully as possible – without revealing or disclosing his identity. As an example, there are many variations on the theme as to how a confidential informant can be described in an affidavit for a search warrant or an arrest warrant.

Describing a Confidential Informant

(a) A confidential informant

(b) A confidential informant who has been reliable in the past

(c) A confidential informant who has been reliable in the past in that he has given a municipal Police Department information in the past which resulted in the arrest of ten people and the conviction of two

(d) Information from a confidential informant who has been extremely reliable in the past in that his information has resulted in the arrest and conviction of five people for counterfeiting and has also resulted in the seizure and confiscation of over a million counterfeit $20 dollar bills

The foregoing is an example of the escalation of source credibility by carefully describing in detail the confidential informant without revealing his identity. Courts will not place any major significance on the mere phrase "confidential informant." Courts must evaluate the reliability of the informant in order to evaluate the credibility of the information he gives. Whenever possible, then, police should describe the confidential informant in as much detail as possible so as to build the source reliability in their arrest and search warrants.

DISCLOSURE OF THE INFORMANT'S IDENTITY. The general rule is that the police do not have to disclose the identity of confidential informants, particularly at the arrest-search level. The right to protect the identity of the informant is an ancient one that comes to us from Common Law, and is a governmental privilege that is based on sound public policy. History and experience dictate that citizens should be encouraged to give information to the police that will help the police protect the community. In order to encourage citizens to go to the police with such information, there is the strongest doctrine against disclosing the informant's identity.

Occasionally, however, there is a rare case where ninety-nine per cent of the probable cause for an arrest is based on hearsay information from a confidential informant. This means, of course, that there is little or no corroboration of the confidential informant's information. In this unique situation there can arise a problem at a suppression hearing concerning the credibility of the officer with regard to the probable cause. At a suppression hearing, the defense has a right to attack the probable cause facts, particularly from the viewpoint of credibility. If nearly all the probable cause is hearsay information, the credibility of that information can be meaningfully attacked only by extensive cross-examination of the police officer to guarantee that such information was, in fact, presented to him from a confidential informant. Whenever the credibility factor hinges predominantly on the reliability of the officer's hearsay information from a confidential informant, then the defense has a right at a suppression hearing to make a searching inquiry concerning the details: how and when the officer received the information, how long the officer had known the informant, and how reliable or unreliable the informant had been in the past.

In this rare situation the court, in the interests of justice, may direct the prosecution to identify the informant so that he can be produced and cross-examined concerning the events. At the option of the prosecution in the event that the prosecution does not wish to disclose the identity of the informant, the court can declare an illegal arrest or an illegal search and seizure. The court would, in effect, declare the arrest or search illegal because the probable cause would not meet a reliability test that the Constitution demands. It is essential to emphasize that disclosure of an informant is considered an extremely unusual demand by a court at the arrest-search level, since the informant-credibility problem arises infrequently.

The informant disclosure problem at the arrest-search level should not be confused with the informant disclosure problem at the trial level. At the trial level courts are much more likely to demand the disclosure of the identity of an informant, particularly where the informant was a material witness to a crime. At the trial level, if the government refuses to identify an informant the court has the power to dismiss the indictment. Consequently, the court at no time has the absolute power to demand disclosure of the informant. The courts' maximum sanctions are to declare an illegal arrest and, at the trial level, to dismiss an indictment where the prosecution refuses to comply with the court's order to disclose the identity of the informant.

FINAL CONSIDERATIONS. Realistically, courts should not be overzealous in requiring law enforcement officers to disclose the identity of confidential informants, either at the arrest-search level or the trial level. There is a danger today of over-emphasizing apparent individual rights and under-emphasizing society's needs. With the dimensions of crime in this country today—particularly organized crime—the informant problem is critical.

One Attorney General of the United States recently testified before Congress that in one federal investigative agency alone 24 confidential informants had been killed in approximately a 38-month period. This same Attorney General mentioned that he had to forego literally hundreds of major prosecutions for organized crime because of a lack of witnesses who would be willing to testify against ruthless men. Courts should consider these hard facts in their determination of whether or not to force the issue with regard to the informant's identity. This is not a legalistic or academic question—it frequently is a matter of life and death. It is only where the interests of justice clearly demand the disclosure of an informant that the courts should direct disclosure. When an individual's rights of confrontation are denied, then the courts must act.

INTERROGATION RULES AND PROCEDURES

THE MIRANDA RULE

Interrogation as a 20th-century police technique has been used rather unevenly. It has been well documented that the traditional police technique of interrogation in the station house has fallen heaviest on the poor and those least able to defend themselves. Two-thirds of the people arrested in this country are classified as indigents, and two-thirds of the arrests in this country are for misdemeanors or less serious offenses. Some legal commentators are quick to point out that the traditional police technique of interrogation in this country has never been used to confront professional, organized or highly sophisticated white collar criminals. There can be little doubt that these factors weighed heavily with the Supreme Court of the United States when it reassessed American police interrogation and insisted on the full protections of the Fifth Amendment's right against self-incrimination at every stage of a criminal proceeding.

The principal impact of the Miranda decision was to place the Fifth Amendment's protection rights against self-incrimination not only in the courtroom but also in the police station . . . and even in the street. Under the Supreme Court's ruling in *Miranda,* the government has to show "by clear and convincing evidence" that a person who has made a confession explicitly waived his Fifth Amendment right aginst self-incrimination. This places upon the prosecution one of the most severe burdens of proof known to the law.

The part of the Miranda Rule which directly affects police interrogation states that whenever an accused person or a suspect is being questioned by the police in the police station, the police must warn the person being questioned, prior to the in-custody interrogation, that:

(a) He has the right to remain silent and say nothing.

(b) If he does make a statement he may stop at any time, and that anything that he says can and will be used against him in court.

(c) He has the right to have an attorney present at the time of the interrogation or that he will have an opportunity to consult with an attorney.

(d) If he cannot afford an attorney, one will be appointed for him prior to any questioning if he so desires.

In-Custody Interrogation

The Supreme Court indicated in *Miranda* that in the future, whenever the police use the technique of in-custody interrogation, they would have to give these Miranda warnings in order that the person being questioned can intelligently waive his right under the Fifth Amendment not to incriminate himself. The second half of the Miranda Rule is that if the warnings are not given, the prosecution cannot prove an intelligent waiver of the Fifth Amendment right against self-incrimination and any statement or confession will not be admissible in evidence against the accused. The reason the Supreme Court now demands the Miranda warnings whenever the police embark on in-custody interrogation is that the Court found not only that in-custody interrogation is a critical stage of a criminal proceeding, but also that the traditional techniques used by police in in-custody interrogation were considered to be destructive of the Fifth Amendment's right against self-incrimination.

Interrogation With the Intent to Arrest

The Miranda Rule applies not only to in-custody interrogation but also to any questioning of a suspect or an accused person when the police intend to deprive that person of a substantial portion of his liberty. This second facet of the Miranda Rule applies to police questioning at any time or at any place. In other words, whenever a police officer intends to arrest someone he must begin to give the Miranda warnings at that moment if he is going to attempt to elicit a statement or a confession that he would hope to introduce as evidence in court.

When an investigation shifts from being investigatory to being accusatory, the warnings must be given.

Therefore, whenever there is a general investigation into an unsolved crime there is no need to give the Miranda warnings. In contrast, when the focus is on an accused person and there is enough substantial evidence or probable cause so that any reasonable person would charge the suspect with a crime, the warnings must be given.

Other Conditions

Field interrogation–in contrast to in-custody interrogation–does not require the Miranda warnings unless the officer intends to arrest the person from whom he is trying to obtain a statement.

A third facet of the Miranda opinion is that the warnings do not have to be given when an attorney is present and representing the accused person. The philosophy contained in the Supreme Court's decision in *Miranda* indicates that it is the attorney's responsibility to protect his client's interests and Fifth Amendment right against self-incrimination during any police interrogation. If a person gives a statement to the police on the advice of counsel, that statement will be admissible regardless of whether or not the Miranda warnings had been given because the lawyer's function at the interrogation is to make sure that his client's constitutional rights are fully protected.

Finally, the Miranda warnings do not apply when statements are volunteered to the police. Whenever an individual volunteers a confession or volunteers admissions to the police, these statements are fully admissible regardless of where they were given. The critical factor here is that the police cannot engage in any questioning. From a prosecution point of view, if someone is volunteering a statement, the best advice is to let him talk and not ask any questions. The moment a police officer begins to ask questions is the time when the Miranda warnings have to be given.

INTERROGATION RULES AT A GLANCE

THE FOUR MIRANDA RULES

1. *You have a constitutional right to remain silent and say absolutely nothing. If you do make a statement, you may stop at any time.*
2. *Anything you say can and will be used against you later.*
3. *You can have a lawyer here to help you while we ask you questions.*
4. *If you don't have a lawyer, one will be appointed for you if you want one now.*

WHEN YOU MUST GIVE THE MIRANDA WARNINGS

IN-CUSTODY INTERROGATION. When a suspect is being questioned by the police in a police station, or when he is put into a police car and questioned, or whenever he is "actually" or "constructively" in police custody, he *must* be given the Miranda warnings.

Examples:

(a) A suspect in a murder case is arrested by the police and taken to a police station for fingerprinting and processing, and is questioned by detectives about the murder. This suspect must be given the Miranda warnings prior to any questioning by the police.

(b) A bank has been robbed, and a man who fits the general description of one of the bank robbers is seen by police officers on a street near where the bank was robbed. The man, when approached by the officers, starts to run and drops a mask. The officers arrest the man and place him in a police car to take him into the police station. This bank robbery suspect is in "actual" custody of the police officers in the police car and the officers must give the Miranda warnings prior to any questions that they ask the suspect on the way to the police station.

(c) Police officers have an arrest warrant for a man alleged to have committed a burglary. The officers go to his apartment and ring the bell, and he opens the door and admits them. Prior to any questioning, the officers must give the Miranda warnings since the burglary suspect is in "constructive" custody of the police officers because of the arrest warrant.

FIELD INTERROGATION WHEN THERE IS AN INTENT TO ARREST. The clearest part of the Miranda Rule is that whenever a suspect is in police custody, either in a police station, a police car, or even out on the street, he *must* be warned of his rights under the Fifth Amendment prior to any questioning by the police.

A second phase of the Miranda Rule requires police officers to warn suspects—no matter where the confrontation between the suspect and the police officer arises—if the officer intends to arrest the suspect or if it can reasonably be inferred that the officer is planning to arrest the suspect.

The Miranda decision states that the police have the duty to advise suspects of their constitutional rights not only when they are in police custody but also whenever the police "intend to deprive someone of his liberty." This means that the police must give a warning at a time when there is probable cause to make an arrest. When the probable cause builds to a point where no reasonable officer could deny that an arrest was imminent, he must, at that point, give the Miranda warnings to the suspect.

Example: An officer sees a man walking along the street late at night in a residential area carrying a couple of portable TV's, a portable radio, and a box. The police officer stops the person in his initial investigation and the person gives evasive answers as to what he is doing. Suddenly, the person admits burglarizing a house nearby. The probable cause for arresting this man appears clearly when he admits burglarizing a nearby house. It is at this point that the officer should discontinue questioning and give him the Miranda warnings before continuing to question him.

WHEN THE MIRANDA WARNINGS DO NOT HAVE TO BE GIVEN

"VOLUNTEERED" STATEMENTS. Whenever a person volunteers incriminating statements to police, no warnings need be given. It does not matter where a person volunteers the statement – they can be made in or out of a police station. The basic rule is that when a person volunteers incriminating information, the police should listen and not ask any questions. If an officer starts to question – he must warn.

WHENEVER A SUSPECT HAS A LAWYER REPRESENTING HIM. The lawyer is expected, according to the Miranda decision, to have a knowledge of constitutional protections for a man undergoing police interrogation. As a result, the burden of insuring compliance with constitutional safeguards now falls on the lawyer rather than on the police.

FIELD INTERROGATIONS INTO UNSOLVED CRIMES. Police officers do not have to give the Miranda warnings when they are making general investigations into unsolved crimes. When police are interviewing a number of suspects in the field, there is generally no requirement for the Miranda warnings. However, when the focus of the investigation narrows to a particular person, the police must give the warnings if they are going to question someone who looks very much as if he is going to wind up being the accused person.

The basic measuring rod to determine whether or not the warnings must be given is probable cause. Where there are a number of facts which would generate a reasonable belief that someone has committed a crime, the police must give the Miranda warnings to that person if they are going to question him. Where there are very few probable cause facts or where there are a number of suspects, field interrogations may generally be conducted without giving the warnings.

INTERROGATION BY A CITIZEN OR BY A PRIVATE SECURITY OFFICER. Since the Bill of Rights applies to the use of force by government officials only, there is no requirement that citizens or private security officers warn people of their constitutional rights under the Fifth Amendment. Private citizens and private security officers are not government officials and whatever they do in the area of interrogation is not regulated by the Constitution. However, if the police have a hand in arranging an interrogation by a private citizen or some other non-governmental person, the issue can become very cloudy. The stronger the appearance of police influence on an interrogation, the more apparent it would become that the warnings should be given.

WHY CONFESSIONS ARE SUPPRESSED

In the last few years, the Supreme Court has established fixed rules requiring the suppression of confessions as a means of enforcing and preserving the individual rights contained in the Fourth, Fifth, and Sixth Amendments. Our Bill of Rights has teeth in it.

In other words, unlike the Russian Constitution or the so-called constitutions of many totalitarian states, if government oversteps its authority in this country it becomes a no-yield transaction. In effect, our Constitution is lethal toward government officials who overstep their lawful delegated authority. The universal rule in this country today is that a law enforcement officer—whether he be a federal or a state officer—must afford to every citizen the full rights of all the Amendments, particularly the Fourth, Fifth, and Sixth. If incriminating statements are made to the police during an illegal search, those statements are inadmissible because they were obtained in violation of the Fourth Amendment right against unreasonable searches and seizures.

If a police officer does not give the Miranda warnings to an accused person in an in-custody interrogation setting, any statement made by the accused person is not admissible at trial because the officer is depriving the person of his Fifth Amendment right against self-incrimination.

If the police attempt to keep an attorney away from his client while they are interrogating him, the suspect's Sixth Amendment right to counsel is violated, and any statement obtained by the police would have to be suppressed.

The Supreme Court has not set up a lot of technical rules concerning police techniques and interrogation; rather, the Court has found effective ways to prevent each individual's constitutional rights from being eroded.

THE WAIVER

Compulsory incrimination is the result of a person's being forced by government to say something for which he can be punished. The Fifth Amendment has been interpreted to relate almost exclusively to testimonial compulsion. As an example, the Supreme Court has indicated that the taking of blood samples in no way affects someone's rights under the Fifth Amendment. A "confession" is broadly defined as someone's admission of all the elements of a crime, while, in contrast, an "admission" is defined as an admission of some elements of a crime or the declaring of facts inconsistent with innocence.

A person may waive his constitutional right not to incriminate himself if he does so knowingly, intelligently, and voluntarily. In other words, a person can, in effect, say, "I know that I have a right under the Fifth Amendment not to say anything which might subject me to punishment, but I don't care." In order that constitutional rights not be whittled away, the Supreme Court demands a high quality of proof by the prosecution to establish a waiver. The Miranda opinion declares that the burden on the government at a suppression hearing for establishing a waiver under the Fifth Amendment is a particularly severe one because the proof of the waiver must be established by clear and convincing evidence. This places a particularly grave evidentiary problem on the prosecution at the suppression hearing.

Because the Fifth Amendment and the Supreme Court require substantial evidence of a "free and voluntary" waiver, law enforcement officers should make every effort to record the factual circumstances of an interrogation. To this end, some police departments are utilizing videotapes of interrogations, since doing this assures the preservation of all the details and circumstances surrounding an interrogation for use at a suppression hearing. Other police departments make sound transcriptions or invite independent, neutral witnesses into interrogations so that they may later testify to the conditions surrounding the interrogation.

It is strongly recommended that police, at a bare minimum, obtain a written waiver of the suspect's Fifth Amendment right against self-incrimination—certainly to establish that he received the Miranda warnings.

It is also highly advisable to make detailed logs of the interrogation; that is, outlining the time the interrogation began, the length of the various interrogations, the length of any interruptions, and all the circumstances surrounding the questioning by the police. At a suppression hearing, all of the circumstances surrounding the obtaining of a confession are important so it is a good idea to record those circumstances by making notations and observations as they relate to a particular interrogation. Since the Miranda decision requires that the Miranda warnings be given prior to any questioning, a particularly important notation for an interrogation log would be to show that the Miranda warnings were given prior to any questioning by the police.

IMMUNITY

There are a number of statutes, state and federal, that provide for giving a person immunity from prosecution so that his testimony may be obtained. Immunity—a creature of statutes—can be granted by the court, usually on application of the prosecutor where the court and the prosecutor believe that it is more important to have the witness's testimony than to punish him.

If a court grants immunity, it means that the person to whom the immunity is granted cannot be prosecuted for any crime that he testifies about. This means that the Fifth Amendment would not be violated. If he is granted immunity—although he is forced to speak—he cannot be punished by the government for anything that he says.

Once the court makes someone immune and orders him to testify, that person must testify or suffer the consequences of a contempt proceeding, based on the refusal of the person to obey a lawful court order to testify. Usually a person who refuses to testify is put in jail and, in effect, given the key to his own release, because he will be released only when he decides to obey the court and testify. There are limitations on the length of time a person can be held in jail on contempt, but generally the court's contempt powers are strong enough to obtain the needed testimony.

Immunity is a powerful weapon in law enforcement's arsenal against highly insulated organized criminals. Since organized crime's first line of defense is intimidation of prosecution witnesses, immunization of witnesses by courts can aid in obtaining desperately needed evidence to break up existing powerful criminal conspiracies.

POLICE INVESTIGATIVE POWERS

Whenever a police officer sees something unusual or suspicious, he has not only the right but also the duty to investigate. It is critical, however, that the officer use only police investigative powers in contrast with police arrest powers.

STOPPING. A police officer should not stop anyone either walking or driving a car unless something unusual or suspicious draws the officer into an inquiry. Police justification for stopping a citizen is evaluated by the courts at the moment the stop is made and not by what turns up after the stop. If a police officer has absolutely no reason to stop a person, even the limited restraint in stopping the person will probably be declared an unreasonable seizure under the Fourth Amendment.

PROTECTIVE FRISK. A protective frisk is not an investigative technique. It can only be used by an officer when he justifiably begins an investigation, stops someone and has a reasonable fear for his safety. The protective frisk cannot be used as a subterfuge to search for incriminating evidence – it may be used only to protect the officer from harm.

QUESTIONING. It is clear that if an officer sees something unusual or suspicious, he has both the right and the duty to investigate. That right and duty includes questioning persons who are acting suspiciously. There is no barrier to questioning because of the Miranda warnings. An officer does not have to warn anyone of his constitutional rights under the Fifth Amendment unless he intends to arrest the person. Also, the Miranda rule does not apply to general investigations into suspicious conduct or unsolved crimes. The Miranda warnings apply to in-custody or station house police interrogation or to interrogations by the police where they intend or should have intended to arrest someone.

In *Terry v. Ohio,* Mr. Justice White, in a concurring opinion, shed some light on the questioning of suspicious persons in a street encounter setting:

"... *There is nothing in the Constitution which prevents a policeman from addressing questions to anyone on the streets.* Absent special circumstances, the person approached may not be detained or frisked but may refuse to cooperate and go on his way. . . . However, given the proper circumstances, such as those in this case, it seems to me a person may be briefly detained against his will while pertinent questions are directed to him. Of course, the person stopped is not obliged to answer, answers may not be compelled, and refusal to answer furnishes no basis for an arrest, although it may alert the officer to the need for continued observation." (Emphasis added.)

DETAINING. When conducting inquiries or investigations in the field—as distinguished from the station house—police have the limited right to detain suspects while their threshold investigation is developing. There is no set formula for how long a police officer may detain someone on the street or in his car. The general rule is that the officer's right to detain increases directly with the number and seriousness of the suspicious facts or circumstances unfolding before the officer. As sinister facts evolve in increasing strength toward establishing probable cause, the officer's right to detain increases in direct proportion. A vital factor here is the seriousness of the crime that the officer believes he is investigating. In investigating crimes of violence, the officer would have great latitude in detaining a suspect.

BINOCULARS AND CAMERAS. So far there have not been any limitations imposed by the courts on the police in the use of binoculars or cameras in their investigations. There have, however, been several severe challenges to the use of these instruments as investigative tools, and it is essential that whenever these devices are employed by law enforcement officers they should be used reasonably. Both binoculars and cameras in the hands of the police can be destructive to individual rights to privacy.

UNDERCOVER AGENTS. Certainly one of the most effective investigative techniques against continuing criminal conspiracies is the use of an undercover agent. Investigations with undercover agents have been particularly significant in the organized crime field. Since one of the principal difficulties in combatting organized crime is getting witnesses, an effective undercover agent produces valuable intelligence information on the criminal group he is investigating and is a willing witness for the prosecution.

The courts have not imposed any general limitations on the use of undercover agents by law enforcement. Recently, however, the American Civil Liberties Union started a drive to require law enforcement agencies to go to the courts whenever they want to "plant" an undercover agent anywhere. This proposal would require the police to go through the same procedures for using undercover agents as are now required by the search warrant process. While the ACLU's efforts in the area have not been adopted by the courts, they do show the trend of the times.

ELECTRONIC EAVESDROPPING

PENN REGISTER. A Penn Register is an electronic device which, when placed on a telephone line, will identify telephone numbers called. The Supreme Court of the United States has not ruled on the legality of this electronic device, but there are several higher federal appellate court decisions that equate the Penn Register techniques with wiretapping. In these cases the use of the Penn Register device has been declared illegal as a violation of Section 605 of the Federal Communications Act. The legal authority is somewhat divided, but it would appear that under existing law, unless there is a statute authorizing court-approved use of the Penn Register, evidence obtained by the police by means of a Penn Register would, in all likelihood, be suppressed.

WIRETAPPING. In June of 1968, the Congress of the United States enacted a statute that authorizes closely supervised, court-approved electronic eavesdropping by federal investigative officers to combat certain serious criminal activity—primarily organized crime. This statute permits both wiretapping and electronic eavesdropping by federal agents under strict federal court supervision.

This new legislation does not empower state law enforcement officers to use electronic eavesdropping devices. In order for state officers to use this investigative technique, there has to be a state statute authorizing the electronic interception of criminal conversations under close court supervision. As an example, New York State has also recently enacted a new electronic eavesdropping statute authorizing state and local police to use electronic listening devices under close court supervision. Therefore, both federal and New York State law would permit state and local officers to use this investigative technique in New York State. In contrast, Pennsylvania has a total ban on wiretapping which would prevent state or local law enforcement officers in Pennsylvania from using electronic listening devices to combat serious crime.

RADIO TRANSMITTING BUG. According to the testimony of scientific experts before Congress, we are now in the third generation of listening devices. Radio transmitters called microcircuits can now be made so small that hundreds can be hidden in an ordinary six-cent postage stamp. The life span of these "bugs" is indefinite since they siphon all the energy they need from a local radio broadcast.

The Supreme Court of the United States, in the Berger decision, indicated strongly that the Fourth Amendment protects our right to privacy in our conversations and clearly established that the use of electronic eavesdropping devices by the police without a court order would be the equivalent of an unreasonable search and seizure of someone's conversation.

One big question is whether or not electronic eavesdropping devices, such as a microcircuit or radio transmitter bug, may be placed, even with a court order, in areas that are not open to the public. From the tenor of recent Supreme Court decisions in this area, it appears that courts can order police to trespass and install listening devices.

WALKING BUG. Another investigative technique is to install a listening device on a person who the police know is going to engage in a criminal conversation regarding a crime. The Supreme Court of the United States has indicated that so long as the witness testifies at trial against the accused, the captured, recorded criminal conversation of the defendant is admissible for corroboration of the government witness.

Law enforcement officers, whether they be federal, state or local, who want to utilize the walking bug investigative technique must obtain prior court approval.

MAIL COVER. In serious cases, the United States postal inspectors will operate a mail cover. This investigative technique entails the recording of details that appear on the outside envelopes of letters. The postal inspectors, without in any way delaying the mail, make a notation of the addressor and addressee of each letter as well as other pertinent data that appears on the outside of the envelopes. Federal courts have ruled that the mail cover is a lawful investigative technique; however, its use—particularly in recent years—has been narrowly limited by the Post Office Department. At the present time requests for mail covers will be honored by the Post Office Department only where there is a particularly serious crime or where there is a fugitive wanted for a grave offense.

LIE DETECTOR TEST. Lie detectors have been used a great deal by investigators as an interrogation technique. The results of the lie detector test are generally not admissible in evidence, so the primary purpose of using a lie detector has tended to limit its effectiveness to the investigative stage as compared with the trial level of a criminal prosecution.

Because of the Supreme Court's disapproval of lie detectors, police should be extremely cautious in using them as aids to interrogation—particularly if the object of the interrogation is to obtain incriminating evidence against the suspect.

BLOOD AND ALCOHOL SAMPLES. The Supreme Court of the United States, in a 5-4 opinion in *Schmerber v. California,* 384 U.S. 757 (1966), approved the compulsory taking of a blood sample by a physician in a hospital where the accused was suspected of drunken driving. The Court found that neither Fourth, Fifth, Six or Fourteenth Amendments were violated in the obtaining of blood samples under the circumstances in the case. The Court stressed the manner in which the blood was taken and the fact that the officer did not have time to get a court order to take the blood sample, and that the taking of the sample was, in effect, an appropriate search incidental to Schmerber's arrest. Once again, the Supreme Court urged caution and restraint.

Note: The Supreme Court has stated that the Fifth Amendment privilege against self-incimination

> ". . . offers no protection against compulsion to submit to fingerprinting, photographing or measurements, to write or speak for identification, to appear in Court, to stand, to assume a stance, to walk, or to make an appropriate gesture."
>
> *United States v. Wade*, 388 U.S. 218, quoting *Schmerber v. California.*

In *Gilbert v. California*, 388 U.S. 263, the Supreme Court of the United States held that the taking of handwriting specimens does not violate constitutional rights of a suspect.

HAIR SAMPLES. Whenever the police want to obtain hair samples or fingernail samples, it is essential for them to go to the courts and get orders permitting them to obtain the samples. This gives maximum protection to the accused, to the police, and to assuring that the evidence will be admissible at trial.

LINEUP. The Supreme Court of the United States has in several opinions demanded fair police practices concerning lineups. If the investigating officers do not comply with the Supreme Court rules, the testimony concerning the pretrial identification will be suppressed. The high Court held, in *United States v. Wade,* 388 U.S. 218, and *Gilbert v. California,* 388 U.S. 263, that pretrial confrontations for the purposes of identification are critical stages of a criminal proceeding and that, therefore, the accused has the right to counsel under the Sixth Amendment. Consequently, attorneys representing accused persons must be advised in advance of the proposed lineup, so that they can protect their clients' constitutional rights and assure fairness in the procedures at the lineup. Failure to comply with the Sixth Amendment right to counsel at the lineup will inevitably result in suppressing testimony concerning the pretrial identification of the defendant.

The Congress of the United States, in the Omnibus Crime Bill enacted in June of 1968, has attempted to nullify this Supreme Court rule regarding pretrial identification of the accused by means of a lineup. This legislative attempt to nullify a constitutional rule will also probably result—according to the experts—in that portion of the Crime Bill being declared unconstitutional.

Police should do everything they can to make lineups as fair as they possibly can, so that the identification evidence elicited will be admissible at trial.

USE OF INFORMANTS. The major legal problem for the prosecution regarding the use of informants is deflecting the attacks by the defense attorney attempting to force the prosecution to identify or produce the informant.

At the investigative and arrest-search level, the defense attorney's success depends in large measure on the percentage of probable cause that the confidential informant supplied to the police. In fact, if ninety-nine per cent of the probable cause justifying a search or an arrest consists of the hearsay accusations of a confidential informant, the only way the reliability of that information can be tested is by identifying and producing the informant for cross-examination. If the confidential informant's contribution to probable cause is a much lower percentage of the probable cause, then the likelihood of a court forcing the identity or the production of the informant would be minimal.

The prosecution does not have to identify or produce a confidential informant even if ordered to do so by a court. On the authority of the ancient governmental privilege to protect informants, the prosecution may refuse to produce the informant, but at the arrest-search level the judge would have to declare the arrest or search illegal.

At the trial level, if a confidential informant was a material witness to a crime, the government must produce the informant or the court will dismiss the indictment.

Another area of caution for the prosecution in the use of informants is to make sure that the informant does not in any way interfere or impinge upon an accused's consultation with his lawyer. In one of the Hoffa cases, *Hoffa v. United States*, 385 U.S. 293 (1966), a paid informant was spying on Hoffa during the course of his trial on charges of violating the Taft-Hartley Act. The informant reported to the federal officers the activities of Hoffa that he witnessed in Hoffa's hotel suite. All of the incriminating statements made by Hoffa to the informant were made when none of Hoffa's lawyers was present.

The best rule here is to make sure that informants do not in any way enter upon the lawful consultations between lawyers and clients.

EVIDENCE FROM PRIVATE PERSONS. If a private person steals or illegally seizes incriminating evidence from someone and turns it over to the police, that evidence is admissible against the accused so long as the police did not in any way participate in the illegal seizure of the evidence. *Burdeau v. McDowell*, 256 U.S. 465 (1921). Citizens, private detectives, store detectives, security guards, and all other persons who are not connected with any official agency of government are not under the strictures of the Fourth Amendment because the Supreme Court of the United States has indicated that this amendment protects the citizen from illegal conduct by government officials only. If a citizen is wronged by another private citizen, his remedy is to sue civilly. It is significant to note that private citizens are not bound by Fifth Amendment rules, either. Therefore, private citizens do not have to give the Miranda warnings if they ask someone questions.

This rule relating to the seizing of incriminating evidence by private citizens has not been reaffirmed by the Supreme Court directly in the last 47 years. This means that the rule concerning private citizens crystallized four decades before the legal explosion in constitutional rights in the 1960's. Whether or not the Supreme Court of the United States, following in the wake of the constitutional rights explosion, will modify or change the Burdeau Rule is anybody's guess.

CHAPTER III

ARREST

ARREST DEFINED

An arrest is, in effect, the beginning of imprisonment, when a man is first taken by government and restrained of his liberty. An arrest by lawful authority takes away a person's freedom and places him in the custody of the law.

The law of arrest is basically uniform in all the 50 states as well as under the federal criminal procedures. The law of arrest in America has not varied significantly from the law of arrest that evolved 350 years ago under the English Common Law. The basic foundations of all our arrest laws are those that were firmly planted in our early Common Law heritage.

An arrest has been defined as:

> "The apprehending or restraining of one's person in order to be forthcoming to answer an alleged or suspected crime."
>
> 4 *Blackstone's Commentaries* 289, p. 1679 (1897 Ed.)

American courts have never had much difficulty in finding dramatic definitions of arrest in our legal heritage, but many judges have had great difficulty in applying hard, realistic facts to these definitions.

It is essential to appreciate that the word "arrest," when appearing in the context of a criminal search and seizure problem, is not the same word as "arrest" as the word is used in civil cases. In false arrest or false imprisonment cases, "*any* restraint upon one's liberty to come and go as he pleases, however slight, is an arrest." *Swetnam v. F. W. Woolworth*

Co., 83 Ariz. 189, 318 P. 2d 364 (1957). The sole test in civil cases of an "arrest" is literally *any restraint.*

FOUR ELEMENTS OF A CRIMINAL ARREST. In a criminal arrest there are four distinct elements that must coalesce to constitute a legal arrest. These four essential elements of a criminal arrest are:

(a) An *intent* by the peace officer to make an arrest.

(b) Real or pretended *authority* to arrest.

(c) A *seizure* or *restraint*, actual or constructive.

(d) An *understanding* by the person being seized that he is being arrested.

In the "criminal arrest" as distinguished from the "civil arrest" situation, all four of these critical factors must be present in one degree or another. These four pivotal facts will always determine whether an arrest has occurred as well as the first vital arrest issue: the *time* the arrest occurred.

In a suppression hearing on a warrantless arrest-search situation, the court has the sole responsibility to determine factually from the circumstances in the case—if there actually was an arrest and assuming there was an arrest, the exact moment the arrest occurred. Arrest, then, is a question of fact for the judge to decide on the basis of the testimony at the hearing.

The way the judge determines whether or not an arrest occurred factually is by applying the law of criminal arrest to the facts in each case. Basically, the court looks to see what the officer's *purpose* was, to see what he *knew* or *observed*, and to see what he *did*. By focusing on these three aspects of the case, the court can intelligently rule on both the fact and the time of arrest.

Of these three determinants to an arrest, the most important from a practical point of view is *what the officer did.* For if an officer uses a police arrest power in a confrontation with a suspicious person, the court must declare the fact of an arrest as the moment the officer used an arrest power.

POLICE ARREST POWERS

(a) *Force*
(b) *Search*
(c) *Seizure or restraint*

Any time a police officer uses one of these three arrest powers he in effect rings the constitutional bell or—if you will—the Liberty Bell. Justification or probable cause for using the police arrest power must be present *before* the power is invoked.

FORCE

When a police officer uses force on a citizen, he has arrested him. Police in this country have no power to use force indiscriminately against citizens. Under law—particularly the Fourth Amendment—an officer may use *reasonable force* for two reasons: to protect himself or to arrest. The use of force also constitutes a seizure or restraint, depending on its intensity. The use of force by police on the citizen is then the strongest irrefutable evidence of an arrest.

SEARCH

A search can be defined as the looking into or prying into hidden places. The term search in the context of the Fourth Amendment implies a governmental investigation or arrest. Searches are intrusions into privacy with the purpose of obtaining incriminating evidence.

Police get the power to search by a search warrant, by consent, or by making a lawful arrest. A search incident to an arrest is permitted basically to protect the officer, and it must be made at the same time as the arrest. Its scope is limited to the accused and the immediate area under his control. Consequently, when an officer starts to make a search on his own, he is using a police arrest power and will be judged by the courts on the facts that occurred prior to the search—not after. A search may never be justified by the incriminating evidence it turns up. In brief then, when a police officer begins a search of someone – on his own – the court must declare an arrest since the officer used an arrest power. The time of the arrest would have to be the moment the search began. The justification for the arrest would be every probable cause fact that occurred chronologically before the search began.

SEIZURE AND RESTRAINT

Seizure and restraint are in reality actual or constructive *control* of a suspect by the police. They are arrest powers. Actual control of a person by an officer would be a *seizure*, while constructive control over a citizen would be a *restraint*. In determining whether a seizure or restraint has occurred, the court must fully explore what the officer intended to do and what he actually did. The most difficult factual decisions concerning arrest are in this area of seizure and restraint. Subtle factual settings, difficult to interpret and offering a wide range of judicial discretion, frequently develop in this area. Cases involving the issue of seizure or restraint offer the greatest legal challenge to the court, the prosecution and the defense. Needless to say, it is an area where technicalities should never reign. Common sense and a realistic attitude toward the Fourth Amendment should determine the issue here.

TIME OF ARREST

At a suppression hearing, the exact moment that a warrantless arrest occurred is frequently the most important preliminary determination for a court. The legality of a warrantless arrest hinges, in large measure, on the probable cause or guilt-laden facts confronting the police officer up to and including, but never after, the actual moment of arrest. At the moment of arrest, probable cause ceases to build. Any after-the-arrest, guilt-laden facts that develop will not be considered by the courts as part of the guilt-laden facts necessary to justify the arrest.

EXAMPLE—BOSURGI CASE—ANALYSIS OF FACTS

(a) Fact of a *known felony*—burglary of a wholesale jewelry store.

(b) Police investigation of the neighborhood.

(c) An anonymous call—information that suspect was trying to sell watches in a neighborhood taproom, plus a detailed description of suspect.

(d) Detectives see Bosurgi in a taproom across from the one mentioned in the anonymous phone call and obtain instant corroboration of the anonymous caller's detailed description of suspect.

(e) The finding of ten watches by the detectives.

(f) The finding of particles of glass in Bosurgi's trousers.

The key problem for the court was to determine from the circumstances surrounding the arrest the exact moment that the arrest of Bosurgi occurred. Did the arrest occur after fact (d)—when the officers commanded Bosurgi to stand up—but before facts (e) and (f) the discovery of the watches and the glass particles? If the arrest occurred before the watches and glass particles were found, then these two highly charged guilt-laden facts could not help justify Bosurgi's arrest. Guilt-laden facts discovered after an arrest cannot be used to justify the arrest.

Facts showing the intent of the officers to arrest and facts demonstrating that a seizure or restraint occurred are the most important factors in determining if an arrest occurred and when the arrest occurred.

In the Bosurgi case, the Philadelphia detectives directed Bosurgi to stand up and turn around and then, after a pat-down search for evidence (not a frisk for the safety of the officers) the detectives felt bulky objects like watches and went into Bosurgi's trousers to seize them.

Justice Benjamin R. Jones applied the law of arrest to these facts:

> Was Bosurgi under arrest at the time of the search of his person? Officers are not required to make any formal declaration of arrest or use the word "arrest" (*Commonwealth v. Holmes*, 344 Mass. 524, 526, 183 N.E. 2d 279,

> 280, 281) nor to apply manual force or exercise "such physical restraint as to be visible to the eye" in order to *arrest* a person. *McAleer v. Good*, 216 Pa. 473, 475, 65 A. 934. An arrest may be accomplished by "any act that indicates an intention to take [a person] into custody and that subjects him to the actual control and will of the person making the arrest." 5 Am. Jur. 2d, Arrest, Sec. 1, p. 695. In the case at bar, Bosurgi was completely in the custody of and under the actual control of the police officers. Moreover, by his actions, Bosurgi submitted to the restraint implicit in an arrest. *Thus Bosurgi was under arrest when the search was made.*
>
> (Emphasis added.)

So the Supreme Court of Pennsylvania concluded that the stolen watches and the glass particles could not be considered as part of the probable cause for Bosurgi's arrest because the arrest in fact occurred before these two vital pieces of incriminating evidence were found. To hold otherwise would set the dangerous precedent of permitting police to justify an arrest by what they turn up later. But the court in *Bosurgi* continued to analyze facts (a), (b), (c), and (d) and held there was sufficient probable cause to justify Bosurgi's arrest before the watches and pieces of glass were found so that the subsequent search by the detectives was reasonable.

Of the circumstances surrounding the arrest, facts showing the intent of the officer to arrest and facts demonstrating that a seizure or restraint occurred, are the most important determinative factors as to whether an arrest occurred and when the arrest occurred.

Since approximately ninety per cent of all arrests are made without arrest warrants in this country, it is undeniably clear that the time an arrest occurs is the first critical step for the prosecution in establishing the probable cause for the arrest. At the suppression hearing involving a warrantless arrest, defense counsel's first line of attack is to establish factually the earliest possible time of arrest. Defense counsel generally take the position that if the accused was stopped by a police officer he was arrested. At that point, of course, the police officer would generally have little or no probable cause to justify an arrest. If the accused makes a devastating admission soon after he is accosted by a police officer, defense counsel's only chance to prevent that damaging admission from justifying the arrest is to convince the court that the moment of arrest occurred by the stopping or accosting of his client by the police. The prosecutor at a suppression hearing involving a warrantless arrest has to argue to the court that the arrest occurred at the last practical moment so that all available guilt-laden facts, such as the damaging admission, may be considered by the court as part of the probable cause justifying the arrest.

Of the four facts that determine if there was an arrest and when it occurred, the element of the intent of the officer and the element of the seizure or restraint are the most important from a practical suppression point of view. This is true because a law enforcement officer nearly always acts in the arrest area by virtue of his police authority and because the accused at the suppression hearing invariably takes the position most advantageous to him—that he thought he was arrested when the officer first looked in his direction. The authority element and the intent of submision to arrest by the accused are generally foregone conclusions at the suppression hearing.

INTENT TO INVESTIGATE OR TO ARREST

Of the four necessary elements in an arrest, the police officer's *purpose* or *intent* when confronting a suspect is of paramount significance in the determination of an arrest. From a realistic point of view, an officer's purpose is projected objectively in arrest situations only by evaluating critically what he said and what he did from the first moment he accosted the accused until the moment it is clear beyond peradventure that the accused was in custody.

Situations in which there can be no doubt when an officer makes an arrest are extremely rare. Police officers generally do not – particularly in the arrest without a warrant category – solemnize an arrest by formal words such as, "Under the Sovereign Laws of the State of Minnesota I hereby arrest you for burglary." Nor, as a matter of practical experience, does the officer at the moment of arrest formally symbolize the arrest by seizing the accused. Arrests most frequently occur without formalities, in the background of quickly emerging facts and in the absence of an iron-clad conclusive arrest fact such as the handcuffing of an accused. The time of the arrest depends, in large measure, on the officer's purpose. Without some conclusive evidence of seizure or restraint, the officer's purpose as demonstrated by his words and his actions, holds the key for the courts to determine when the arrest in fact occurred.

From many recent cases, both state and federal, there is a newly emerging legal principle that focuses upon the distinction between an officer's purpose to investigate and his purpose to arrest. Where it is apparent from the officer's action that he is investigating something suspicious rather than nothing, the courts are taking the position that officers have not only the right but also the duty to investigate. Officers pursuing facts with genuine investigative purpose are not being penalized by the court's finding of an early arrest. A police officer who investigates suspicious facts or unusual conduct gets four additional specific investigative powers so far as the courts and the Fourth Amendment are concerned. The right to stop, the right to frisk for safety, the right to detain, and the right to question – without having the court declare a technical arrest – are the four powers given to officers to pursue suspicious or unusual conduct where there are insufficient guilt-laden facts to justify an arrest. As the suspicious facts grow, any judicial doubts of the officer's genuine investigative purpose disappear. The officer's stop-frisk, detention, and questioning powers are strengthened without the penalty of a premature technical arrest being declared. It is rapidly becoming axiomatic that courts encourage investigation by the police to prevent crime and to protect the citizen. But investigation does not include the seizing of people without cause or without sufficient facts so that the crime can be found out later.

When the officer's arbitrary arrest purpose shows through, when the officer's naked purpose is to arrest and find the crime later, then courts impose their full sanctions on the officer by construing the technical moment of arrest at the earliest possible moment.

From a professional police point of view, law enforcement officers should attempt to squeeze every ounce of investigation available when confronted with difficult street situations. Street interrogation, limited street detention, rapid relaying of information, and genuine invitations for identification or explanation are all encouraged by the courts.

SEIZURE OR RESTRAINT REVISITED

The law of arrest uniformly holds that virtually any restraint by a police officer, no matter how slight, when coupled with an intent by the officer to arrest, constitutes a technical arrest. What law enforcement officers fail to realize is that the courts automatically infer a police officer's intent to arrest where officers demonstrate they are operating on "Gestapo" hunches rather than investigating facts. When a confrontation of a police officer with a citizen gives the appearance of arbitrary, unreasonable conduct by the officer, usually slight restraints will be interpreted by the courts as a technical arrest.

Seemingly the greatest variable in the arrest concept and one that troubles police, lawyers, and courts alike is in this area of seizure or restraint. While an arrest can occur only where there has been a "taking into custody," control may be constructively assumed by the police without actual force, and in some cases without any visual restraint. Of course, a physical touching of the accused person is not essential, either. Seizure or restraint can arise from any act, from brute force to police command. Factual variations are virtually unlimited. Grabbing a suspect, laying hands on a suspect—no matter how lightly—preventing a suspect from leaving, forcing a suspect into an enclosed place, taking someone against his will to a place where he is unwilling to go, stopping someone and demanding to know what he has in a package, commanding someone to throw up his hands, and extending "royal invitations" to come and see the Captain, can all be interpreted as actions manifesting an intent by a police officer to take someone into custody. All of these actions, in varying degrees, demonstrate seizures and restraints. But it is important to consider that these kinds of actions are not judged by the courts in isolation. They are judged by reviewing them in the context of their surrounding circumstances.

One indestructible axiom emerges: when police officers are investigating – following up guilt-laden facts – without utilizing arrest powers of force, or search or seizure, the courts will *not* construe technical arrests against them. Conversely, when officers operate forcefully on minimal or nonexistent threshold facts, courts are quick to construe seemingly inconsequential restraints as technical arrests. This assures the citizen freedom from unnecessary, unwarranted police intrusion into his privacy.

When the officers are on a witch-hunt – without sufficient suspicious circumstances to investigate anything – courts will determine that a technical arrest has, in fact, occurred. Invoking full police powers on loose suspicion and unfounded conjecture is never condoned by the courts. It is in this background that constitutional rights to be let alone assume their full proportion.

The element of seizure or restraint as contained in the law of arrest looms more ominously for the police in cases in which the officers lack suspicious facts. Slight restraint, such as stopping cars, in a background of no suspicious facts, will be construed by the courts to constitute an arrest, while strong restraint or even seizure in a setting of strong suspicious facts may not be declared an arrest by the courts. Where there are suspicious facts, officers must investigate; an emergency exists, and the police must be free to act without fear of legal technicalities.

ARREST WITH A WARRANT

Police should obtain an arrest warrant whenever possible. In this way, the officer avoids taking the law – or the citizen's fate – into his own hands.

An arrest warrant, the product of an impartial judicial officer, determines that an arrest should be made and orders its execution. Prior justification – probable cause under oath – is the part of the arrest warrant that shields the citizen and guarantees justice through the Fourth Amendment.

Arrests without arrest warrants should be made only when there is an emergency requiring immediate police action. It is not a fatal defect if police fail to get an arrest warrant – or even a search warrant – where there is time to do so, but this omission is very important in a discussion of the totality of circumstances determining the reasonableness of the arrest or search.

CONCLUSION

Arrest today is a "doomsday" device. Police records and computers indelibly put the "mark of Cain" on any citizen who is arrested. His criminal record will pursue him all the days of his life. Educational and employment opportunities narrow drastically for anyone who has been arrested in this country and with our frontier now gone, the man with a record has nowhere to go but down.

Police arrest powers, then, in modern 20th-century America are indeed awesome powers. These police arrest powers have both the power to protect society and the power to destroy the citizen. The Fourth Amendment was designed to limit the chances of a citizen being destroyed – unfairly or unjustly. The courts have the responsibility to make sure the Fourth Amendment works to protect the citizen and, at the same time, assure the security of society.

CHAPTER IV

SEARCH AND SEIZURE

THE SEARCH WARRANT

Important: Whenever you want to search a person or a place and can get a search warrant—*get a search warrant.*

If you have time, *get a search warrant.*

If you have any hesitation about marginal or thin probable cause, *get a search warrant.*

If you want to search an entire building or an entire apartment, you must *get a search warrant.*

If you want to search somewhere and you do not anticipate making an arrest, you must *get a search warrant.*

WHEN YOU DON'T NEED TO GET A SEARCH WARRANT

If you make a lawful arrest you may search the person and the immediate area under his control to protect yourself and to prevent the destruction of evidence.

If you make a lawful arrest of a man driving a car, you may search his person and the entire car without a warrant if you search immediately at the time of the arrest, whether the arrest is for a misdemeanor or a felony. You have this power in order to protect yourself and to prevent the destruction of evidence.

If emergency circumstances exist, such as the necessity of saving a life or of capturing a dangerous criminal by hot pursuit, you may search without a warrant.

WHAT YOU NEED TO GET A SEARCH WARRANT

PROBABLE CAUSE

Probable cause is an absolute necessity when obtaining a search warrant. Probable cause, which consists of facts or apparent facts that are reliable and would generate a reasonable belief that crime has been committed, must be set forth in the affidavit for the search warrant. The Fourth Amendment requires that the essential facts establishing criminality be set forth specifically in the affidavit. The affidavit for a search warrant is, in effect, an application, under oath, for a search warrant.

Since probable cause is deduced from a combination of facts, it is important for the police officer to set forth in his affidavit every sinister and guilt-laden fact that he has knowledge of. From a probable cause point of view, a search warrant affidavit becomes increasingly strong with each added fact.

Probable cause facts are generally sinister, guilt-laden facts in combination which persuasively generate a reasonable belief that someone has committed a crime or that contraband, stolen property, the instrumentality of a crime, or evidence of a crime are at a particular place.

There are many recurring factual variations on the probable cause theme. Some of the principal ones are:

TIME AND PLACE. Facts about the time and place where suspicious conduct begins to unfold can be particularly significant as far as probable cause is concerned. If, for instance, a mysterious car is seen in the vicinity of a shopping center at about three o'clock in the morning, these facts are particularly powerful as far as probable cause is concerned.

INFORMATION. Information may come from informants, from fellow officers, or from a variety of other sources. Any kind of reasonably trustworthy information of a general accusatory nature that is received from other people contributes substantially toward establishing probable cause. At the arrest-search level, information is the primary building block of probable cause and there is virtually no restriction on the use of this type of probable cause by the police at this level of a criminal proceeding.

SURVEILLANCE. Any facts observed by police surveillance or by anyone else can contribute toward establishing probable cause. Recurring factual patterns of daily conduct such as those found in a numbers operation are particularly significant factors of probable cause when coupled with police expertise about the functioning of a gambling operation.

PRIOR KNOWLEDGE. Any prior knowledge that an officer has concerning a person or crime contributes toward establishing probable cause. It is particularly significant to realize that a criminal arrest or a conviction record has been universally recognized by the courts as an element of probable cause. While this type of evidence is prejudicial and inadmissible at trial, it is nonetheless completely relevant and admissible at the arrest-search level.

FLIGHT. The fact of flight from a police officer is universally recognized as a guilt-laden probable cause fact.

ADMISSIONS. Any admissions to police officers before an actual arrest are also facts which the courts recognize as establishing probable cause. Not only are admissions factors in showing probable cause, but evasive answers constitute probable cause facts as well

These are just a few of the general factual variations that many courts have declared to be elements establishing probable cause. It is the combination of facts such as these that persuasively establish the "reasonable belief" necessary for obtaining warrants.

WHAT YOU CAN SEARCH FOR

You can get a search warrant for and seize the following types of property:

THE FRUITS OF A CRIME. (Stolen or embezzled property.)

THE INSTRUMENTALITY OF A CRIME. (Property designed, used, or intended to be used as a means of committing a crime.)

CONTRABAND. (Property which is unlawful to possess, such as narcotics.)

EVIDENTIARY PROPERTY. (Property which would aid in apprehending and convicting criminals, such as blood-stained clothing. There must be a logical connection between the evidentiary property seized and criminal behavior.)

Be sure to state which kind of property you are searching for.

WHERE YOU CAN SEARCH

A search on authority of a search warrant gives the officers the power to make a complete and thorough search of the entire premises described in the warrant. The only restriction here is that the search must be performed in a manner consistent with the type of property the search warrant indicates the premises is being searched for. For instance, a search of bureau and desk drawers cannot be made under the authority of a search warrant for stolen TV sets.

WHAT YOU CAN SEIZE

So long as the manner of the search is consistent with the property being searched for, (for example, floor boards should not be ripped up looking for a stolen elephant from the circus!) any property connected with any crime, even though not described or listed in the search warrant, may be seized and will not be suppressed.

Contraband, stolen property, the instrumentality of crimes, or evidentiary property connected with a crime, even though not described in a search warrant, may nonetheless be seized by police if they find them in good faith while executing a search warrant for some other kind of property. If, while executing a search warrant for narcotics, police find something such as stolen TV sets, courts are in complete agreement that the TV sets may lawfully be seized by the police and will not be suppressed.

HOW TO DRAFT SEARCH WARRANT AFFIDAVITS

IDENTIFY THE PREMISES. The location where the search is to be made has to be absolutely clear. The purpose of describing the premises is to state in advance the definite area that is to be searched. Care must be taken so that there is no confusion about similar property in the area. Addresses must be right. A slight error in the address can completely nullify the search warrant.

In multiple-occupancy dwellings such as apartments or rooming houses, the particular apartment or room to be searched must be named specifically. While it is not essential to name the owner or occupant, police should do so if they are sure of his name since it reduces the likelihood of a mistake. If there is any likelihood of an error, a diagram of the place to be searched should be drawn.

IDENTIFY THE PROPERTY. Police must describe what is being searched for and what is to be seized. If the property is contraband, like narcotics, police can be somewhat general. Other property, such as stolen property, the instrumentality of a crime, or evidentiary property must be described in detail. The more detailed and accurate the description the better.

AFFIDAVIT UNDER OATH. The Fourth Amendment demands "probable cause under oath." Therefore, it is absolutely essential that the officer who gets the warrant swear that the facts establishing probable cause are true. This oath requirement for a search warrant is never dispensed with. It is a fatal flaw if the officer obtaining the warrant is never placed under oath. The oath requirement is not a super-technicality of the Fourth Amendment. The oath requirement is essential because it prevents accusations of "shadowy faceless accusers" who would otherwise not come forward into the light of day to make their charges.

PROBABLE CAUSE. The essential facts justifying the search must be set forth with particularity in the affidavit for the search warrant. This does not mean that search warrant affidavits should be long and technical. It means that search warrant affidavits should be short and persuasive.

In actually drafting search warrant affidavits, police should keep in mind the following guidelines:

Use the First Person Singular. In preparing search warrant affidavits, the officers should use the first person singular, "I." This keeps the facts pivoted upon the officer and satisfies the requirement that the officer set forth the facts from his own personal knowledge. One problem that recurs in a number of actual search warrant affidavits is the fact that when the officer fails to use the first person singular the facts have a tendency to float into outer space. The facts must be within the personal knowledge of the officer and he must swear that they are true to the best of his knowledge, information and belief. The best way to begin these affidavits is: "I, Officer Brown, ..."

Present Probable Cause. The sinister facts which combine to establish probable cause should be set forth clearly, consisely, and persuasively. The best method of setting forth the facts is chronologically. It is important to remember that since probable cause is established by the combination of guilt-laden facts, it is best to set forth all the sinister facts and circumstances known by the officer.

Avoid Police "Mandarin." Police "Mandarin" is a protective language barrier utilized by some police officers, particularly when testifying. It is noted for its precision which, regrettably, never establishes clarity. Police "Mandarin" was adopted by some law enforcement officers in the days before police professionalization to protect themselves from searing cross-examination by defense lawyers. While it worked in the old days, it has unfortunately been outflanked by professionalization of the police. The cardinal rule for police is to speak and write persuasively when challenged at the arrest-search level. Fog-bound, stilted, formalistic language, whether spoken or written, should be avoided.

Be Specific. In preparing probable cause affidavits, the officers should be as specific as possible as to the time that information was received or the time a surveillance was made. With regard to surveillance, it is important to indicate *who* made the surveillance.

Show the Source of Information. When a law enforcement officer is relying on information as part of his probable cause to justify a search, he should state the source of the information whenever possible. The Supreme Court of the United States has indicated clearly that one of the tests used by courts to evaluate the truthfulness of information obtained from others is to know as much as possible about the person who gave the information. Hearsay information relied upon by officers in the preparation of affidavits for search warrants is only as believable as its source. Whether the information comes from a saint or a sinner, a citizen or a child, an FBI agent or a snake oil salesman is particularly important to the courts in evaluating the likelihood of the truthfulness of the information. Therefore, whenever possible, the officer should indicate the source of the information he is relying upon in the probable cause affidavit.

If the source of the information is an informant, there are varying methods by which the officer can describe the informant without revealing his identity. As an example, the officer would set forth that he received information "from a confidential informant," "a confidential informant who has been reliable in the post," or "a confidential informant who has been reliable in the past in that he has supplied information to the police that resulted in the arrest of thirteen people and the conviction of two." As the description of the informant becomes stronger and more detailed, his information becomes more and more believable as far as the courts are concerned.

Corroborate Hearsay Information. A second test used by the courts to test the truthfulness of hearsay information used at the arrest-search level is whether or not the police have independently corroborated the information that was given to them. Where the source of information is weak, police investigation corroborating that information must be strong. When an officer receives information from any source he should attempt to independently corroborate any of the facts asserted in the information. Each time an officer is able to corroborate a fact contained in the information, he is establishing to the court's satisfaction the truth contained in the hearsay information.

"I Believe There is Presently . . ." It is essential for the officer who has obtained a search warrant to affirmatively state that he believes the contraband, stolen property, instrumentality of the crime, or evidentiary property in connection with the crime is now at the location to be searched. The officer's belief is based on the probable cause facts that he asserts in his probable cause affidavit.

Three General Hints. Finally, the three cardinal rules of preparing search warrant affidavits are:

Be brief.
Be specific.
Be persuasive.

EXECUTING A SEARCH WARRANT

WHO MUST BE PRESENT. A search warrant can be directed to a specific officer or to a class of officers (for example, to any officer in the Philadelphia Police Department). If an officer is mentioned specifically in a search warrant, he must be present at the time the search is made. Other officers not named in the warrant may assist in the search.

The person whose home or apartment is being searched does not have to be there at the time of the search. Searches may be and frequently are made with no one at home.

HOW TO GET IN

Peaceful Entry. So long as the officers who are executing a search warrant do not use force in obtaining entrance, there is no need to announce their authority and purpose. Stealth and stratagems to gain entrance may be used by the police and so long as no force is used, the officers need not announce their authority and purpose.

Forceful Entry. Whenever law enforcement officers use force to gain entrance to make a search, they must, under federal and state law, announce their authority and purpose. The announcement can be as brief as, "Police – search warrant," but it must be made before force is used to gain entrance. If the police are using subterfuge to gain entrance and have to combine it with force, they must, before they begin to use force, announce their authority and purpose. Some states have statutes which permit the judge who issues the search warrant to authorize a forceful entry without announcing authority and purpose. Whenever the issuing authority authorizes this type of an entry, the officers need not comply with the knocking and announcing of authority and purpose.

The rule requiring officers to knock and announce their authority and purpose comes from the Common Law and was basically designed to protect the lives of the officers executing a search warrant. Today many states are enacting meaningful legislation which would permit the officers to make forceful entries without knocking and announcing their authority and purpose whenever their lives would be in jeopardy or when there would be a great likelihood that evidence could be destroyed.

Multiple Entry. Once the officers executing the search warrant have announced their authority and purpose, the officers may enter the property to be searched at as many points as they desire.

LIMITATIONS UNDER A SEARCH WARRANT. Generally, police may search only premises, not people, under the authority of a search warrant. If someone commits a crime while they are making a search police may, of course, arrest him and search him incidental to the arrest, but a search warrant for premises gives the officer no right to search anyone on the premises.

There are two types of search warrants, one for premises and one for persons. If officers are executing a search warrant for a person they may search only the person.

The time of the search is limited to a reasonable amount of time. Unduly long searches appear to the courts as harassment and stand a great risk of being declared unreasonable. Some searches will, however, take a great deal of time to perform. Each case is decided on its own facts.

RESPONSIBILITY TO PERSON WHOSE HOME IS SEARCHED. Give the person whose premises were searched a copy of the warrant and a signed inventory of the property seized. If no one is there, leave a copy of the warrant and a signed inventory of the property seized.

RETURN TO ISSUING AUTHORITY. Return the original search warrant to the issuing authority after listing the inventory of items seized.

CONCLUSION

In our free society every citizen has an absolute right to privacy. When the police decide to use the full force of government and threaten that privacy they must, under our system of law, have prior justification. The Fourth Amendment dictates that this prior justification be "probable cause, under oath." This constitutional phrase protects the citizen against unwarranted, unfair police intrusions.

The Supreme Court of the United States has emphatically stated that it prefers law enforcement officers to obtain search warrants through the courts rather than have the officers take the law into their own hands, in effect, and search without warrants. To encourage police to get search warrants, the Supreme Court has indicated that it will review affidavits for search warrants in a nontechnical, commonsense, and realistic manner. The professional law enforcement officer must make every effort to master the technique of preparing search warrant affidavits in order to assure that incriminating evidence will not be suppressed needlessly. The art of drafting search warrant affidavits is not difficult provided the officer applies himself intelligently and professionally to the task. The key to the problem, like most of the perplexing problems facing the police today, is greater professional knowledge.

SEARCH OF THE PERSON

SEARCH OF THE PERSON WITH A SEARCH WARRANT FOR THE PERSON

GET A SEARCH WARRANT IF YOU HAVE TIME. If you have time to get a search warrant for the person, it is the best possible way to assure that incriminating evidence will not be suppressed.

Attempts to rely on an arrest-search situation are hazardous both for the officer and for the incriminating evidence since defense counsel have the best potential for suppressing evidence in an arrest-search situation.

Attempts to seize incriminating evidence by consent are also dangerous because there is a substantial burden on the prosecution at a suppression hearing to show that the consent was freely and voluntarily given. For this reason police should not rely too heavily on the use of consent search techniques. The consent search should be used only as a last means.

If the person named in the search warrant refuses to be searched in public or if it would be impractical to search the person in public, you may use reasonable force to detain the person and make reasonable arrangements to perform the search.

Note: It is important to realize that even if the police officers have had time to get a search warrant for the person, it is not a fatal flaw if they fail to get one. The mere fact that officers have had time to get warrants will never of itself result in the suppression of incriminating evidence. From a tactical point of view of getting incriminating evidence into the case at trial, the search warrant offers by far the greatest likelihood that there would be no chance of suppressing the evidence.

WHAT MAY BE SEIZED UNDER A SEARCH WARRANT FOR THE PERSON. In addition to seizing what is described in the search warrant for the person, you may also make a reasonable search of the person and seize any other evidence, even though it is not described in the search warrant, if it represents contraband, stolen property, or the instrumentality or the fruits of any crime. Of course, this also includes weapons carried in violation of law.

In executing a search warrant for the search of a person, you may make entry in the same manner as executing search warrants for premises or in the execution of an arrest warrant. Reasonable force may be used to effectuate the search.

SEARCH INCIDENTAL TO ARREST

GENERAL RULES. Whenever an officer has sufficient probable cause to arrest someone for a past or present felony or a present misdemeanor, he may search the person he has arrested basically to protect himself and to prevent the destruction of evidence.

When taking a person into lawful custody, you may search the arrested person not only for weapons, contraband, for fruits and instrumentalities of crimes, but also for evidence connected with the crime.

The legality of the search will depend almost entirely on the lawfulness of the arrest.

A search incidental to an arrest may only be made where the offense committed permits you to take the person into full physical custody. Generally, there may be no search incidental to an arrest for minor summary offenses where the person is not taken into custody.

WHY YOU ARE ALLOWED TO SEARCH WHEN YOU ARE MAKING AN ARREST

To protect yourself.

To prevent the destruction of evidence.

To prevent the person arrested from escaping.

An officer is empowered to make a search only when he is making a lawful arrest and, therefore, when an officer makes a search on his own he is using an arrest power.

The legality of the officer's actions are judged by applying constitutional standards as of the exact moment the officer invokes his arrest powers. Justification or probable cause for the arrest is measured *only* by the sinister or guilt-laden facts that have developed up until the split second that the officer uses one of his three fundamental arrest powers. When an officer uses force, makes a search on his own, or exercises seizure or restraint over someone, an arrest occurs as of that moment. No guilt-laden facts that occur *after* the officer has invoked his arrest powers can be used to justify the officer's using his awesome arrest power.

THE ARREST MUST BE LAWFUL. In order for a search incidental to an arrest to be lawful, it is necessary for the arrest itself to be lawful. The validity of the search hinges almost entirely on the lawfulness of the underlying arrest. If for any reason an arrest is unlawful, any incriminating evidence that is found will be suppressed.

Note. Searches made incidental to arrest *without* warrants are almost always attacked by defense lawyers at suppression hearings because defense counsel have a broad area of attack and a good chance of getting evidence suppressed. If you can, *always get a search warrant.*

THE ELEMENTS OF A LAWFUL ARREST. Probable cause to justify the arrest must exist as of the moment the officer invokes an arrest power.

An arrest for a felony or a misdemeanor committed in the presence of the officer, or for a felony committed out of the presence of the officer is lawful.

Note. If an officer arrests for a misdemeanor committed out of his presence it is an unlawful arrest. That is, an officer must personally observe through one of his five senses part of the misdemeanor occurring if he is to make a lawful arrest for that misdemeanor. If the officer did not observe the commission of the misdemeanor, the arrest is unlawful and any incriminating evidence obtained would be suppressed.

The arrest must be bona fide. "Sham" arrests, or arrests where the officer's purpose is to search for evidence and not really to take a person into custody, are unlawful and any evidence obtained by means of a "sham" arrest will be suppressed.

If an officer has made a physical trespass in order to obtain probable cause to justify an arrest, the probable cause obtained by the police officer's physical trespass will be rejected by the courts. Unless there is sufficient probable cause independent of the probable cause obtained by police trespass, the evidence will be suppressed. In cases of serious police trespass, there is a grave risk that the evidence will be suppressed solely on the magnitude of the police trespass.

Time of the Search. The search incidental to an arrest must be made at the time the arrest occurs. Since the purpose of the search incidental to an arrest is basically to protect the officer and to prevent the destruction of evidence, the search must be made contemporaneous with the arrest. Searches made hours after the arrest are generally held by the courts to be illegal and unreasonable. The unalterable time sequence is that the arrest must be made *first* because until it has been made there is *absolutely no right to search.* "Contemporaneous" means that a search must be made immediately or as soon as possible after the arrest.

Scope of the Search. The scope of the search incidental to an arrest is severely limited in that the police may search only the person arrested and the area within his immediate control. These limitations are caused by the fact that the officer really only gets the power to make a search incidental to an arrest to protect himself and to prevent the destruction of evidence. In arresting someone, the officer may:

Search the arrested person completely.

Search objects in the actual possession of the arrested person. Suitcases, purses, or anything carried by someone being arrested may be searched incidental to his arrest.

Search areas within the person's immediate control. All of the immediate physical surroundings where a person is arrested are considered by law to be, in effect, an extension of his person and therefore may be searched incidental to an arrest. If the man is sitting at a desk when he is arrested, the desk may be searched.

Objects in constructive possession. Where the person arrested has such objects as locker keys or safe deposit box keys in his possession, the keys may be seized if it is believed that they are connected with the crime. The best practice is to then obtain a search warrant for the search of the locker or safe deposit box. However, if there is an emergency situation and the officer does not have time to get a search warrant for the locker or safe deposit box, he may make the search on the basis that whatever is in the locker or safe deposit box is within the constructive possession of the person being arrested.

Objects in body cavities. Officers must exercise great care when it is necessary to make searches of body cavities. In every case where it is possible, the police should have such searches conducted by physicians. In cases where it is impossible to have doctors aid in the search, the officer must act as reasonably as possible and realize that the greatest right to privacy exists in maintaining bodily integrity. The conditions surrounding the search into the body cavities, the manner of the search, the amount of force, and an urgent need to prevent the destruction of evidence are all facts which the courts will carefully scrutinize in determining whether or not evidence will be suppressed.

Manner of the Search. Courts must inquire into the manner in which the search incidental to an arrest is conducted by the police. If excessive force is used or if the method of search is completely unreasonable, the officers have exceeded their power and the search will be declared unconstitutional. For example, one New York case of an unreasonable search and seizure resulted when an officer stripped and searched a man in the doorway of a building, searching for incriminating articles.

Who Should Make the Search. Whenever possible, the officer who makes the arrest should conduct the search himself. The danger involved when other officers – other than the arresting officer – make the search is that contemporaneousness is lost.

WHAT MAY BE SEIZED IN A SEARCH INCIDENTAL TO AN ARREST

Weapons, stolen property, instrumentalities of the crime, and contraband, as well as evidentiary articles may be seized by the police when searching incidental to an arrest.

ITEMS RELATING TO ANY CRIME. Officers' seizure powers include seizing any instrumentalities, fruits, contraband, and evidence of crimes different from the offense for which the arrest was made. Officers may seize these additional items even though they initially do not have the right to search for them.

PERSONAL OBJECTS. Clothing worn by a person at the time he is arrested may be seized lawfully by the police if there is a likelihood that laboratory examination will connect the clothing with the crime. Other clothing, such as hats, masks, and other items used to hide someone's identity may be seized as instrumentalities of the crime.

Even personal property may be seized initially since the person arrested will be placed in jail and the police have the duty to protect his property.

USING FORCE TO SEARCH A PERSON

Whenever an officer uses force to conduct a search of the person incidental to an arrest, the court at a suppression hearing will make a careful inquiry to assure that the use of force by the officer was reasonable. Only such reasonable force as is necessary to accomplish the search will be permitted. Each case will hinge upon its own unique circumstances. Generally proper, reasonable force is considered to be the minimum amount of force needed to accomplish the desired result.

Always use as little force as you possibly can in searching incidental to an arrest.

ARREST AND SEARCHES INCIDENTAL TO ARREST IN MOTOR VEHICLES

An officer who makes an arrest of a person in or immediately adjacent to a motor vehicle may search incidental to the arrest the *entire* vehicle *if he makes the search immediately.* This means that where an officer makes a lawful arrest of someone in or next to a car, the officer may search the entire car, including the glove compartment and the trunk, if he conducts the search immediately at the scene of the arrest. If the officer attempts to search or conducts the search at a place other than the place of arrest, there is grave danger that any incriminating evidence that the officer found will be suppressed.

WHAT MAY BE SEIZED BY THE POLICE WITHOUT A SEARCH WARRANT

OBJECTS IN PLAIN VIEW. Whenever you see stolen property, contraband, the instrumentalities of a crime, or evidence of a crime in plain view, you may seize them. Incriminating items that are out in the open may be seized independently, and the seizure does not require justification by a search warrant or by a lawful arrest. A search is defined as "the prying by police into hidden places." Since no search is involved in an officer's seeing something in plain view, he does not have to justify his seizure of objects in plain view by a search warrant or by a lawful arrest.

ABANDONED PROPERTY. If someone abandons property, he discards his right to privacy in the property that he abandons. When property is abandoned, no one has any further property right in it and it may be seized by the police without the basis of a lawful arrest or a search warrant.

OBJECTS OBTAINED BY A FRISK. A frisk, or the "patting down" of a person for weapons, *is a search.* The frisk is a serious invasion of someone's privacy. Its purpose is not to search but to protect the officer. The justification needed to frisk someone is, first, that the officer must be drawn into an inquiry by suspicious activity, and, second, that the officer must reasonably fear for his safety. When an officer frisks he is using an investigative power and not an arrest power. So long as the officer's purpose was to protect himself when he made a frisk, weapons or other incriminating evidence that the officer thought might be a weapon will not be suppressed.

THE CITIZEN'S PRIVACY

The use of the arrest power by government is the most devastating exercise of governmental power on the citizen.

Under our Constitution, a citizen can only be arrested for cause. Consequently, whenever an arrest occurs, courts are required by the Fourth Amendment to inquire closely into the facts and circumstances surrounding the arrest to insure that the full force of government was not used excessively, thereby destroying someone's sacred constitutional rights.

When an officer makes an arrest based on probable cause he acquires the right to make a search to protect himself and to prevent the destruction of evidence. Our tradition of law under the Fourth Amendment places severe limitations on the time and scope of the search incidental to an arrest, recognizing that governmental searches utterly demolish a citizen's privacy. Our Constitution places different limitations on the exercise of police powers of arrest, search, and seizure in preserving the most fundamental necessity for a free society—the right to privacy.

SEARCH OF PREMISES

You must have a warrant to search premises. In order to make a search of premises, you generally must have a warrant. Police have never been empowered by law to make searches independently and indiscriminately. The police power of search comes fundamentally from the courts. There are, however, four exceptions to the rule that police must have search warrants to search premises. These four exceptions are narrowly construed by the courts to assure that they are not misused. They came into existence by necessity and permit police to search premises without a warrant under certain limited conditions.

WHEN YOU CAN SEARCH WITHOUT A WARRANT

You may search premises or property without a warrant only under certain conditions:

Emergencies. When there is no time to get a search warrant and when time is of the essence, the police may enter and search premises where there is an urgent need for immediate action. The police response to cries for help within a house would be an example of this exception to the search warrant rule.

Hot Pursuit. Whenever the police are chasing an escaping criminal or an escaping suspect they are permitted—without warrants—to follow him inside a house and make a search of that house.

Contraband. Whenever the police know that contraband such as narcotics or counterfeit money is going to be removed or destroyed, they have emergency powers to act without warrants.

Search Incidental to Lawful Arrest. Whenever the police make an arrest they may search the person arrested and the property or area within his immediate control. The law authorizes this search to protect the arresting officers and to prevent the destruction of evidence. The search incidental to arrest is limited to the immediate area that the person is arrested in, and is limited in time—it must be done at the same time as the arrest.

WHEN YOU NEED A WARRANT TO SEARCH

Whenever you are in doubt concerning whether or not you need a search warrant and when you have time, *always get a search warrant.*

Get a search warrant when you are searching in houses, buildings or curtilage.

Houses. The Fourth Amendment has been interpreted to provide protection for all dwellings, whether private homes, apartments, hotel rooms, or rooms in a boarding house. Business places and offices are also fully protected.

Houses that are temporarily unoccupied are still protected under the Fourth Amendment and you must have a search warrant to make a search.

Landlords, owners of property, or managers of hotels or motels cannot validly consent to searches of property. Police should be extremely reluctant to rely on consent from property owners and should, whenever possible, get search warrants to search tenants' premises.

Whenever a person checks out of a hotel or rooming house permanently, he no longer has a right to privacy in the room, and a search can be made without a warrant.

Curtilage. Curtilage, a concept that comes to us from Common Law, is generally considered to be that area of open space surrounding a dwelling which is so immediately adjacent to the dwelling that it is considered part of the house.

Since searches cannot be made by the police without warrants in curtilage areas, it is essential that whenever there is any doubt about whether or not the area to be searched is within the curtilage of the dwelling, you should get a search warrant. Examples of curtilage are areas nearby or adjacent to a house that are fenced in, and trash can areas close to the house.

Open Fields. At law, "open fields" begin where the curtilage ends. Outhouses, woods, or caves in open fields can be searched without a warrant. Usually, it is safe to consider a hundred yards from a dwelling "open fields."

WHAT YOU MAY SEARCH FOR. When making a lawful search of premises, the police may search for contraband, fruits of a crime, weapons and instrumentalities of a crime, and evidence directly related to a crime.

WHAT TO DO IF OTHER INCRIMINATING EVIDENCE IS FOUND. When making a search of premises for certain specified incriminating evidence under a search warrant, if the police find other incriminating evidence relating to a different crime, that evidence also may be lawfully seized and will not be suppressed. For example, if the police have a search warrant for narcotics and discover counterfeit money in their search of a house, the counterfeit money may be seized by the police and will not be suppressed.

In searches incidental to an arrest of a person in a house the same rule applies. That is, if other incriminating evidence is found near the person being arrested, that evidence may be seized and will not be suppressed.

HOW TO CONDUCT A SEARCH OF PREMISES. The most important factor for the police to remember when executing a search warrant for premises or when searching a person incidental to an arrest is that the Fourth Amendment prohibits general, exploratory searches. If the search, either by the authority of a search warrant or incidental to an arrest, is conducted so that it appears to be a general exploratory search for incriminating evidence, the risk of suppression of the evidence is great.

Courts will usually make detailed inquiries into the methods of the search. For example, if the police are searching for a large object according to the search warrant and search into small areas when they are making the search, there is every indication that this will be held to be a general exploratory search. Fishing expeditions or inquisitorial searches for incriminating evidence are not tolerated under the philosophy of the Fourth Amendment.

SEARCH OF VEHICLES

STOPPING CARS

Under the Fourth Amendment, the police must have a reason to stop a car. Although stopping a car is a very limited invasion of the driver's right to privacy, the police officer, who represents the force of government, may not lawfully make even this limited invasion of the driver's privacy unless he has a reason.

Courts have held that if an officer stops a car for absolutely no reason, a technical arrest has occurred and any incriminating evidence discovered by the officer after stopping the car would be suppressed. Therefore, the first rule with regard to vehicles is: *You must have a reason to stop a car.*

VEHICLES ARE "EMERGENCIES." The Supreme Court has specifically declared that the great mobility of motor vehicles makes them, in certain situations, police emergencies. The courts have recognized that when confronted with a problem concerning an automobile, police must act immediately or not at all. The officer who is investigating someone in a car rarely gets a second chance. His time is limited and his decision final. Consequently, the courts view investigations focusing on people in mobile cars as extreme situations where police judgments, of necessity, must come quickly.

SEARCHING VEHICLES WITHOUT A WARRANT. Even though the mobile motor vehicle is viewed in certain situations by the courts as a police emergency, the law is that searches of vehicles without warrants may be made by the police only when they have probable cause to believe that someone in the car has committed a crime, or that the vehicle contains contraband or the fruits of a crime. Only when the police have probable cause to make the search may they make a search of a motor vehicle, and then the search should be made immediately.

WHEN DOES PROBABLE CAUSE STOP?

The police authority to search motor vehicles without warrants rests on probable cause. Between the time that a car is stopped by a police officer and the time that the officer uses an arrest power, the officer should be alertly gathering probable cause facts. Observations, admissions, or other events occurring between the time a car is stopped and the time the officer uses an arrest power should be used to build probable cause for the eventual arrest-search.

Under the Fourth Amendment a police officer has the power to stop an automobile when he has reason to stop it, to frisk the driver if the officer reasonably fears for his safety, and to question and detain the driver if suspicious circumstances warrant it. However, if the officer uses one of his arrest powers, such as using force on the driver or beginning a search of the car, probable cause stops building. The officer is judged by the courts as of the moment he uses his arrest power.

Therefore, police should fully exploit their investigative powers of stopping, frisking, questioning, and detaining in stopping cars under suspicious circumstances before they use their arrest powers of force, search, seizure, and restraint.

While an officer uses his investigative powers he may collect suspicious facts to build probable cause. In contrast, the moment the officer uses one of his arrest powers probable cause stops.

Example. Listed below is a sequence of events which shows the building of probable cause from the time of the car stop until the officer uses an arrest power:

(a) Police officer on highway patrol sees a new Ford Mustang being driven erratically (reason to stop car).

(b) Officer stops the Mustang and notices that while the car is neat and clean, the driver is a bearded, disheveled beatnik type.

(c) As he approaches the car, the officer notices that the window vent on the driver's side is broken.

(d) As the officer looks inside the Mustang he notices that there are no keys in the ignition.

(e) The officer asks the driver for an owner's card and driver's license and the driver has neither.

(f) The officer questions the driver about the car and the driver answers evasively.

(g) The officer checks the car and gets a radio report that it has been reported stolen.

(h) At this time, the officer finds that the license plate on the car is stolen.

(i) The officer arrests the driver for stealing the car and searches the car.

This example demonstrates how probable cause can build persuasively from the time of stopping the car until the officer uses an arrest power. While there is probably sufficient probable cause to arrest the driver from point (d) on, the probable cause gets stronger and stronger until finally it is irrefutable. The worst mistake a police officer can make in stopping cars is to search the car as soon as he stops it. This is a classic example of the premature use of a police arrest power which would result in the suppression of incriminating evidence.

USING FORCE TO SEARCH. Using excessive force to stop an automobile or using unreasonable force in searching a car will result in the suppression of incriminating evidence. The reasonableness of searches and seizures can turn on the amount of use of force by the officers. The cardinal rule is always to use as little force as you possibly can to accomplish your purpose.

NO RIGHT TO SEARCH PASSENGERS. Although the police may have evidence of probable cause justifying a search of a vehicle, they do not necessarily have the power to search passengers. Passengers may only be searched if they are being arrested in connection with a crime or if the officer has definite evidence that they are concealing incriminating evidence. However, if the officer has any reasonable fear for his safety, he should frisk them.

SEARCHING A NON-MOBILE VEHICLE. A motor vehicle in police custody should be searched only on the authority of a search warrant. Since the mobility of the car is ended when it is in police control, the emergency characteristics cease. Consequently, if a vehicle is in police custody or if its condition renders it immobile, police must obtain a search warrant to make a search of the car.

SEARCHING A VEHICLE INCIDENTAL TO AN ARREST. The most important factor in searching automobiles incidental to an arrest is that the search must be conducted *immediately*. The law requires that the arrest be made of a person in or near the car and that the search be made *contemporaneous* with the arrest. When a car is being searched incidental to arrest *the entire car*, including the trunk, may be searched provided the search is done right away.

ARRESTING FOR TRAFFIC VIOLATIONS. The general rule is that in arresting for traffic violations the police cannot conduct an incidental search since there are no fruits, instrumentalities, or contraband usually connected with traffic violations. Police should not use traffic violations as a means of searching for incriminating evidence. Courts are constantly alerted to abuses in this area where vehicle arrests are used as pretexts for incriminating searches. Such searches are completely unlawful. However, in arresting for drunken driving an officer could make a search for liquor. Also, whenever the officer reasonably fears for his safety he may make a frisk for concealed weapons.

ROADBLOCKS FOR CARS. Although roadblocks have been judged lawful by the courts for general police purposes, they cannot be used indiscriminately by the police as a general means of searching for incriminating evidence. Although the police may have the right to set up roadblocks, the prosecution does not have the right to get all incriminating evidence that was obtained by roadblock searches into evidence. Police may have to set up roadblocks and search cars in limited emergency conditions, but the incriminating evidence that they find in this manner will generally be suppressed.

There is an exception, however, where the police information focuses on a particular kind of car because of specific, reliable probable cause information. Arrests and searches made under these circumstances have been upheld by the courts.

"MAY I LOOK IN YOUR TRUNK?" Police have often used the method of asking a driver after they have stopped him, "May I look in your trunk?" If incriminating evidence is found in the trunk when this police technique is used, it would be very difficult to get it into evidence. The request to look in someone's trunk should be used only when all other avenues of investigation are exhausted. The old "May I look in your trunk?" technique should only be used by the police in a last desperate effort to find incriminating evidence.

CONSENT SEARCH

A legally valid consent to search is a waiver of a person's rights under the Fourth Amendment to be searched only on the authority of a lawful search warrant. It is similar to the familiar waiver of one's right against self-incrimination under the Fifth Amendment.

The general rule concerning consent is that the person giving consent must fully understand the nature of his consent—that he is waiving his constitutional rights under the Fourth Amendment—and that the consent must be freely and voluntarily given. The burden is on the prosecution at a suppression hearing to establish that any purported consent to search was *understandably, freely, and voluntarily* given, and that the consent was *specific and absolutely clear.* In addition, the prosecution must establish that the consent was obtained from the right person.

Consent can be obtained orally or in writing. From a tactical point of view, it is of much greater advantage to the prosecution to have a specific written consent to search rather than an oral one.

CAN CONSENT BE IMPLIED? Consent to search—the waiver of an individual's rights and privileges under the Fourth Amendment—can never be implied, either by silence or by tacit nonresistance. A consent to search must be specific, affirmative, and clear. A person giving consent must actually and affirmatively indicate that he consents to a search.

WHEN SHOULD CONSENT BE USED? Police should be very reluctant to use consent—particularly oral consent—as a means of obtaining incriminating evidence. Consent is a constitutional waiver. The Fourth Amendment cases place a particularly heavy burden on the prosecution to establish that the consent was absolutely freely and voluntarily given—with a full understanding that Fourth Amendment rights were being waived.

Moreover, consent must be obtained from the right person—someone who has a right to privacy in the area to be searched. The general rule is that parents cannot give consent for the search of areas in the exclusive possession of their children, and that employers generally are not able to give valid consent to search areas exclusively used by employees.

Because these burdens to establish a valid consent are—from a tactical point of view—particularly severe for the prosecution at a suppression hearing, the criminal investigator should use the consent technique only as a last resort.

The person giving consent to search must understand his rights before the courts will hold that he has validly waived his right to a search. Under the doctrine of the "warrant machinery" of the Fourth Amendment, a person must actually know about his Fourth Amendment rights. Police officers who are obtaining consents – written or oral – should advise the person who is giving the consent of his specific Fourth Amendment rights so that a foundation will be made for a Fourth Amendment waiver *knowingly and intelligently* given.

A person giving consent to search must do so freely and voluntarily. An extremely heavy burden is placed on the prosecution at a suppression hearing involving consent searches to establish that the consent was given absolutely freely and voluntarily. Coercion, expressed or implied, will invalidate consent. Even slight coercion, such as an overbearing manner by the officer, could invalidate consent. The burden of proof is so great here that there is almost an implied doctrine against a court accepting a consent as a free and voluntary waiver of Fourth Amendment rights.

BURDEN ON THE PROSECUTION. At a suppression hearing, the burden is on the prosecution to establish that the consent was lawful. This burden is a particularly severe one and difficult for the prosecution to sustain. A variety of attacks are available to defense counsel at a suppression hearing when the government has relied on a consent search. Defense counsel's classic attacks are attempts to show that the consent was not given with full understanding, that the consent was coerced, or that it was obtained from the wrong person.

VOLUNTARY OR INVOLUNTARY? The true test of a consent to search is a developing of all the circumstances surrounding the consent. Where the person was when he consented (if under arrest and he has not confessed, there is almost a nonrebuttable presumption that the consent was involuntary); how many officers requested consent; whether or not there was a show of force; whether or not the person was advised of the nature of the investigation; and whether or not he was advised of his Fourth Amendment rights.

Another important factor involved in consent is the age of the person who gives consent. If the law enforcement officers are relying on a consent given by a child or a juvenile, the burdens to establish that the consent was understandably, freely and voluntarily given are almost insurmountable for the prosecution.

CONSENT FROM THE RIGHT PERSON. In general, a law enforcement officer must obtain consent from the person whose privacy is being invaded or who is the object of the incriminating search.

There is a second rule which provides that where there are people who have equal rights to privacy in a particular area, then a lawful, valid consent may be obtained from either one of the parties.

As an example, there are circumstances where a parent can give consent to the police to make a search of a living room area for incriminating evidence to be used against a child. This is true because both the parent and the child would have a right to privacy in the living room. The same rule applies generally to husbands and wives and employers and employees. However, where there is an area that is used exclusively or almost exclusively by a child, spouse, or employee, then no one can give a valid consent for a search of that area except the person with almost exclusive rights to privacy in it. As an example, a bureau drawer that a child uses exclusively could not be lawfully searched on the authority of the parent's consent. The bureau drawer would represent a tiny pocket of privacy for the child alone and only his valid consent could waive Fourth Amendment rights in that area.

Therefore, the general cautious rule is that parents cannot give consent for searches of children's areas of privacy, nor employers for employees, nor landlords for tenants, nor husbands for wives. The right to privacy under the Fourth Amendment is a personal one and in the areas where someone's right to privacy is particularly great only that person with the right to privacy in that area can waive Fourth Amendment rights.

HOW TO OBTAIN A VALID CONSENT

(a) Advise the person whose consent is being sought of the general nature of the investigation—if you can—and the purpose for the search for incriminating evidence.

(b) Advise the person whose consent is being sought that under the Fourth Amendment he has an absolute right to be searched only on the authority of a search warrant issued by a judge and that a judge will issue a search warrant only where there are enough facts available for him to believe that a crime has been committed and that the area to be searched is connected with the crime.

(c) Be sure to advise the person from whom consent is being sought that he can absolutely and unconditionally refuse to permit the search, and that any evidence found can be used against him.

(d) Avoid any show of force or anything that could be interpreted as even the mildest or slightest coercion. It is essential that the consent be freely and voluntarily given.

(e) Get consent from the right person. Consent must be obtained from the person who has a right to privacy in the area to be searched or against whom the incriminating search is directed, or from a person who has a valid and equal right to privacy in the area to be searched.

(f) Obtain a written consent in preference to an oral consent whenever possible.

WRITTEN CONSENT. Because of the likelihood of having a consent declared unlawful at a suppression hearing, it is much more desirable from a prosecution point of view to have a written consent.

Written consent freezes credible, reliable facts justifying the search in time, crystallizes the advice and warnings given by the police, and makes it difficult for manufactured assertions by the defense to succeed. It is much more difficult for defense counsel at a suppression hearing to attack a written consent than an oral consent, and the defense lawyer's attack has to be directed at the written waiver or consent rather than at the officer.

Example:

> On April 31, 1969, I, Roderick Roe, was advised by Officer John Doe that he had received reliable information that I have a recently stolen television set in my living room. Officer Doe further informed me that under the Fourth Amendment my home could be searched only on the authority of a search warrant issued by a judge and that a search warrant would be issued by a judge only where there were sufficient facts presented to him, under oath, that would lead to a reasonable belief that there was stolen property in my home. Officer Doe told me that I did not have to agree or consent to have my living room searched and that I could absolutely refuse to consent to this search.
>
> I hereby freely and voluntarily—knowing my rights under the Fourth Amendment—waive and consent to the search of my living room for this allegedly stolen television set.
>
> No threats or promises or representations of any kind have been made to me by this officer.
>
> Signed: /s/ Roderick Roe
>
> Witnessed: ________________ ________________

Whenever possible, get a search warrant. Do not rely on consent searches.

Caution: Consent searches are particularly difficult to uphold when consent is obtained from children or juveniles.

WITHDRAWN CONSENT. If a person first consents to a search and then withdraws his consent before the search is made, there is no consent. Consent, therefore, can be withdrawn at any time before the search is made. If consent is withdrawn, the officers should immediately get a search warrant.

CHAPTER V

THE SUPPRESSION HEARING

PRELUDE TO TRIUMPH OR TRAGEDY OF LAW

The war against crime, like 20th-century warfare, is of necessity a limited war. Just as our military strategists must be restrained from unleashing doomsday devices like the hydrogen bomb, so police must be restrained from overkill with their doomsday devices. For just as surely as H-bombs can destroy our world, mass arrests and searches can destroy our freedom.

If it is true that law enforcement officers are at war with the criminal to protect the peace of the citizen, then it is certainly true today that most of the decisive legal battles in this war against crime are being fought not at trial, but at the suppression hearing.

Throughout most of the country, the first and last critical encounter in a criminal case traditionally was at trial. This is no longer true. Now the pre-trial suppression hearing is the first critical encounter between the prosecution and the defense, and it frequently determines whether or not there will be a trial at all. Without the incriminating evidence of the crime, even the most skilled prosecutors cannot advance to trial.

If there is to be a trial, what happened at the suppression hearing will in large measure ultimately determine if justice is to triumph.

The suppression hearing, then, is truly the prelude to the triumph or tragedy of law. To assure justice, everyone with an important role at the suppression hearing—the judge, the prosecutor, the defense attorney, and especially the police officer—should know all he can about the tactics and strategies of this important battle for evidence. For justice—particularly criminal justice—is not a game that should be resolved by the relative skills of the adversaries or the manufactured weights of the technicalities but rather by truth.

THE SUPPRESSION OF EVIDENCE RULE

WHAT DOES IT MEAN? The Suppression of Evidence Rule means that incriminating evidence obtained by police who exceed the scope of their powers according to the Constitution can never be used against the accused at trial. When evidence is suppressed by the court it never gets through the courtroom doors at the time it is most needed—when the defendant is on trial for his crime.

Physical evidence is suppressed when it is seized by police in violation of the rules of the Fourth Amendment, and testimonial evidence—confessions—are suppressed whenever the police interrogation tactics violate the requirements of the Fifth Amendment.

Today, when evidence is suppressed, justice is defeated. Nevertheless, if a police officer knows his power according to the Constitution, knows the law, and recognizes the citizen's constitutional rights, incriminating evidence should never be suppressed and justice should never be defeated.

WHERE DID THE SUPPRESSION RULE COME FROM? The Suppression Rule is a court-made rule that first appeared on the American scene in 1914. The important factor here is to recognize that when the Suppression Rule was created in 1914 it was created by federal judges and held to apply only to federal law enforcement officers. From 1914 to 1961, the Rule of Suppression under the Fourth Amendment remained predominantly a federal Rule of Suppression in terms of legions of reported cases.

Many of the states—almost half of them—created court-made suppression rules in their own jurisdictions, but there was no uniform national Rule of Suppression until 1961, when the United States Supreme Court decided *Mapp v. Ohio.*

HOW DID THE SUPPRESSION RULE BECOME THE RULE IN ALL FIFTY STATES? The Supreme Court of the United States, until approximately the 1920's, held emphatically that the first ten amendments to the United States Constitution placed restraint only on federal power and not on state power. In other words, a citizen's relationship with the federal government was traditionally determined by the first ten amendments to the United States Constitution, and a citizen's relationship with his state government was determined by the Fourteenth Amendment to the United States Constitution as well as any constitutional guarantees contained in his own state constitution.

Beginning in the 1920's, the Supreme Court of the United States began to imply that the constitutional guarantees contained in the first ten amendments were contained, by inference, in the Fourteenth Amendment. In 1922, the Court held that the First Amendment's guarantee of freedom of speech was by implication contained in the Fourteenth Amendment, and that New York City police officers could not silence a soapbox orator in Central Park. Between 1922 and 1961, the Supreme Court of the United States selectively incorporated, by inference, nearly all of the guarantees of the first ten amendments into the Fourteenth.

In *Mapp v. Ohio,* in 1961, the Supreme Court of the United States declared that the protections against illegal searches and seizures of the Fourth Amendment were implicitly contained in the Fourteenth, and by a stroke of the pen in the Mapp decision, all 50 states acquired the Suppression Rule. This historic development in which the Supreme Court gradually found all of the safeguards of the first ten amendments to be contained in the Fourteenth Amendment is known as the "encorporation doctrine."

WHAT IS THE EFFECT OF THE SUPPRESSION RULE'S BEING PLACED ON ALL THE 50 STATES? The Supreme Court decision in *Mapp v. Ohio* which, in effect, gave all the states the federal Suppression Rule, created the first explicit, national, uniform standards in constitutional and criminal law. Now police officers all over the nation operate under exactly the same rules as far as interfering with a citizen's privacy is concerned.

The introduction of the Suppression Rule to state law enforcement systems has required all state and local law enforcement officers to know the law or to suffer the frustration of losing cases. The most important side effect of the Mapp decision is that it is rapidly professionalizing all of the police in America. With increased demands for knowledge of law and other vital facets of law enforcement work, police all over the nation are rapidly shifting their goals. They are also interacting more with lawyers and other key members of the criminal justice team.

The most significant effect of the Supreme Court's decision in *Mapp v. Ohio* is to provide national, uniform protection to each citizen's constitutional rights, so that each citizen, no matter who he is or where he is, will be treated with equal justice before the law.

THE ANATOMY OF A FOURTH AMENDMENT SUPPRESSION HEARING

WHAT IS IT? A Fourth Amendment suppression hearing is an adversary pretrial criminal evidentiary hearing before a judge sitting without a jury. Its purpose is to determine whether the incriminating evidence obtained by the prosecution was obtained lawfully. Lawful in this area means obtained in harmony with the requirements of the Fourth Amendment. From a practical point of view, the word "lawful" concerns the issue of whether the police exceeded the power given to them by law when they obtained the incriminating evidence.

A PRETRIAL CRIMINAL HEARING. A suppression hearing has to be conducted prior to the trial of the criminal case, because the whole issue at a suppression hearing is whether or not the incriminating evidence discovered by the police will be admissible in evidence at the trial. In the federal system a defendant may move to suppress evidence at any time before the trial and in exceptional circumstances may even move to suppress during the trial. Most state law provides that motions to suppress must be filed ten days or more before trial.

AN EVIDENTIARY HEARING. At a suppression hearing testimony is taken by a court stenographer and later transcribed and made a permanent part of the record in the case. It is essential to record the testimony at a suppression hearing because the trial court and every appellate court, state or federal, that might possibly review the suppression decision is bound by the transcribed testimony of the witnesses who appeared at the suppression hearing. Reviewing courts particularly are unable to look outside the record for facts. Because of this, it is essential for both the prosecution and the defense to make the best possible record at the suppression hearing so that both the prosecution and the defense fully assert their relative positions on the suppression issue.

AN ADVERSARY PROCEEDING. The basic characteristic of the American system of criminal justice is its adversary nature. Under our system of law, the state as prosecutor and the defendant meet as equals in a criminal prosecution, and neither side is to ask or give quarter.

A suppression hearing is an adversary proceeding. That is, there are ideally speaking, two equal combatants, the prosecution and the defense, meeting as equals to develop facts for the court to determine whether or not the evidence was obtained lawfully. Sometimes suppression hearings tend to be conducted in a somewhat relaxed atmosphere, particularly since there is no jury present. Prosecutors, defense lawyers, and witnesses should always realize that they are engaged in a deadly serious adversary battle, a battle to get evidence in or to keep evidence out.

A HEARING BEFORE A JUDGE SITTING WITHOUT A JURY. The most significant difference between a suppression hearing and a trial is the fact that a jury is not present during a suppression hearing. The absence of the jury at the suppression hearing makes a profound impact on the traditional rules of evidence.

Evidence at law is defined as the means or methods by which facts are established or disproved. The rules of evidence were designed at Common Law to protect juries from weak, prejudicial, or untrustworthy testimony, and this grand design to insulate jurors from being misled is the dominant characteristic of our rules of evidence today.

Modern rules of evidence prevent the prosecution from injecting into the trial any prejudicial evidence such as a defendant's prior convictions. Today the rules of evidence also block untrustworthy testimony by means of the Hearsay Rule. The Hearsay Rule of Evidence basically prevents witnesses from testifying to what other people said, since the trustworthiness of what other people say can generally be proved or disproved by having that person as a witness subject to cross-examination.

Since there is no jury present at a suppression hearing, all of the traditional rules of evidence are jettisoned. This means that the rules of evidence such as the rule against the admission of prejudicial evidence and the Hearsay Rule do not bar any testimony at a suppression hearing. Everything is admissible.

There are absolutely no restrictions on the kind of evidence that can come into a suppression hearing. There are no limitations as to the admissibility of testimony at a suppression hearing. The only necessity is that witnesses be placed under oath and that they tell the truth.

Since the normal protective evidentiary barriers are down at a suppression hearing and all evidence, hearsay or otherwise, is admissible, the judge, the prosecutor and the defense lawyer must overfocus on the reliability of the evidence. This means that the three key figures at a suppression hearing must be ever vigilant to assess the reliability of the evidence presented. This is true because the Fourth Amendment requires reliable, persuasive facts under oath to justify the use of police arrest, search and seizure powers.

AN INQUIRY INTO POLICE CONDUCT. The fundamental inquiry at a suppression hearing is to ascertain what the officer did to get the evidence and the factual justification for the officer's action. Although the court decisions are filled with conclusions such as "reasonable" or "unreasonable" or "legal" or "illegal" the basic standard that the courts apply in deciding whether or not to suppress incriminating evidence under the Fourth Amendment is to see if the officer exceeded the limits of his constitutional powers.

As an example, if the police officer obtained a search warrant the basic inquiry at a suppression hearing would be whether or not the search warrant that he prepared contained sufficient probable cause facts, testified to under oath, that would justify the search.

As a second example, where a police officer has obtained incriminating evidence by means of a protective frisk the inquiry at a suppression hearing would be focused on the initial justification that drew the officer into an inquiry of the accused and the reasonableness of the officer's fear for his own safety.

As a third example, in an arrest-search situation the inquiry at a suppression hearing would be focused on the exact moment that the police officer used his arrest powers and whether or not at that moment there was sufficient probable cause to justify the arrest-search.

BURDENS OF PROOF. There is no Supreme Court decision that directly establishes who has the burden of proof at a suppression hearing. Some other courts, both state and federal, have indicated that where the incriminating evidence has been seized by the authority of a search warrant the burden of proof is on the defendant to show that the search warrant is invalid or illegal. Where the incriminating evidence was seized at an arrest that was authorized by an arrest warrant, it would also seem reasonable to put the burden of proof on the defendant to establish that the arrest warrant or that the arrest itself was illegal.

In contrast, where the police officer obtains incriminating evidence by means of a protective frisk or an arrest without any kind of warrant, then the burden should be on the prosecution to develop the lawfulness of the protective frisk or the lawfulness of the arrest. Where the theory of the prosecution is that the incriminating evidence was obtained by consent, the burden should also be on the prosecution to establish the lawfulness of the consent.

In summary, this means that whenever the police have gone to the courts for judicial approval concerning an arrest or a search, there should be a presumption of legality and the burden should be on the defendant to show illegality of the warrant process. In contrast, where the police officer obtained the incriminating evidence on his own, whether it be by a protective frisk, arrest or consent, since he has taken the law into his own hands the burden should be on the prosecution to establish the lawfulness of the police conduct.

ORDER OF PROOF. Although the Supreme Court of the United States has not given any direction as to the order of proof at a suppression hearing, some courts have decided and it would appear reasonable that the party with the burden of proof should proceed first. At any rate, the order of proof is not a critical factor at a suppression hearing since the examination of witnesses, both on direct and cross-examination, can and should be permissively broad. A suppression hearing is a rare legal proceeding these days in that it is a diligent search for the truth with no holds barred. That is, there are no technicalities or barriers to the admissibility of evidence at a suppression hearing. Because the whole purpose of a suppression hearing is to get at the truth without any restrictions, judges should allow broad latitude in direct and cross-examination. Leading questions should be blocked only where an attorney is making an attempt to "stack" the record.

There is one cautionary note, however: suppression hearings should be kept to the central issue of lawfulness of police conduct in obtaining incriminating evidence. Any diffuse "fishing expeditions" by the defense that are patently motivated for the purpose of pretrial discovery should be cut off by the court.

Finally, since a suppression hearing is a critical stage of a criminal proceeding, both the defendant and his attorney should be present at the suppression hearing.

THE SUPPRESSION BATTLEGROUND

DEFENSE STRATEGIES. At a suppression hearing the defense's basic attitude should be: *What did the officer do?* In other words, the defense focuses on every act performed by the officer in the escalating events that led to the discovery of incriminating evidence. The defense lawyer at a suppression hearing is attempting to show that the police officer exceeded the scope of his powers by showing that the officer's conduct was not justified by the circumstances or by establishing that the police used illegal tactics to get the incriminating evidence. In effect, then, the normal strategy of a defense lawyer is to focus on each action of the investigating officer and to attempt to convince the court that the officer was not justified in doing what he did.

PROSECUTION STRATEGIES. In sharp contrast, the prosecution should emphasize and *develop all the facts* known or observed by the officer that would justify the seizure of incriminating evidence. Basically, the prosecution has the responsibility of marshalling all the facts that would justify an investigation or establish probable cause for warrants or for an arrest. Since there are no rules of evidence acting as a barrier, the prosecution is not limited in any way in establishing the probable cause facts that would justify the officer's seizure of incriminating evidence.

A second facet of the prosecutor's strategy at a suppression hearing is that the prosecution *must, prior to* the suppression hearing, have developed a theory for admitting the incriminating evidence. The prosecution must devote some time and energy to prior planning so that in advance of the suppression hearing a theory is developed that would justify the seizure of the incriminating evidence.

DEFENSE TACTICS

The mission of the defense attorney is a direct one. He is attempting to keep the incriminating evidence out.

DEFENSE ATTACKS ON THE SEARCH WARRANT. The defense attorney has six lines of attack that he can make on a search warrant. Five of these attacks relate to fatal defects contained in the warrant itself or the manner in which the warrant was obtained, while the sixth attack relates to the manner in which the search warrant was executed. Four out of the six attacks by a defense attorney on a search warrant are aimed directly at the search warrant itself. The other two attacks are directed at the officer.

Attacks on the Warrant

(a) Lack of *probable cause.*

(b) Lack of *particularity* (such as describing the wrong premises on the face of the warrant).

(c) *Age of the probable cause* contained in the warrant. Basically, the rule is that if the last observation or the last probable cause fact occurred more than 30 days before the search warrant was issued, the probable cause information is too stale and the likelihood that the incriminating evidence would still be at the location indicated in the warrant would be unlikely.

(d) *Reliability* of the probable cause. Where the probable cause for the search warrant is largely hearsay, such as accusations by an informant, the defense can attack the reliability of the probable cause in the search warrant and attempt to convince the court that the only way to establish the truth of the probable cause accusations is to produce the confidential informant.

Attacks on the Officer. (a) Failure of the officer to have been placed *under oath.* (The Fourth Amendment requires that search warrants be issued only on the basis of probable cause "under oath." If an officer does not swear that the facts were true before a judicial officer who issues the warrant, the search warrant never takes its first breath as a legal document.)

(b) *Entry.* (The basic federal rule, by statute, and throughout the states by virtue of the development of the Common Law, is that police officers executing search warrants must knock and announce their authority and purpose before they make a forceful entry into the premises that they are searching.) Some states, such as New York, provide that in an emergency situation where an officer's life is in danger or there is a likelihood that evidence will be destroyed, the officers, when authorized by a judicial officer, may make a forceful entry without knocking and announcing their authority and purpose. If this rule of entry is violated – even though the search warrant is completely valid – the judge must, under existing law, suppress the evidence.

DEFENSE ATTACKS ON AN ARREST-SEARCH

MOMENT OF ARREST. The defense attorney at a suppression hearing where the incriminating evidence has been obtained by an arrest-search will try to show that the officer used his arrest power prematurely. Central to this attack is the desire of the defense counsel to establish that the accused was arrested early in the police-citizen confrontation. The rule is that as soon as a police officer exercises one of his arrest powers (of force, search, seizure, or restraint), his probable cause is judged by the courts as of the split second that he invoked an arrest power. The officer will be unable to justify the use of his arrest power by any incriminating evidence that he discovered after he used his arrest power. This means that the defense lawyer will constantly be asking the officer *what he did*, not *what he knew*.

INSUFFICIENT PROBABLE CAUSE. In an arrest-search situation, the major defense attack is generally an attempt to convince the court that there was not sufficient probable cause to justify an arrest. If the defense lawyer can persuade the court that the police officer used one of his arrest powers prematurely, the opportunity for developing probable cause is cut off, and the court would be forced to the position of declaring an unlawful arrest. When the officer takes the law into his own hands and arrests and searches someone without judicial approval, courts require strong probable cause justification for his action.

TIME OF THE SEARCH. A police officer is given the right to make a search at the time he makes an arrest, basically to protect himself and to prevent the destruction of evidence. In an arrest-search situation, time is of the essence. Because the officer is given the right to search to protect himself and to preserve evidence, he must make the search *immediately*. The search must be contemporaneous with the arrest. As an example, if the police officer arrests someone in a car and does not search the car until two hours after the man has been in a police lockup, the search would be unlawful because it would violate the simultaneous search requirement of the Fourth Amendment.

SCOPE OF THE SEARCH. The scope of the search incident to a lawful arrest is limited by the courts to the defendant himself and the area under his immediate control. The scope of the search is limited because a suspect that is taken into custody could harm the officer only with something that he had on his person or something that was near him. Therefore, if the police arrest someone in his living room they may not search his attic incident to that arrest. The one exception is that if the suspect runs through his apartment or house in an attempt to get away from the police, the police may search every area where he ran in an attempt to preserve evidence.

FELONY-MISDEMEANOR ATTACK. A police officer may arrest for a felony or a misdemeanor committed in his presence, but he may not arrest for a misdemeanor committed out of his presence. If defense counsel can establish that the officer arrested a suspect for a misdemeanor that was not committed in the officer's presence, the arrest is unlawful and any incriminating evidence that was seized would have to be suppressed.

TRESPASSING OFFICERS. If the police are trespassers while they are in the process of collecting their probable cause, none of the probable cause that they obtain while they are trespassing will be permitted to assist in justifying the arrest.

SHAM ARREST. Police may not arrest a suspect as a sham because they really want to search him. In one leading case, some police officers in Alaska arrested a taxicab driver for minor motor vehicle violations—two days after they had occurred—so that they could search his cab for narcotics. If the defense can establish a sham arrest, the evidence has to be suppressed.

RELIABILITY. Where the probable cause for an arrest is largely hearsay, such as information from an informant, the defense can attack the reliability of the probable cause for the arrest and attempt to convince the court that the only way to establish the truth of the probable cause accusations is to produce the confidential informant.

ENTRY ATTACK. If the police make an illegal forceful entry, evidence must be suppressed.

POLICE PARTICIPATION IN STEALING INCRIMINATING EVIDENCE. If the police initiate or assist third parties or citizens to steal incriminating evidence, the alliance is illegal because it violates the Fourth Amendment. If defense counsel can persuasively prove a sinister alliance between the police and the private citizen who took the incriminating evidence illegally from the accused, the incriminating evidence has to be suppressed.

POISONOUS FRUIT ATTACK. Where a police investigation is based on incriminating evidence that was illegally obtained, the evidence itself is suppressed, as well as all other evidence that grew out of or was subsequently developed from the original illegal evidence by later police investigation.

This rule of suppression is known as the "poisonous fruit doctrine." It means that if the trunk of the tree, or the incriminating evidence that was the very foundation of the investigation, was illegally obtained by the police, then the tree and all its fruit (other evidence) are poisonous – and have to be cut down.

Defense counsel are always eagerly searching for the poisonous tree at a suppression hearing. If they find one, the whole criminal investigation collapses.

When the problem of the poisonous fruit doctrine arises, the prosecution conceding the initial illegality can hold the case against the accused together by establishing that the incriminating evidence against the accused came not from the poisonous tree but from independent leads that developed from other sources during the investigation.

The poisonous fruit attack by the defense is unquestionably the most devastating of all attacks on incriminating evidence. The prosecution must counterattack on the basis that the incriminating evidence in the case came from completely untainted sources or from investigative leads independent of the "primary taint." The bitter reality is that poisonous trees of evidence not only kill the poisonous fruit of subsequent investigation, but also implant terminal disease in the underlying criminal prosecutions.

THE PROTECTIVE FRISK. When incriminating evidence is seized by a police officer by means of a protective frisk, the defense attack has to establish that the officer did not have sufficient prior justification for stopping the accused. A second facet for the defense to develop is that the officer did not reasonably fear for his safety or that the officer was really attempting to make a search for incriminating evidence. If the defense attorney can establish that the frisk was a mass frisk, or routine or unnecessary, the incriminating evidence would have to be suppressed.

CONSENT SEARCH. The law requires that a consent to search be given freely and voluntarily by the citizen. A severe burden is placed on the prosecution to establish by clear and persuasive evidence that the person who gave consent gave it willingly. One fact that the defense attorney will focus on will be whether or not the officer advised the person from whom he obtained consent of his constitutional right under the Fourth Amendment. A second fact to develop is whether or not the officer indicated the nature of the investigation and the purpose for which the consent search was to be made. Absence of either or both of these facts is not fatal, but it is best to advise the suspect of his Fourth Amendment rights and to explain the nature of the investigation.

A very powerful attack can be made by defense counsel when consent to search is obtained from parties other than the accused. Here the critical factor is that the police must obtain consent from the right person; that is, someone who has a right to privacy in the area that is to be searched.

The consent battle in a suppression hearing more frequently than not revolves around the issue of credibility of the prosecution and defense witnesses. Consequently, it is essential whenever possible for the police to obtain a written consent rather than a mere oral consent.

If an officer says he has a warrant but doesn't have one or has a defective warrant, acquiescence to the authority of the alleged or asserted warrant is not consent.

PROSECUTION TACTICS

HOW TO GET INCRIMINATING EVIDENCE IN AT TRIAL. It is vital that the prosecution have a legal theory that would justify the seizure of the incriminating evidence before the suppression hearing begins. Basically, there are at least a dozen potential legal theories for the prosecution to use in attempting to get incriminating evidence in at trial. They are:

(a) The *search warrant*

(b) A *lawful arrest* pursuant to an *arrest warrant* or a *warrantless arrest*

(c) *Consent*

(d) The *protective frisk*

(e) Incriminating evidence in *open* or *plain view*

(f) *Abandoned property*

(g) Seizure of incriminating evidence by *private persons* without police participation

(h) *Custodial searches*

(i) Incriminating evidence seized by authority of *special statutes* (such as the Federal Counterfeit Statute that permits federal treasury agents to search for counterfeit money if they have probable cause to believe that it is at a certain location)

(j) Incriminating evidence seized by *border searches*

(k) Incriminating evidence found by police in *open fields*

(l) Incriminating evidence found by police who were engaged in a bona fide *police emergency*

The prosecution, then, has to plan which one of these twelve theories they will rely on to get the incriminating evidence in at trial. Sometimes they can rely on two or three of these theories simultaneously. As an example, if a search warrant appears legally insufficient, the prosecution can not only argue the legality of the seizure of the evidence on the authority of a search warrant, but they can also rely on an arrest-search theory—if someone was arrested when the incriminating evidence was discovered.

The doctrine of abandoned property or abandoned rights to property (where a man checks out of a hotel or room) frequently supplies the opportunity for multiple prosecution theories at a suppression hearing. In other words, it is not inconsistent for the prosecution to rely on several legal justifications or theories for getting the evidence in. As a matter of fact, the resourceful prosecutor will build evidence supporting theories on as many of these 12 lawful grounds for admission as he possibly can.

THE ANATOMY OF A FIFTH AMENDMENT SUPPRESSION HEARING

The Supreme Court of the United States, in *Jackson v. Denno,* 378 U.S. 368 (1964) declared that whenever a defendant in a federal or state criminal case moves to suppress a confession, there must be a preliminary suppression hearing out of the presence of the jury so that the court can ascertain whether or not the confession was freely and voluntarily given. This means that a Fifth Amendment suppression hearing is conducted virtually under the same conditions as a Fourth Amendment suppression hearing. However, the full focus of the legal inquiry in the Fifth Amendment suppression hearing is into all the facts and circumstances of the manner in which the confession was obtained.

For more than thirty years, the Supreme Court of the United States has been reviewing state cases concerning the admissibility of confessions in criminal cases. In 1936, in *Brown v. Mississippi,* 297 U.S. 278, the Supreme Court, drawing upon the Due Process clause of the Fourteenth Amendment, reversed a conviction where Brown, a murder suspect, had been tied to a tree, whipped, and twice hanged by a rope from a tree in order to obtain a confession. In more than three dozen cases the Supreme Court of the United States has overturned convictions obtained by local and state law enforcement officers on the grounds that they violated the constitutional guarantees of the Fourteenth Amendment.

DEFENSE ATTACKS ON THE CONFESSION

THE MIRANDA ATTACK. Today the main attack of defense counsel on a confession at a Fifth Amendment suppression hearing is the Miranda attack. In *Miranda v. Arizona,* 384 U.S. 436, the Supreme Court of the United States outlined four mandatory warnings that must be given prior to in-custody interrogation or prior to police questioning when they intend to arrest. If the interrogating officers do not give the Miranda warnings to the accused, the prosecution will not be able to establish a free and voluntary waiver of the right against self-incrimination and the confession must be ruled inadmissible.

In June of 1968, the Congress of the United States enacted, and the President signed, the Omnibus Crime Control and Safe Streets Act of 1968. Title 2 of this Act is a legislative attempt to annul the Miranda Rule in criminal prosecutions by Federal law enforcement officers and provides that a federal judge, in determining the issue of voluntariness of a confession, shall take into consideration all of the circumstances surrounding the giving of the confession.

> including (1) the time elapsing between arrest and arraignment of the defendant making the confession, (2) whether such defendant knew the nature of the offense with which he was charged or of which he was suspected at the time of making the confession, (3) whether or not such defendant was advised or knew that he was not required to make any statement and that any such statement could be used against him, (4) whether or not such defendant had been advised prior to questioning of his right to the assistance of counsel, and (5) whether or not such defendant was without the assistance of counsel when questioned and when giving such confession.

The critical part of the statute is:

The presence or absence of any of the above-mentioned factors is to be taken into consideration by the judge and need not be conclusive on the issue of voluntariness of the confession.

(Emphasis added.)

This is a legislative attempt to reverse the mandatory requirement of the Miranda warnings. Most legal commentators believe that this part of the statute will be declared unconstitutional by the Supreme Court of the United States, since the Miranda warnings rule is directly based on constitutional grounds.

The bill also provides for the abandonment of the federal McNabb-Mallory Rule. The bill would permit six hours of reasonable federal interrogation. The McNabb-Mallory Rule is based on a federal rule of criminal procedure that requires an accused person to be brought before a United States Commissioner without any unreasonable delay.

In the more than twenty years of federal decisions concerning the McNabb-Mallory Rule, the time for interrogation by federal officers has been narrowed down, for all practical purposes, to two hours. This destruction of the McNabb-Mallory Rule by the Congress of the United States may well survive the constitutional gauntlet since the rule was not based on the Fourth Amendment but rather on a federal rule of criminal procedure.

ATTACK ON THE CIRCUMSTANCES OF THE INTERROGATION. The voluntariness of a confession is determined after the Miranda hurdle, on the basis of the totality of the circumstances surrounding the interrogation. The place where the accused was questioned, the extent of the questioning, the time the questioning endured, the number of interrogators, and whether or not the accused was held incommunicado, are all significant circumstances that should be explored by defense counsel at a Fifth Amendment suppression hearing.

Of course, if the person being interrogated is harmed, threatened, or harassed by police interrogators, the confession will be ruled involuntary.

The age, education, condition, and intelligence of the person being interrogated are also vital circumstances in the battle to establish the voluntariness of a confession and the validity of a waiver.

In summary, then, the defense attack at a Fifth Amendment suppression hearing will be an in-depth attempt to develop all of the circumstances surrounding the interrogation of the accused. Harsh, unfair, or inhuman treatment of the accused during interrogation is wrong not only because it is directly against the very foundations of our rule of law, but also because it is strictly a "no-yield" transaction as far as getting incriminating confessions in at the trial.

PROSECUTOR'S RESPONSIBILITY AT A FIFTH AMENDMENT SUPPRESSION HEARING

The law is that the burden is on the prosecution to establish by clear and convincing evidence that the accused waived his Fifth Amendment right against self-incrimination at the time he confessed to the crime. This places a tremendous burden on the prosecution. In order to meet this responsibility, it is recommended that innovative ways be sought to preserve the setting at the interrogation. Video-tapes, tape recorders, and neutral or impartial witnesses at the interrogation are all ways to preserve and present persuasive evidence of the voluntariness of the waiver and the fairness of the police interrogation techniques.

THE POLICE OFFICER AS A WITNESS AT THE SUPPRESSION HEARING

PRIOR PREPARATION. Before an officer testifies at a suppression hearing, it is essential for him to meet and discuss the case with the prosecutor. If the officer does not have an opportunity to discuss the case with the prosecutor, he should fully prepare himself by having an understanding of the theory to get the evidence in and by anticipating the probable lines of cross-examination by the defense attorney.

Prior preparation in most cases—particularly in arrest-search situations—means that the officer must develop every ounce of probable cause facts to justify the arrest. Only combinations of probable cause facts will justify an arrest or a search and, therefore, the officer must be ready to testify about them.

As an example, in a prosecution in the Eastern District of Pennsylvania for interstate theft of a motor vehicle, a police officer, unfortunately, had to take the witness stand at the suppression hearing without the opportunity of consulting with the prosecutor. The suppression hearing came suddenly—just at the last minute before trial—and the prosecutor, who was new and inexperienced, did not have the vaguest idea of what a suppression hearing was all about. The young prosecutor was caught completely off-guard.

The defense was attempting to suppress a driver's license and some other cards that had been taken from the defendant, as well as the stolen car itself. Since this stolen car case was an arrest-search situation, the burden was on the prosecution to establish justification for the arrest by showing probable cause.

The new prosecutor had to do what all young lawyers have to do when they are confronted with something new in a courtroom: he had to go on and fake it.

The arresting officer was called as a witness. The prosecutor asked him that age-old question: "Officer, what are the facts in this case?"

The officer identified himself as a Philadelphia police officer and indicated that at about 2:30 a.m. he was driving a police red car in North Philadelphia—a high crime area—that the defendant was driving slowly and could not spell his name, so he was arrested for stealing a car. After obtaining only these sketchy facts, the prosecutor turned the officer over to the defense for cross-examination. At this point it was quite clear that the prosecution had not sustained its burden requiring establishing justification for the arrest by persuasive probable cause. Neither the young prosecutor nor the officer was aware that they had not made a *prima facie* showing of a lawful probable cause arrest. The two facts that a man was driving slowly and that he couldn't spell his name could not add up in any language to justification to arrest for a stolen car.

The prosecution had definitely missed the boat, but they were to be saved by an over-zealous, underskilled defense lawyer. The defense lawyer exhibited tremendous forensic skill at cross-examination, but what he failed to realize was that his questioning of the officer under these circumstances was extremely disastrous for his client.

The defense attorney picked up a book and was leafing through it—Hamlet-like. This immediately aroused the Judge's curiosity and he leaned forward with eager anticipation. Finally, after a prolonged pause, the defense lawyer looked up at the police officer on the witness stand and said, "I can't seem to find it, Officer. Is it a crime in Pennsylvania to drive slowly?" This question represents excellent technique for a defense lawyer in arguing to the court, but it was definitely the wrong question to ask this officer. In arguing to the judge, it is effective for a defense lawyer to isolate a fact from the other probable cause facts and hold it up to ridicule and scorn. But that is argument, and this was cross-examination.

The officer responded that he knew that it was not a crime in Pennsylvania to drive slowly, but that the way the defendant was driving had really aroused his curiosity. He testified that, driving in his red car, he followed the defendant for about eight blocks. He said that the defendant was driving about six miles an hour and stopped at six green lights. He said that the defendant kept looking back toward the red car all this time.

What happened here was that the defense lawyer, by his question on cross-examination, began to develop in detail the probable cause facts justifying the arrest. Unbelievably enough, he was doing what the prosecutor should have done!

Defense counsel blundered on. He did not even realize that the officer's last answer was beginning to undercut the defense charge of an unlawful arrest. Dramatically, he stormed to the exhibit table, picked up the driver's license and saw, to his amazement, that the name on the driver's license was "Brown." Recalling that the officer said that the accused could not spell his name, the defense lawyer swung around on the officer and shouted, "Officer, you realize that you are under oath, don't you?" This attack startled the officer and captured the judge's whole-hearted interest. The officer, momentarily confused, responded with a weak "yes" and the defense attorney, in an even louder voice shouted to the witness, "You realize that you can go to jail if you don't tell the truth, don't you?" The officer was recovering his composure and this time he answered "yes" with some conviction.

"Nonetheless, Officer," shouted defense counsel, "you mean to tell this Court . . . under oath . . . that my client could not spell his name . . . B-R-O-W-N?"

The officer hesitated for a moment as all eyes in the courtroom froze on him. Finally he said, "I didn't say he couldn't spell 'Brown.' He couldn't spell the first name on that license —it was 'E-p-h-r-a-i-m.' "

This time the defense lawyer realized that he had been gathering the probable cause facts to justify the arrest for the prosecution, and he was literally staggered by the police officer's answer.

The officer then added that the driver's license was a New York license, that there was a round space for a picture to be placed on the license, that the defendant had a square picture in that round space, and that right away the officer thought it was a phony license. Another probable cause fact came leaping into the record with this volunteered statement.

Now the defense attorney realized he had completely undone himself. He had established the prosecution's justification for the arrest by his inept cross-examination. The judge leaned forward, looked down at the defense lawyer and said softly, "Are you satisfied?" The judge was satisfied—he declared the arrest lawful and held the search incidental to that arrest as a reasonable one. The defendant was later convicted of interstate theft of a motor vehicle.

CONDUCT AS A WITNESS. A police officer who is to be a witness at a suppression hearing should be neat, courteous, and professional. The appearance of a witness and the manner in which he testifies is always important in a courtroom. The police witness should never take an antagonistic attitude toward the defendant, the defense lawyer, or anyone else in the courtroom. He should be polite, answer "Yes, sir" and "No, sir" and be particularly respectful when addressing the court.

A law enforcement officer who is a professional knows the law, anticipates the probable lines of cross-examination, and keeps his answers short so that he does not over-extend himself by volunteering information. At most suppression hearings the officer's principal responsibility is to testify to all the probable cause facts that would justify the seizure of the incriminating evidence.

The officer should always remember that in a suppression hearing both the prosecution and the defense are constantly battling for the "atmosphere" of the case. Suppression cases are frequently decided on the total impact of the facts. Major factors in a suppression hearing are the seriousness of the crime that is being investigated, whether or not there was a police emergency, what investigative tactics the officer used, what the officer's purpose was in doing what he did, and what justification he had for taking action.

FINDINGS OF FACT. It is advisable for both the prosecution and the defense to request the court to make findings of fact when ruling on the suppression issue. This protects both the prosecution and the defense positions on appeal.

Finally, police officers should be aware that the court measures police conduct against the best citizen, not the worst. Since an accused is presumed to be innocent until proved guilty, the judge must approach the police activity as it would affect a good, law-abiding citizen. The judge's standard then is objective—he cannot subjectively think of just this one defendant. He must think of the impact of the police activity on all law-abiding citizens.

COMMENTARIES ON SUPREME COURT DECISIONS

Cases Involving

The Fourth Amendment
The Fifth Amendment
The Sixth Amendment

CHAPTER VI

CASES INVOLVING THE FOURTH AMENDMENT

The right of the people to be secure in their persons, houses, papers, and effects, against unreasonable searches and seizures shall not be violated, and no warrants shall issue but upon probable cause, supported by oath or affirmation, and particularly describing the place to be searched and the persons or things to be seized.

Fourth Amendment to the United States Constitution

THE RIGHT TO PRIVACY

HISTORY OF THE RIGHT. The Fourth Amendment protects the right to privacy. That right is older than the Bill of Rights, older than the Constitution, even older than the Common Law. The right to privacy is as old as the history of man.

Privacy – the right to be left alone – is the central concept in free society. Privacy supplies the only setting where an individual can live in dignity.

In Colonial times, Americans were particularly concerned by Redcoat invasions of their privacy. The Bostonians complained that "our houses and even our bed chambers are exposed to be ransacked. Our boxes, chests and trunks broke open, ravaged and plundered by wretches, whom no prudent man would venture to employ even as menial servants."

In Virginia, Patrick Henry complained, "Excise men may come in multitudes; for the limitation of their numbers no man knows. They may, unless the general government be restrained by a bill of rights, or some similar restriction, go into your cellars and rooms, and search, ransack, and measure everything you eat, drink and wear. They ought to be restrained within proper bounds."

James Otis of Massachusetts denounced the infamous Writ of Assistance as "the worst instrument of arbitrary power, and the most destructive of English liberty and the fundamental principles of law, that was ever found in an English law-book."

As Jacob W. Landyski has stated in his book, *Search and Seizure and the Supreme Court:*

> In a very real sense, the Fourth Amendment embodies a spiritual concept: the belief that to value the privacy of home and person and to afford Constitutional protection against the long reach of government is no less than to value human dignity, and that this privacy must not be disturbed except in case of overriding social need, and then only under stringent safeguards. As Justice Brandeis so eloquently summed up the essence of the Amendment:
>
>> The makers of our Constitution undertook to secure conditions favorable to the pursuit of happiness. They recognized the significance of man's spiritual nature, of his feelings and of his intellect. They knew that only part of the pain, pleasure and satisfaction of life are to be found in material things. They sought to protect Americans in their belief and thoughts, their emotions and their sensations. They conferred, as against government, the right to be let alone as the most comprehensive of rights and as the right most valued by civilized men.

DIMENSIONS OF PRIVACY

Mr. Justice Douglas in his dissent in the Hayden case focused on the dimensions of privacy in a free society:

> The personal effects and possessions of the individual . . . are sacrosanct from prying eyes, from the long arm of the law, from any rummaging by police. Privacy involves the choice of the individual to disclose or reveal what he believes, what he thinks, what he possesses. The article may be a nondescript work of art, a manuscript of a book, a personal account book, a diary, invoice, personal clothing, jewelry, or whatnot. Those who wrote the Bill of Rights believed that every individual needs both to communicate with others and to keep his affairs to himself. The dual aspect of privacy means that the individual should have the freedom to select for himself the time and circumstances when he will share his secrets with others and decide the extent of that sharing. This is his prerogative–not that of the States. The Framers, who were as knowledgeable as we, knew what police surveillance meant and how the practice of rummaging through one's personal effects could destroy freedom.

The right to privacy, however, must yield under certain circumstances, when there is justifiable or probable cause for reasonable police intrusion. Reasonable police investigation to solve crime or to protect life is certainly not prohibited by the Fourth Amendment.

SAFEGUARDS

When reasonable police investigation escalates to the point where it begins to invade the inner sanctum of someone's privacy, the police must act within the framework of certain Fourth Amendment constitutional safeguards. These constitutional safeguards were designed to protect the right of privacy from unfair, unjust, and unreasonable government investigations.

First the Fourth Amendment requires a law enforcement officer to obtain arrest and search warrants whenever he reasonably can. This requirement interposes as a safeguard to privacy an independent and impartial judge between the police and the suspect to make sure that there is probable cause or justification for the arrest or for the search.

Second is the requirement of probable cause under oath or pre-existing facts justifying the arrest or search.

Specifying crime, person, place, and object to be seized is a third constitutional safeguard to the right to privacy.

One of the major recurring themes of the Supreme Court of the United States in the area of search and seizure is an undisguised attempt to encourage law enforcement officers to obtain search warrants whenever possible. In the case of the *United States v. Ventresca*, 380 U.S. 102 (1965), Mr. Justice Goldberg began his discussion of the law regarding search warrants stressing the essential fact that in the Ventresca case the search was made pursuant to a search warrant:

> We began our analysis of this constitutional rule mindful of the fact that in this case a search was made pursuant to a search warrant. In discussing the Fourth Amendment policy against unnecessary invasions of privacy, we stated in *Aguilar v. Texas*, 378 U.S. 108:
>
> > An evaluation of the constitutionality of a search warrant should begin with the rule that "the informed and deliberate determinations of magistrates empowered to issue warrants . . . are to be preferred over the hurried action of officers . . . who may happen to make arrests." . . . The reasons for this rule go to the foundations of the Fourth Amendment.

The Court then emphasized its strong preference for search warrants by indicating that in a doubtful or marginal case, a search under a warrant would be sustained whereas the same search without one would fail. The Court's reasoning for preferring a search warrant had been stressed by Mr. Justice Jackson in *Johnson v. United States*, 333 U.S. 10:

> The point of the Fourth Amendment, which often is not grasped by zealous officers, is not that it denies law enforcement the support of the usual inferences which reasonable men draw from evidence. Its protection consists in requiring that those inferences be drawn by a neutral and detached magistrate instead of being judged by the officer engaged in the often competitive enterprise of ferreting out crime. Any assumption that evidence sufficient to support a magistrate's disinterested determination to issue a search warrant will justify the officers in making a search without a warrant would reduce the Amendment to a nullity and leave the people's homes secure only in the discretion of police officers.

When time or circumstances make it impossible for a law enforcement officer to get an arrest or search warrant, some of these Fourth Amendment safeguards are by-passed on the grounds of necessity. Regardless of necessity or emergency, the constitutional safeguard of probable cause is *never* dispensed with.

THE MEANING OF PROBABLE CAUSE. Probable cause is the oldest and certainly one of the most important concepts in criminal law. Actually, from a practical point of view, the words "probable cause" are and have been for more than two thousand years the two most important words in criminal law. Probable cause provides for the citizen, as well as for the police a fixed, predetermined standard in the critical areas of arrest and search. To the citizen and to the police there is no more important concept in our entire legal system.

Probable cause is loosely defined as *facts or apparent facts that would lead a reasonable man to believe that someone has committed a crime.* While in some countries, such as the Soviet Union, a citizen may be arrested and held indefinitely without the police justifying the arrest by a single fact, the Fourth Amendment demands that citizens be arrested in this country only for cause based upon facts. This concept of probable cause has acquired its legal potency in the United States because it has constitutional dimensions and because it is interpreted in the final analysis by impartial judges rather than by the citizens or the police. The severe penalty that the courts impose on police officers who fail to abide by the spirit of the Fourth Amendment is the suppression of evidence. Police anywhere in the country, whether state or federal, who seize evidence illegally can never use it in any criminal courtroom.

The law enforcement officer who does not thoroughly understand this standard of probable cause is in the unenviable position of a man who does not know what he is doing. For in order to make a valid arrest, with or without a warrant, or in order to make a search, a police officer must have probable cause. In order to prepare arrest and search warrants, a police officer must know how to articulate probable cause. Equally important to the law enforcement officer, particularly at this time, is the fact that if he is sued civilly for false arrest or false imprisonment, the most important issue at his trial is the probable cause upon which he acted. In a civil rights criminal prosecution against an officer, the critical issue at trial is the nature of the officer's probable cause. Obviously, a thorough knowledge and understanding of the standard of probable cause is essential for all law enforcement officers.

The law of probable cause is such that while there is no restriction on the police with regard to the kind of facts that they may use to justify an arrest, there is nonetheless a compelling necessity to justify the use of the police arrest power. At the arrest level or the probable cause stage of a criminal proceeding, there are no rules of evidence. There are no rules of exclusion, such as the Hearsay Rule, or rules concerning prejudicial evidence. Everything is admissible, whether it is information from a third party or a criminal record or an indication of criminal associations. Decisions in the probable cause area indicate strongly that courts assess the justification for an arrest by the combination of circumstances known to the officer at the time he makes an arrest. If the combination of circumstances is strong enough to generate a reasonable belief that a crime has been committed and that the officer is arresting the likely culprit, the arrest will be lawful. It is only when the police act without cause that courts must strike down the illegal police conduct by suppressing evidence.

The Suppression Rule

MAPP, *Petitioner v.* STATE OF OHIO

(367 U.S. 643 – Decided June 19, 1961)

FACTS. Hard facts make hard cases. In *Mapp v. Ohio*, the factual setting that developed at the suppression hearing revealed that the arresting officers' tactics were in direct conflict with the most important values of the Fourth Amendment. Mr. Justice Clark, who delivered the majority opinion, indicated that Miss Mapp had been convicted in Ohio for possessing obscene material and succinctly recited the facts of the case:

> On May 23, 1957, three Cleveland police officers arrived at appellant's residence in that city pursuant to information that "a person (was) hiding out in the home, who was wanted for questioning in connection with a recent bombing, and that there was a large amount of policy paraphernalia being hidden in the home." Miss Mapp and her daughter by a former marriage lived on the top floor of the two-family dwelling. Upon their arrival at that house, the officers knocked on the door and demanded entrance but appellant, after telephoning her attorney, refused to admit them without a search warrant. They advised their headquarters of the situation and undertook a surveillance of the house.
>
> The officers again sought entrance some three hours later when four or more additional officers arrived on the scene. When Miss Mapp did not come to the door immediately, at least one of the several doors to the house was forcibly opened and the policemen gained admittance. Meanwhile Miss Mapp's attorney arrived but the officers, having secured their own entry, and continuing in their defiance of the law, would permit him neither to see Miss Mapp nor to enter the house. It appears that

Miss Mapp was halfway down the stairs from the upper floor to the front door when the officers, in this high-handed manner, broke into the hall. She demanded to see the search warrant. A paper, claimed to be a warrant, was held up by one of the officers.

She grabbed the "warrant" and placed it in her bosom. a struggle ensued in which the officers recovered the piece of paper and as a result of which they handcuffed appellant because she had been "belligerent" in resisting their official rescue of the "warrant" from her person. Running roughshod over appellant, a policeman "grabbed" her, "twisted (her) hand," and she "yelled (and) pleaded with him" because "it was hurting." Appellant, in handcuffs, was then forcibly taken upstairs to her bedroom where the officers searched a dresser, a chest of drawers, a closet and some suitcases. They also looked into a photo album and through personal papers belonging to the appellant. The search spread to the rest of the second floor including the child's bedroom, the living room, the kitchen and a dinette. The basement of the building and a trunk found therein were also searched. The obscene materials for possession of which she was ultimately convicted were discovered in the course of that widespread search.

At the trial no search warrant was produced by the prosecution, nor was the failure to produce one explained or accounted for. At best, "There is, in the record, considerable doubt as to whether there ever was any warrant for the search of defendant's home."

EXTENSION OF THE SUPPRESSION RULE. It was on these facts, or the lack of them, that the Supreme Court of the United States placed the Suppression Rule upon all 50 states. The Supreme Court indicated that the Fourth Amendment is contained, by inference, in the Fourteenth, and that from the day of its decision, June 19, 1961, any evidence that was illegally obtained by the police would be inadmissible in any courtroom in the country. Basically, the Mapp case demonstrates a complete lack of probable cause to justify the arresting of Miss Mapp. Of course, at the time the police applied force and searched her apartment, she was unmistakably under arrest.

Since there was no search warrant and no consent for the search in the Mapp case, the prosecution was placed in the difficult position of attempting in some measure to justify the search of Miss Mapp's apartment by her arrest. The rule is that if the police lawfully arrest a person they may make a search incidental to that arrest for the primary purpose of protecting themselves. In this case when the police used force and made a search, they were utilizing arrest powers and they had to justify the use of those powers as of the minute that they started to use them. The only factual justification that they had for taking any action against Miss Mapp at all was the loose "information," which could certainly never justify the arrest of anyone.

Mr. Justice Clark quoted from prior Supreme Court opinions:

> The criminal goes free, if he must, but it is the law that sets him free. Nothing can destroy a government more quickly than its failure to observe its own laws, or worse, its disregard of the charter of its own existence . . . Our government is the potent, the omnipresent teacher. For good or for ill, it teaches the whole people by its example. . . . If the government becomes a lawbreaker, it breeds contempt for law; it invites every man to become a law unto himself; it invites anarchy.

Finally, Mr. Justice Clark eloquently stated why the Supreme Court of the United States felt that it had to impose the Suppression Rule on the states:

> The ignoble shortcut to conviction left open to the State tends to destroy the entire system of constitutional restraints on which the liberties of the people rest. Having once recognized that the right to privacy embodied in the Fourth Amendment is enforceable against the States, and that the right to be secure against rude invasions of privacy by state officers is, therefore, constitutional in origin, we can no longer permit that right to remain an

empty promise. Because it is enforceable in the same manner and to like effect as other basic rights secured by the Due Process Clause, we can no longer permit it to be revocable at the whim of any police officer who, in the name of law enforcement itself, chooses to suspend its enjoyment. Our decision, founded on reason and truth, gives to the individual no more than that which the Constitution guarantees him, to the police officer no less than that to which honest law enforcement is entitled, and, to the courts, that judicial integrity so necessary in the true administration of justice.

Search Warrants

AGUILAR, *Petitioner v.* STATE OF TEXAS

(378 U.S. 108—Decided June 15, 1964)

FACTS. On January 8, 1960, Officers Strickland and Rogers from the Narcotic Division of the Houston Police Department prepared a state search warrant to search for narcotics in Aguilar's home. The critical probable cause section of their affidavit recited:

> Affiants have received reliable information from a credible person and do believe that heroin, marihuana, barbiturates and other narcotics and narcotic paraphernalia are being kept at the above described premises for the purpose of sale and use contrary to the provisions of law.

The search warrant was issued by a local justice of the peace and the officers, after knocking on Aguilar's door and announcing their authority and purpose, seized the defendant in the act of attempting to dispose of a packet of narcotics. At Aguilar's trial in a Texas state court, his defense lawyer objected to the seizure of the narcotics on the ground that the search warrant was invalid. Defense counsel argued that the probable cause for the search warrant had not been spelled out in the affidavit.

Mr. Justice Goldberg, in speaking for the majority of the Court, emphasized the purpose of the search warrant:

> An evaluation of the constitutionality of a search warrant should begin with the rule that "the informed and deliberate determinations of magistrates empowered to issue warrants . . . are to be preferred over the hurried action of officers . . . who may happen to make arrests." *United States v. Lefkowitz,* 285 U.S. 452, 464. The reasons for this rule go to the foundations of the Fourth Amendment. A contrary rule "that evidence sufficient to support a magistrate's disinterested determination to issue a search warrant will justify the officers in making a search without a warrant would reduce the Amendment to a nullity and leave the people's homes secure only in the discretion of police officers." *Johnson v. United States,* 333 U.S. 10, 14. . . . Thus, when a search is based upon a magistrate's, rather than a police officer's, determination of probable cause, the reviewing courts will accept evidence of a less "judicially competent or persuasive character than would have justified an officer in acting on his own without a warrant" . . . and will sustain the judicial determination so long as "there was substantial basis for (the magistrate) to conclude that the narcotics were probably present . . ."

THE SUPREME COURT DECISION. The majority of the Court held that the probable cause affidavit in this Texas search warrant was insufficient because it did not provide *any factual basis* for the justice of the peace's determination that probable cause existed. The affidavit was fatally defective in that it contained no affirmative information that affiant spoke with personal knowledge and that it did not indicate the source of the complainant's belief. Primarily, the probable cause affidavit was defective because it did not set forth a sufficient factual basis upon which a finding of probable cause could be made. The justice of the peace in the Aguilar case could certainly not judge for himself the persuasiveness of the facts relied upon by the Houston narcotics officers to show probable cause, because they had not placed any facts in their affidavit.

For the law enforcement officer, the Aguilar case signifies the absolute necessity of outlining concisely and persuasively the essential facts relied upon to justify the search. The probable cause affidavits in search warrants *must* contain factual allegations and assertions so that the person authorizing the warrant can make an independent judgment to issue the warrant based on the facts presented by the officer.

The preference for using search warrants to obtain evidence is so strong that if the warrants are drawn properly there is little or no likelihood that the evidence obtained by the search warrant will ever be suppressed. Secondly, at a suppression hearing the defense has to attack the search warrant itself rather than the officer who obtained the warrant.

DEFECTS IN WARRANTS. There are basically only three major fatal defects with regard to a search warrant, and each one of the critical areas of default can easily be avoided by the officer if he knows the law. The first fatal defect is that if the officer is not under oath when he presents the essential facts to the issuing authority, the search warrant never takes its first breath as a living legal document. The Fourth Amendment to the United States Constitution requires "probable cause be under oath," and since this is a constitutional requirement it cannot be dispensed with. The reason for the oath requirement is to prevent accusations by faceless informants rising to a level of probable cause. The requirement that the officer be under oath when he presents his facts to the issuing authority is not burdensome; all that the officer has to do as he hands the search warrant and affidavit to the issuing authority is to say, "I swear the facts are true."

The second fatal defect in a search warrant is the one that is pointed up by the Supreme Court of the United States in the Aguilar case; that is, failing to set forth the essential facts justifying the search. The probable cause section of a search warrant affidavit should present the guilt-laden facts underlying the search persuasively so that the judicial officer who issues the search warrant has a sufficient factual foundation to determine that a search should be made. If the officer merely uses terms such as "information" and "surveillance" without stating what the information or surveillance was, then he is not presenting any facts to the court issuing the warrant—he is merely presenting conclusions.

The third fatal defect is the failure to find whatever is being sought at the place described in the search warrant. Most law enforcement officers are fully aware of this fact. In other words, if a search warrant is issued for a dwelling at 310 South Narberth Avenue, that warrant is no authority to search 315 South Narberth Avenue. The incriminating evidence must be found at the place described in the warrant, and the judicial authority to search under the search warrant is *only* for the place described in the warrant.

United States *v.* Ventresca

(380 U.S. 102—Decided March 1, 1965)

FACTS. In the summer of 1961, federal alcohol and tobacco tax officers of the Internal Revenue Service focused an extensive investigation on a house at 148½ Coburn Avenue in Worcester, Massachusetts.

In a short time, the investigators uncovered an illegal still run by Ventresca, and now the federal officers had to swing into action. A well prepared raid on the still was planned and the agents obtained a search warrant to search 148½ Coburn Avenue. The affidavit for the warrant recited in some detail the facts establishing probable cause.

Affidavit for Search Warrant

BEFORE W. ARTHUR GARRITY, Worcester, Massachusetts. The undersigned being duly sworn deposes and says:

That he has reason to believe that on the premises known as a one-family light green wooden frame dwelling house located at 148½ Coburn Avenue, Worcester, occupied by Giacomo Ventresca and his family, together with all approaches and appurtenances thereto, in the District of Massachusetts, there is now being concealed certain property, namely an unknown quantity of material and certain apparatus, articles and devices, including a still and distilling apparatus setup with all attachments thereto, together with an unknown quantity of mash, an unknown quantity of distilled spirits, and other material used in the manufacture of non-tax-paid liquors; which are being held and possessed, and which have been used and are intended for use, in the distillation, manufacture, possession, and distribution of non-tax-paid liquors, in violation of the provisions of 26 USC 5171 (a), 5173, 5178, 5179 (a), 5222 (a), 5602, and 5686.

And that the facts tending to establish the foregoing grounds for issuance of a Search Warrant are as follows:

SEE ATTACHED SHEET

/s/ WALTER A. MAZAKA
Investigator, Alcohol and Tobacco Tax Div., Internal Revenue Service

Sworn to before me, and subscribed in my presence, August 31st, 1961

/s/ W. ARTHUR GARRITY
United States Commissioner

Based upon observations made by me, and based upon information received officially from other Investigators attached to the Alcohol and Tobacco Tax Division assigned to this investigation, and reports orally made to me describing the results of their observations and investigation, this request for the issuance of a search warrant is made.

On or about July 28, 1961, about 6:45 P.M., an observation was made covering a Pontiac automobile owned by one Joseph Garry. Garry and one Joseph Incardone put thirteen bags of sugar into the car. These bags of sugar weighed sixty pounds each. Ten such bags were put into the trunk, and three were placed in the rear seat. Those in the rear seat were marked "Domino." The others appeared to have similar markings. After the sugar was loaded into the car, Garry together with Incardone drove it to the vicinity of 148 Coburn Avenue, Worcester, Massachusetts, where the car was parked. Sometime later, the car with its contents was driven into the yard to the rear of 148 and between the premises 148 and 148½ Coburn Avenue. After remaining there about twenty-five minutes, the same two men drove in the direction of Boston.

On August 2, 1961 a Pontiac car owned by Garry, and driven by Garry with Incardone as a passenger, was followed from Boston to Worcester. The car appeared heavily laden. The car was again driven into the driveway of 148 and 148½ Coburn Avenue to the rear of the yard and between the above-numbered houses.

On August 7, 1961 at least six sixty-pound bags of Domino Sugar were loaded into the Pontiac owned by Garry. The loading was done by Garry and Incardone. The car traveled from Boston to Worcester, then to Holden, and returned with its contents and entered the driveway at 148 and 148½ Coburn Avenue, where the car was parked at the rear between the two houses.

On August 11, 1961 new empty metal or tin cans were transferred from a car owned by Incardone to the Pontiac owned by Garry on Highland Street in Hyde Park. The Pontiac was driven by Garry with Incardone as a passenger to Worcester, and into the yard at 148 and 148½ Coburn Avenue to the rear and between the two numbered premises.

On August 16, 1961 the Pontiac was observed. In the back seat bags of sugar were observed covered with a cloth or tarpaulin. A sixty-pound bag of sugar was on the front seat. Garry was observed after loading the above-described sugar into the car placing a carton with various five-pound bags of sugar on the top of the tarpaulin. The car was then driven by Garry with Incardone as a passenger to Worcester together with its contents into the yard at 148 and 148½ Coburn Avenue to the rear of and between the two houses. About Midnight on the same night, the Pontiac driven by Garry with Incardone as a passenger was seen pulling up to the premises at 59 Highland Street, Hyde Park, where Garry lives. Garry opened the trunk of his car, and removed ten five-gallon cans therefrom, and placed them on the sidewalk. He then entered the house, and opened a door on the side. Incardone made five trips from the sidewalk to the side of the house carrying two five-gallon cans on each such trip. It appeared that the cans were filled. On each of these trips, Incardone passed the two cans to someone standing in the doorway. Immediately after the fifth such trip, Garry came out of the door and joined Incardone. They walked to the sidewalk, and talked for a few moments. Incardone then drove away, and Garry went into his home.

On August 18, 1961 Investigators smelled an odor of fermenting mash on two occasions between 4:00 A.M. and 5:00 A.M. The first such odor was detected as they walked along the sidewalk in front of 148 Coburn Avenue, and the second such odor was detected from the side of 148 Coburn Avenue. At or about the same time, the Investigators heard certain metallic noises which cannot be further identified by source or sound.

On August 24, 1961 the Pontiac was observed parked at a bowling alley and coffee shop off Route 9. The back of the car contained what appeared to be boxes covered by a cloth or tarpaulin, but which cannot be more specifically identified. On the front seat of the car was observed a sixty-pound bag of Revere Sugar. Garry and Incardone were observed in the restaurant or coffee shop eating. Later the car was seen driven to the rear of 148 between 148 and 148½ Coburn Avenue, Worcester.

About Midnight the Pontiac was observed pulling up in front of Garry's house at 59 Highland Street, Hyde Park. Garry was driving, and Incardone was a passenger. They both got out of the car. Garry opened the trunk, and then entered his house. From the trunk of the car there was removed eleven five-gallon cans which appeared to be filled. Incardone made six trips to a door on the side of the house. He carried two five-gallon cans on each trip, except the sixth trip. On that trip he carried one can, having passed the others to somebody in the doorway, and on the last trip he entered the house. He remained there at least forty-five minutes, and was not observed to leave.

On August 28, 1961 Garry drove Incardone in his car to Worcester. On Lake Ave. they met Giacomo Ventresca, who lives at 148½ Coburn Avenue, Worcester. Ventresca entered the car driven by Garry. The car was then driven into the yard to the rear of 148 and between 148 and 148½ Coburn Avenue. An observation was made that empty metal cans, five-gallon size, were being taken from the car owned by Garry, and brought into the premises at 148½ Coburn Avenue, which was occupied by Ventresca. Later, new cans similar in size, shape and appearance were observed being placed into the trunk of Garry's car while parked at the rear of 148 and in front of 148½ Coburn Avenue. The manner in which the cans were handled, and the sound[s] which were heard during the handling of these cans, were consistent with that of cans containing liquid.

On August 30, 1961, at about 4:00 A.M., an odor of fermenting mash was detected while Investigators were walking on the sidewalk in front of 148 Coburn Avenue. At the same time, they heard sounds similar to that of a motor or a pump coming from the direction of 148½ Coburn Avenue.

The foregoing information is based upon personal

knowledge and information which has been obtained from Investigators of the Alcohol and Tobacco Tax Division, Internal Revenue Service, who have been assigned to this investigation.

/s/ WALTER A. MAZAKA

This search warrant contained innumerable facts—but it had one critical weakness. Mr. Justice Douglas centered on it in his dissent in *Ventresca.* The essential facts, Mr. Justice Douglas said, were recited in 12 paragraphs within the affidavit, but only the first and last paragraphs described who was actually making the observations that established the facts. Since facts are only as credible as their source, Mr. Justice Douglas reasoned, a court could not possibly know from the affidavit how credible the facts were.

At Ventresca's suppression hearing the search warrant was declared valid and the evidence seized by the agents was admitted. The federal appellate court reversed Ventresca's conviction on the grounds that the search warrant was invalid because of the lack of identification of sources.

The Supreme Court of the United States then reversed the appellate court and held the search warrant lawful.

Search Warrant Formula for Success—Common Sense

After documenting its preference for search warrants in *Aguilar,* the Court focused on the practical problem of how affidavits for search warrants should be tested and interpreted by the courts. The critical question for the Supreme Court was whether search warrant affidavits should be held to a high legal standard. Should search warrant affidavits be reviewed by a legal technician's standard or should there be some lesser test used by the courts in interpreting them? The Supreme Court in *Ventresca* emphatically declared that search warrant affidavits should be tested and interpreted by the courts in a non-technical, commonsense fashion. The Court stated:

> These decisions reflect the recognition that the Fourth Amendment's commands, like all constitutional requirements, are practical and not abstract. If the teachings of the Court's cases are to be followed and the constitutional policy served, affidavits for search warrants, such as the one involved here, must be tested and interpreted by magistrates and courts in a commonsense and realistic fashion. They are normally drafted by nonlawyers in the midst and haste of a criminal investigation. Technical requirements of elaborate specificity once exacted under common law pleadings have no proper place in this area. A grudging or negative attitude by reviewing courts toward warrants will tend to discourage police officers from submitting their evidence to a judicial officer before acting.

The Ventresca decision also realistically cautions law enforcement officers that when they prepare search warrant affidavits in which part of the probable cause relates to surveillance or information, it is essential for the officer preparing the affidavit to indicate concisely not only what the surveillance or information was but also *who* conducted the surveillance or related the information. Mr. Justice Douglas cautioned the police in his dissenting opinion in *Ventresca:*

> If hearsay evidence is to be relied upon in the preparation of an affidavit for a search warrant, the officer or attorney preparing such an affidavit should keep in mind that hearsay statements are only as credible as their source and only as strong as their corroboration. And where the source of the information is in doubt and the corroboration by the affiant is unclear, the affidavit is insufficient.

Since the Fourth Amendment requires probable cause under oath, it is particularly important to establish the truthfulness of information that officers rely on as part of their probable cause for search warrants. If the source of the information is weak, the police investigation corroborating that information must be strong. Since hearsay information plays such a substantial role in police investigations, it is essential for the professional law enforcement officer to develop a skilled technique in corroborating information that is relayed to him. Corroboration is required by the courts in order to assure the truthfulness of the hearsay information.

CONCLUSION. The Supreme Court, therefore, announced unequivocally in the Ventresca decision its preference for police to obtain search warrants from the courts and declared that affidavits for search warrants would be reviewed by all the courts in the land in a commonsense, realistic, and nontechnical manner. The Court instructed both state and federal courts not to invalidate a search warrant by interpreting affidavits in a hypertechnical legal fashion and that in any doubtful or marginal cases, the search warrant should be upheld.

In the closing words of the Ventresca decision, Mr. Justice Goldberg indicated that the Supreme Court is alert to the problems of law enforcement officers and is hopeful that law enforcement officers, whenever possible, will go to the courts for search warrants. If law enforcement officers follow the spirit of the Fourth Amendment by going to the courts for search warrants, individual liberties will be fully protected and respect for the law will be greatly promoted:

> . . . This Court is equally concerned to uphold the actions of law enforcement officers consistently following the proper constitutional course. This is no less important to the administration of justice than the invalidation of convictions, because of disregard of individual rights or official overreaching. In our view the officers in this case did what the Constitution requires. They obtained a warrant from the judicial officer "upon probable cause, supported by Oath or affirmation, and particularly describing the place to be searched, and the . . . things to be seized." It is vital that having done so their actions should be sustained under a system of justice responsive both to the needs of individual liberty and to the rights of the community.

Compulsory Blood Samples

ARMANDO SCHMERBER, *Petitioner v.* STATE OF CALIFORNIA

(384 U.S. 757—Decided June 20, 1966)

FACTS. Armando Schmerber was convicted in the Los Angeles Municipal Court for the criminal offense of drunken driving. The evidence showed that Schmerber and a friend had been drinking at a tavern and a bowling alley and that they left the bowling alley at about midnight on November 12, 1964. Shortly after the two drove away in the car, the car skidded across the road and struck a tree. Both Schmerber and his friend were injured and were taken to a nearby hospital for treatment.

The record unequivocally indicated that Schmerber had been arrested at the hospital while he was receiving treatment for his injuries. At the hospital, at the direction of a Los Angeles police officer, a blood sample was withdrawn from Schmerber's body by a physician on duty at the hospital. Schmerber contended at the trial that he refused to allow the blood sample to be withdrawn on the advice of his lawyer and that the compulsory taking of his blood by the doctor at the direction of the police officer violated his right not to be unreasonably searched and seized under the Fourth Amendment, his privilege against self-incrimination under the Fifth Amendment, his right to counsel under the Sixth Amendment, and his right to due process under the Fourteenth Amendment. The trial court refused to suppress the blood sample and admitted it together with oral testimony indicating that the chemical analysis of Schmerber's blood revealed a proportion of alcohol in his blood at the time of his offense which indicated intoxication. On this, together with other evidence, Schmerber was convicted for the misdemeanor of drunken driving.

THE FOURTEENTH AMENDMENT. Mr. Justice Brennan, in speaking for the majority of five justices of the Supreme Court of the United States, had no difficulty with Schmerber's claim that his rights under the due process clause of the Fourteenth Amendment were violated by the withdrawal of his blood and the admission of the analysis in evidence against him. The Court focused on the critical fact that the extraction of Schmerber's blood was made by a physician in a simple, medically accepted manner in a hospital enviornment. Since the Supreme Court held earlier, in *Breithaupt v. Abram*, 352 U.S. 432 (1957), that it was not a violation for police officers to have a doctor remove a blood sample from an unconscious defendant, the Court rejected Schmerber's due process argument by affirming their ruling in *Breithaupt*.

THE FIFTH AMENDMENT. The Supreme Court then considered in some detail the allegations that the taking of the blood at the direction of the police violated Schmerber's Fifth Amendment privilege against self-incrimination. First, Mr. Justice Brennan noted:

> It could not be denied that in requiring petitioner to submit to the withdrawal and chemical analysis of his blood the State compelled him to submit to an attempt to discover evidence that might be used to prosecute him for a criminal offense. He submitted only after the police officer rejected his objection and directed the physician to proceed. The officer's direction to the physician to administer the test over petitioner's objection constituted compulsion for the purposes of the privilege. The critical question, then, is whether petitioner was thus compelled "to be a witness against himself."

The Court continued, stressing the constitutional foundation of the right against self-incrimination:

> Government—state or federal—must respect the dignity and integrity of its citizens. In order to maintain a "fair state-individual balance," the government must

shoulder the entire load and respect the inviolability of the human personality in our accusatory system of criminal justice.

The Court stated that the police purpose in withdrawing the blood was to use it to incriminate the defendant as evidence of his criminal guilt.

Mr. Justice Brennan then strongly emphasized the fact that the history of the Fifth Amendment clearly delineated that the privilege against self-incrimination relates only to *oral* or *testimonial compulsion.* The protection of the Fifth Amendment is offered to prevent the cruel, simple expedient of compelling a man to convict himself from his own mouth.

The Supreme Court held that the Fifth Amendment privilege against self-incrimination offers no protection against compulsion to submit to fingerprinting, photographing, or measurements, to write or speak for identification, to appear in court, to stand, to assume a stance, to walk, or to make a particular gesture. All of these activities merely make the suspect the source of "real or physical evidence" and do not violate the Fifth Amendment privilege against self-incrimination. In sum, the majority opinion implies that testing accused persons during interrogation, such as lie detector tests, may actually be directed toward eliciting responses which are essentially testimonial. To compel persons to submit to testing, such as lie detector tests, since it is an attempt to determine his guilt or innocence on the basis of psychological responses, would, according to the majority, seem to violate both the spirit and history of the Fifth Amendment. This language bodes ill for the continued use of lie detector tests as an interrogation technique.

Mr. Justice Brennan, speaking for the majority, indicated that even if the blood test evidence were an incriminating product of compulsion, it was not Schmerber's oral testimony and it consequently could not be held inadmissible on the grounds of the Fifth Amendment.

The Court next turned to Schmerber's contention that his right to counsel under the Sixth Amendment was violated by the officer's directing the doctor to take the blood sample without his consent, a refusal which was based on the advice of his lawyer. The Court reasoned that since Schmerber was not entitled to assert his Fifth Amendment privilege to prevent the blood sample from being taken, he had no greater right to assert his Fifth Amendment privilege because his lawyer erroneously advised him that he could. The Court held therefore that the taking of the blood sample here did not violate Schmerber's right to counsel under the Sixth Amendment.

THE FOURTH AMENDMENT. Finally, the Court turned to the question as to whether Schmerber's Fourth Amendment right against unreasonable search and seizure was violated by the officer's directing the doctor to remove a blood sample. Mr. Justice Brennan unequivocally indicated that the taking of the blood sample clearly constituted a "search" of the person and was within the purview of the Fourth Amendment. Since the Court, in effect, was dealing with a police intrusion into a human body, as contrasted with the typical case of a police intrusion into someone's home, the Court announced that it was approaching the unique problem of searches into the body for the first time. The Court held that there was sufficient probable cause for the Los Angeles police officer to arrest Schmerber and charge him with driving an automobile while under the influence of an intoxicating liquor. The Court then discussed the probable cause justifying Schmerber's arrest:

> The police officer who arrived at the scene shortly after the accident smelled liquor on petitioner's breath, and testified that petitioner's eyes were "bloodshot, watery, sort of glassy appearance." The officer saw Schmerber again at the hospital within two hours after the accident. The officer testified that Schmerber was in the same condition and had the same symptoms of drunkenness at the hospital. The officer testified that he informed Schmerber that he was under arrest, that he was entitled to the services of an attorney, that he could remain silent, and that anything Schmerber told him could be used against him in evidence.

Having found the arrest lawful based on the probable cause and the guilt-laden facts confronting the officer, the Court next considered whether or not a blood sample was the type of evidence that the police could marshal in an investigation. The history of the Fourth Amendment indicates that the police may seize fruits or evidence of crime, instrumentalities of crime, and concealed weapons. These historical rules, according to the majority of the Supreme Court, have little applicability to searches involving intrusion beyond the body's surface. Mr. Justice Brennan wrote:

> The interest in human dignity and privacy which the Fourth Amendment protects forbid any such intrusions on the mere chance that desired evidence might be obtained. In the absence of a clear indication that in fact such evidence will be found, these fundamental human interests require law officers to suffer the risk that such evidence may disappear unless there is an immediate search. . . .
>
> The importance of informed, detached and deliberate determinations of the issue whether or not to invade another's body in search of evidence of guilt is indisputable and great. . . .

The Court reasoned that the officer in the Schmerber case was confronted with an emergency and that he would not have been able to obtain a search warrant under the circumstances, since by the time he got it the alcohol content in the blood would have dropped and, in effect, the evidence would be destroyed.

The Court held:

> Given these special facts, we conclude that the attempt to secure evidence of blood-alcohol content in this case was an appropriate incident to Schmerber's arrest. The blood test was administered in a humane and reasonable manner, and the taking of the blood was reasonable when projected against the history and purpose of the Fourth Amendment.

In conclusion, Mr. Justice Brennan, for the majority, emphasized the unique factors in the Schmerber case and stated:

> It bears repeating, however, that we reach this judgment only on the facts of the present record. The integrity of an individual's person is a cherished value of our society. That we today hold that the Constitution does not forbid the States minor intrusions into an individual's body under stringently limited conditions in no way indicates that it permits more substantial intrusions, or intrusions under other conditions.

Informants

GEORGE MCCRAY, *Petitioner v.* STATE OF ILLINOIS

(386 U.S. 1042—Decided March 20, 1967)

ISSUE. The Supreme Court of the United States, in the McCray case ruled on the validity of an arrest by a police officer without a warrant where the probable cause for the arrest was based almost entirely on information from an unidentified informant.

FACTS. In the early morning hours of January 16, 1964, two Chicago police officers met with an informant in an unmarked car. The informant told the officers that on that same morning he had been "Boobie George" selling narcotics and that he had narcotics with him. Both officers knew that "Boobie George" was an alias for George McCray, whom one of the officers had arrested previously. The informant told the police officers that McCray was in the vicinity of the officers, near 47th and Calumet Streets in Chicago. The officers drove with the informant to the immediate area where the informant indicated the defendant would be, and the informant pointed him out. McCray spotted the police car and hurriedly walked away between two buildings. The officers stopped McCray, advised him that they had information that he had narcotics with him, and placed him in the police car. The officers then searched McCray and found heroin in a cigarette package.

The defense took the position at the suppression hearing that the officers had to name their informant. The defense argued, in effect, that since the police had not seen McCray actually commit a crime and since they did not have an arrest warrant for him, the police had taken the law in their own hands, basing their actions on an informant's tip. The defense argued further that the police superseded the magistrate, and that the identity of the informant had to be disclosed because the defense could not show an absence of probable cause by any other means. The defense relied on the language of the Supreme Court in *Beck v. Ohio*, 379 U.S. 89, 96:

> An arrest without a warrant bypasses the safeguards provided by an objective predetermination of probable cause, and substitutes instead the far less reliable procedure of an after-the-event justification for the arrest or search, too likely to be subtly influenced by the familiar shortcomings of hindsight judgment.

The defense's position was that unless the identity of the informant were disclosed and the informant produced, the result would be that the policeman himself would conclusively determine the validity of his own arrest.

RELIABILITY OF THE INFORMANT. The critical question for the prosecution at the suppression hearing was to establish the reliability of the informant either by demonstrating that he had been reliable in the past or by corroborating his information independently. In the McCray case, one of the officers testified that he had arrested McCray previously, that he knew he was involved in narcotics, and that he knew he used the alias of "Boobie George." The officer also indicated that the informant had been reliable in the past, that he had known the informant for approximately a year, and that the informant had given him information regarding narcotics fifteen or sixteen times at least. The officer testified specifically that the information given by this informant had proved to be accurate in the past and had resulted in numerous arrests. On cross-examination the officer was even more specific as to the informant's previous reliability, giving the names of people who had been convicted as a result of the informant's information. A second officer testified that he had known the informant for five years and had received information approximately fifty times from him, and the informant in his judgment was completely reliable. The prosecution pointed out that the informant in this case was neither a participant in the crime nor was he actually present at the time of arrest.

Both officers were asked on cross-examination the identity of the informant. The prosecutor objected and claimed the informant privilege. The judge presiding at the suppression hearing sustained the prosecutor's objection and refused to force the officers to identify their informant.

In 1957, the Supreme Court of the United States in *Roviaro v. Unted States,* 353 U.S. 53, outlined in some detail the doctrine of the informant privilege:

> What is usually referred to as the informer's privilege is in reality the Government's privilege to withhold from disclosure the *identity* of persons who furnish information of violations of law to officers charged with enforcement of the law. . . . The purpose of the privilege is the furtherance and protection of the public interest in effective law enforcement. The privilege recognizes the obligation of citizens to communicate their knowledge of the commission of crimes to law enforcement officials and, by preserving their anonymity, encourages them to perform that obligation.
>
> The scope of the privilege is limited by its underlying purpose. Thus, where the disclosure of the contents of a communication will not tend to reveal the identity of an informer, the contents are not privileged. Likewise, once the identity of the informer has been disclosed to those who would have cause to resent the communication, the privilege is no longer applicable.

> A further limitation on the applicability of the privilege arises from the fundamental requirements of fairness. Where the disclosure of an informer's identity, or of the contents of his communication, is relevant and helpful to the defense of an accused, or is essential to a fair determination of a cause, the privilege must give way.
> (Emphasis added.)

THE SUPREME COURT DECISION. Mr. Justice Stewart delivered the opinion of the Supreme Court in *McCray* and initially focused on the validity of McCray's arrest and search. The Court held that each of the officers in the case described in detail what the informant had actually said about McCray and why each officer thought that the information was reliable. Mr. Justice Stewart indicated that the testimony informed the Court of the "underlying circumstances from which the informant concluded that the narcotics were where he claimed they were, and some of the underlying circumstances from which the officer concluded that the informant . . . was 'credible' or his information 'reliable.'"

Mr. Justice Stewart then turned his attention to the question with constitutional dimensions – whether or not the identity of the informant should have been divulged.

Quoting the language of Chief Justice Weintraub of the Supreme Court of New Jersey in *State v. Burnett,* 201 A.2d 39, Mr. Justice Stewart emphasized the fact that this was a suppression hearing and not a trial:

> If a defendant may insist upon disclosure of the informant in order to test the truth of the officer's statement that there is an informant or as to what the informant related or as to the informant's reliability, we can be sure that every defendant will demand disclosure. He has nothing to lose and the prize may be suppression of damaging evidence if the State cannot afford to reveal its source, as is so often the case. And since there is no way to test the good faith of a defendant who presses the demand, we must assume the routine demand would have to be routinely granted. The result would be that the

State could use the informant's information only as a lead and could search only if it could gather adequate evidence of probable cause apart from the informant's data. Perhaps that approach would sharpen investigatorial techniques, but we doubt that there would be enough talent and time to cope with crime upon that basis. Rather we accept the premise that the informer is a vital part of society's defensive arsenal. The basic rule protecting his identity rests upon that belief.

We must remember also that we are not dealing with the trial of the criminal charge itself. There the need for a truthful verdict outweighs society's need for the informer privilege. Here, however, the accused seeks to avoid the truth. The very purpose of a motion to suppress is to escape the enculpatory thrust of evidence in hand, not because its probative force is diluted in the least by the mode of seizure, but rather as a sanction to compel enforcement officers to respect the constitutional security of all of us under the Fourth Amendment. *State v. Smith*, 37 N. J. 481, 486 (1962). If the motion to suppress is denied, defendant will still be judged upon the untarnished truth.

The Fourth Amendment is served if a judicial mind passes upon the existence of probable cause. Where the issue is submitted upon an application for a warrant, the magistrate is trusted to evaluate the credibility of the affiant in an *ex parte* proceeding. As we have said, the magistrate is concerned, not with whether the informant lied, but with whether the affiant is truthful in his recitation of what he was told. If the magistrate doubts the credibility of the affiant, he may require that the informant be identified or even produced. It seems to us that the same approach is equally sufficient where the search was without a warrant, that is to say, that it should rest entirely with the judge who hears the motion to suppress to decide whether he needs such disclosure as to the informant in order to decide whether the officer is a believable witness.

Mr. Justice Stewart next cited the leading *Treatise on Evidence* compiled by Professor Wigmore:

> A genuine privilege, on . . . fundamental principle . . ., must be recognized for the *identity of persons supplying the government with information concerning the commission of crimes.* Communications of this kind ought to receive encouragement. They are discouraged if the informer's identity is disclosed. Whether an informer is motivated by good citizenship, promise of leniency or prospect of pecuniary reward, he will usually condition his cooperation on an assurance of anonymity—to protect himself and his family from harm, to preclude adverse social reactions and to avoid the risk of defamation or malicious prosecution actions against him. The government also has an interest in nondisclosure of the identity of its informers. Law enforcement officers often depend upon professional informers to furnish them with a flow of information about criminal activities. Revelation of the dual role played by such persons ends their usefulness to the government and discourages others from entering into a like relationship.
>
> That the government has this privilege is well established, and its soundness cannot be questioned.
>
> 8 Wigmore, *Evidence* 2374

Finally, Mr. Justice Stewart dispatched a variety of constitutional attacks by the defense and firmly supported the prosecution's right to invoke the informant privilege:

> In sum, the Court in the exercise of its power to formulate evidentiary rules for federal criminal cases has consistently declined to hold that an informer's identity need always be disclosed in a federal criminal trial, let alone in a preliminary hearing to determine probable cause for an arrest or search. Yet we are now asked to hold that the Constitution somehow compels Illinois to abolish the informer's privilege from its law of evidence, and to require disclosure of the informer's identity in every such preliminary hearing where it appears that the officers made the arrest or search in reliance upon facts supplied

by an informer they had reason to trust. The argument is based upon the Due Process Clause of the Fourteenth Amendment, and upon the Sixth Amendment right of confrontation, applicable to the States through the Fourteenth Amendment. *Pointer v. Texas,* 380 U.S. 400. We find no support for the petitioner's position in either of those constitutional provisions.

The arresting officers in this case testified, in open court, fully and in precise detail as to what the informer told them and as to why they had reason to believe his information was trustworthy. Each officer was under oath. Each was subjected to searching cross-examination. The judge was obviously satisfied that each was telling the truth, and for that reason he exercised the discretion conferred upon him by the established law of Illinois to respect the informer's privilege.

Nothing in the Due Process Clause of the Fourteenth Amendment requires a state court judge in every such hearing to assume the arresting officers are committing perjury. "To take such a step would be quite beyond the pale of this Court's proper function in our federal system. It would be a wholly unjustifiable encroachment by this Court upon the constitutional power of States to promulgate their own rules of evidence . . . in their own state courts. . . ."

The petitioner does not explain precisely how he thinks his Sixth Amendment right to confrontation and cross-examination was violated by Illinois' recognition of the informer's privilege in this case. If the claim is that the State violated the Sixth Amendment by not producing the informer to testify against the petitioner, then we need no more than repeat the Court's answer to that claim a few weeks ago in *Cooper v. California:*

> Petitioner also presents the contention here that he was unconstitutionally deprived of the right to confront a witness against him, because the State did not produce the informant to testify against him.

This contention we consider absolutely devoid of merit.

On the other hand, the claim may be that the petitioner was deprived of his Sixth Amendment right to cross-examine the arresting officers themselves, because their refusal to reveal the informer's identity was upheld. But it would follow from this argument that no witness on cross-examination could ever constitutionally assert a testimonial privilege, including the privilege against compulsory self-incrimination guaranteed by the Constitution itself. We have never given the Sixth Amendment such a construction, and we decline to do so now.

CONCLUSION. The McCray case not only protects the informant privilege but also presents to the officer the necessity for establishing the past reliability of the informant. Where the informant is not produced, the truthfulness of the information supplied to the officer will depend principally on the informant's previous reliability or upon the independent corroboration of his information by the police. Since so many arrests depend in large measure upon informant information, it is essential for the professionally minded police officer to know that the burden is on him to establish the reliability of the information.

McCray, then, stands for the proposition that an arrest by police officers without a warrant, based on information by an unidentified but reliable informant, is valid, and that the informant's identity need not be disclosed at the suppression hearing, particularly where his reliability is established by the prosecution's evidence.

Hot-Pursuit Arrest

WARDEN, MARYLAND PENITENTIARY, *Petitioner* *v.* BENNIE JOE HAYDEN

(387 U.S. 294 – Decided May 29, 1967)

ISSUE. The Hayden case involved a clear-cut case of police emergency. Within five minutes after an armed robbery, police officers in hot pursuit of the armed bandit closed in on his home. They had neither an arrest nor a search warrant.

This case is important because it discusses, in some detail, three critical questions with regard to arrest and search by police officers without warrants. First – the police *entry* without a warrant; second – the *scope* and *purpose* of the search incidental to the defendant's arrest; and third – the objects which could be *seized* by the police at the time of the defendant's arrest.

FACTS. On the morning of March 17, 1962, an armed robber held up the Diamond Cab Company in Baltimore, Maryland, and escaped on foot with nearly $400.

Two cab drivers in the vicinity of the holdup followed the robber to 2111 Cocoa Lane in Baltimore. One of the drivers alerted the Company dispatcher by radio that the robber was a Negro, 5 feet 8 inches tall, wearing a light cap and a dark jacket, and that he had gone into the house on Cocoa Lane.

The dispatcher immediately relayed this information to the Baltimore Police. Within minutes, the police surrounded the house. An officer knocked on the door and told the woman who answered – a Mrs. Hayden – that a robber had entered her house. The officer requested permission to search the house for the robber, and Mrs. Hayden did not object.

The officers then entered the house and spread out simultaneously to search the cellar and the first and second floors. Hayden, the defendant, was found upstairs in a bedroom. He was pretending that he was asleep. As the officer arrested him, the other officers searching the house reported that there was no other man in the house.

About that same time, an officer, hearing rushing water in the bathroom, discovered a shotgun and a pistol in the flush tank. A second officer who was "searching the cellar for the man or the money" found a jacket and trousers like the ones the robber had worn in the washing machine. Ammunition for the guns was found in Hayden's bedroom, and so was a light cap. The guns, the ammunition, and the clothing were seized by the arresting officers and offered in evidence against the defendant at the trial. Hayden was convicted for this armed robbery and the Maryland courts upheld his conviction. Then Hayden attempted to get habeas corpus relief in the Federal District Court of Maryland, but that court refused to take jurisdiction.

Hayden appealed this habeas corpus denial to the Court of Appeals for the Fourth Circuit and that federal appellate court reversed Hayden's conviction on the ground that the *clothing* was improperly admitted into evidence since it had "evidential value only" and was not subject to seizure by the police. The Supreme Court of the United States reversed the Fourth Circuit's ruling and held that the entry, the search, and the seizure involved in the case were lawful and reasonable under the Fourth Amendment.

THE ENTRY. Mr Justice Brennen, in speaking for the majority of the Court in the Hayden case, stated that the police entry here without an arrest or search warrant was lawful because of the police emergency involved in the hot pursuit of this armed robber. The Court emphasized that the facts made it clear that the police officers acted properly;

> . . . The police were informed that an armed robbery had taken place, and that the suspect had entered 2111 Cocoa Lane less than five minutes before they reached it. They acted reasonably when they entered the house, and began to search for a man of the description they had been given, and for weapons which he had used in the robbery or might use against them. The Fourth Amendment does not require police officers to delay in the course of an investigation if to do so would gravely injure their lives or the lives of others. Speed here was essential. . . .

SCOPE OF THE SEARCH. The general rule with regard to the scope of search or the areas that may be searched incidental to an arrest is that the police may only search the person being arrested and the area within his immediate control. *Harris v. U.S.*, 331 U.S. 145. Ordinarily, when a man is arrested in one room of his home, only that room may be searched incidental to his arrest, since that is the only area under his immediate possession and control.

In this case, as soon as the officers entered Hayden's home, they spread out and searched the entire house. The scope of the search incidental to Hayden's arrest was the whole house. Since Hayden was arrested in an upstairs bedroom, the defense – asserting the general rule – claimed that the police had exceeded their authority and searched too extensively.

The Court rejected this argument and held that because of the hot-pursuit emergency "only a thorough search of the house for persons and weapons could have insured that Hayden was the only man present and that the police had control of all weapons which could be used against them or to effect an escape."

Here, the search of Hayden's home was prior to or immediately contemporaneous with Hayden's arrest. The clear purpose of the police search of the entire home was to find a dangerous criminal. Because of these critical facts, the Supreme Court stated a commonsense exception to the general rule limiting the scope of search incidental to an arrest:

> . . . The permissible scope of search must, therefore, at the least, be as broad as may reasonably be necessary to prevent the danger that the suspect at large in the house may resist or escape.

Police officers are given the right to make a search incidental to arrest, to protect themselves and to prevent the destruction of evidence. This is why the general rule restricts the scope of the search to the area within the immediate control of the person being arrested. As an example, if a man is arrested in his living room, it is highly unlikely that he could harm an officer with a weapon concealed in his attic for the obvious reason that he couldn't get to it.

The Hayden search is distinguished from ordinary arrest-search situations because it involved a hot-pursuit arrest. The purpose of the search in *Hayden* was to find the suspect and to secure weapons. It was clearly the emergency situation that permitted the police an enlarged scope of search in this case.

SEIZURE. Since approximately 1886, American case law and American statutes have established that law enforcement officers may seize only three kinds of objects. Historically, only instrumentalities of crime, stolen property, or contraband may be seized by the police. The articles of Hayden's clothing seized by the Baltimore police do not fit in any of these three categories.

In the past, it had been held uniformly that items of evidential value only, such as clothing, could not lawfully be searched for or seized by government officers. This rule limiting what may be seized by the police has been called the "mere evidence" rule. Mr. Justice Brennen indicated in this case that the reason for the rule limiting the seizure of evidence is that *"limitations upon the fruit to be gathered tend to limit the quest itself. U.S. v. Poller*, 43 F, 2d 911. . . ." The "mere evidence" rule has been associated historically with searches for private papers. The leading case supporting the "mere evidence" rule stated that search warrants "may not be used as a means of gaining access to a man's house or office and solely for the purpose of making search to secure evidence to be used against him in a penal proceeding . . ." *Gouled v. U.S.*, 225 U.S. 309.

The "mere evidence" rule was founded on a property law concept that in order for the government to seize property, the government had to have a superior right to possession of that property. Clearly, the government would have a valid claim of superior interest in property that was stolen or contraband or an instrumentality of a crime. In *Hayden* the Supreme Court of the United States categorically rejected this property law concept of the "mere evidence" rule, holding:

> We have recognized that the principal object of the Fourth Amendment is the protection of privacy rather

> than *property*, and have increasingly discarded fictional and procedural barriers rested on property concepts.
> (Emphasis added.)

The Supreme Court went further in *Hayden* and emphatically rejected the entire "mere evidence" rule by concluding that the Constitution does not restrict searches and seizures to these three traditional categories.

Mr. Justice Brennen emphasized the need for the evidence that is seized to be connected logically with the crime:

> *Schmerber* settled the proposition that it is reasonable within the terms of the Fourth Amendment, to conduct otherwise permissible searches for the purpose of obtaining evidence which would aid in apprehending and convicting criminals. The requirements of the Fourth Amendment can secure the same protection of privacy whether the search is for "mere evidence" or for fruits, instrumentalities or contraband. There must, of course, be a nexus—automatically provided in the case of fruits, instrumentalities or contraband—between the item to be seized and criminal behavior. *Thus in the case of "mere evidence," probable cause must be examined in terms of cause to believe that the evidence sought will aid in a particular apprehension or conviction*. In so doing, consideration of police *purposes* will be required. . . . But no such problem is presented in this case. The clothes found in the washing machine matched the description of those worn by the robber and the police therefore could reasonably believe that the items would aid in the identification of the culprit.
> (Emphasis added.)

EPILOGUE. The Hayden case is important to law enforcement officers because the Supreme Court of the United States has focused fully for the first time on police emergency powers. In cases involving hot pursuit, the overriding *purpose* of the officers is to protect lives and to apprehend a dangerous criminal. Because of this purpose, the Supreme Court has acknowledged that a police officer has broader searching powers in a hot-pursuit case than he would have in a standard arrest situation. The broader searching power is given to the police officers in limited emergency cases as a matter of practical necessity. *Hayden* establishes this doctrine conclusively.

Hayden destroys a doctrine that has been a unique principle of the American law of search and seizure for nearly a hundred years. The Supreme Court has indicated in this case that the "mere evidence" rule is anachronistic, and it has jettisoned the rule. This means that police officers may obtain search warrants for or may search and seize, incidental to arrest, objects that do not fit in the three traditional categories of fruits of the crime, instrumentalities, and contraband. The Hayden case gives police the authority to seize *any evidence* that would logically connect the suspect with the crime.

There is, however, one caveat for the police. Throughout history and today, there has been, and is, a great abhorrence of government officials rooting through a citizen's private papers. Police officers should realize that a citizen's personal private papers have the highest priority in terms of the right to privacy.

Mr. Justice Douglas, in his dissent in *Hayden,* indicated that he believes that there is an inner zone of privacy that the Fourth Amendment protects against any invasion "by the police through raids, by the Legislature through laws or by the Magistrate through the issue of warrants." Douglas believes that any invasion of personal private papers is of itself "unreasonable" within the meaning of the Fourth Amendment. Justice Douglas's strong language should act as a warning to the professionally minded police officer. The warning is that under the Fourth Amendment, the area where the right to privacy is the strongest is in the area of private papers. Consequently, the police must realize that when they rummage through someone's private papers, they had better have the gravest justification for it. The right to privacy in a free society demands the utmost protection for private papers, for it is not too great a step from failing to have privacy in our personal papers to failing to have privacy in our thoughts.

Inspections

Roland Camara, *Appellant* v. Municipal Court of the City and County of San Francisco

(387 U.S. 523—Decided June 5, 1967)

> The poorest man may in his cottage bid defiance to all the forces of the Crown. It may be frail—its roof may shake—the wind may blow through it—the storm may enter—the rain may enter—but the King of England cannot enter. All his forces dare not cross the threshold of the room and tenement!—Pitt the Elder

ANATOMY OF THE INSPECTION TECHNIQUE. For more than two hundred years, states have empowered their officers to make inspections without warrants of homes, businesses, and properties in order to promote the general welfare. As early as 1722, Pennsylvania enacted laws authorizing official inspection of flour and bread, and later added laws providing for inspections of both pork and hemp. In 1761, Pennsylvania enacted a law permitting government inspection in order to regulate and repair sewerage systems. While these laws did not relate to criminal behavior, penalties were created for resisting inspections.

As the years flowed on, more and more areas became subject to governmental inspections for the public good. For nearly two hundred years, the practice of inspections without warrants was tacitly accepted by the American people. However, in the late 1950's, with the category of needs for inspections increasing, the constitutionality of routine governmental inspections without court authorization came under seige. In 1959, a closely divided Supreme Court rejected the argument that these inspections were unauthorized invasions of privacy in violation of the Fourth Amendment.

These inspections—which are authorized by local law—represent the traditional exercise of lawful police powers to maintain minimum health and welfare standards. However noble the motive, it is nevertheless apparent that each time an inspector knocks on any door, it is the full force of government knocking, and with each knock someone's privacy is about to be invaded.

FACTS. Roland Camara leased an apartment in San Francisco and refused to allow a city inspector to enter and inspect his apartment without a search warrant. The City of San Francisco, under a local ordinance, brought criminal action against Camara for refusing to permit the warrantless entry and inspection of his apartment. Camara was convicted and his conviction was upheld in the California courts.

The United States Supreme Court reversed Camara's conviction and held that the Fourth Amendment's protection against unreasonable searches and seizures applies even to routine inspections for violations of housing, health, fire, or sanitation codes.

In a companion case, *See v. City of Seattle,* 387 U.S. 541, the Supreme Court held that the Fourth Amendment's protection against unreasonable searches and seizures also applied to "similar inspections of commercial structures." The Court did make the distinction that commercial structures which are open to the general public may, however, be inspected by government officials without search warrants.

BALANCING THE VALUES—SOCIETY'S NEED AND THE INDIVIDUAL'S PRIVACY. Mr. Justice White, speaking for a unanimous Court in *Camara,* initially focused on the recent past before turning to the problem presented by this case:

> In *Frank v. Maryland,* 359 U.S. 360, this Court upheld by a 5 to 4 vote a State conviction of a homeowner who refused to permit a Municipal health inspector to enter and inspect her premises without a search warrant. In *Ohio ex rel Eaton v. Price,* 364 U.S. 263, a similar conviction was affirmed by an equally divided Court. Since those closely divided decisions, more intensive

> efforts on all levels of government to contain and eliminate urban blight have led to an increasing use of inspections while numerous decisions of this Court have more fully defined the Fourth Amendment's effect on state and municipal action . . .
>
> In view of the growing nationwide importance of the problem, we noted probable jurisdiction in this case to reexamine whether administrative inspection programs, as presently authorized and conducted, violate the Fourth Amendment's rights as those rights are enforced against the States through the Fourteenth Amendment.

After an honest reappraisal of the inspection technique, the majority in *Camara* shattered the dual thesis supporting a warrantless inspection that had been upheld in the Frank case. The Frank concepts—that routine inspections of private property are "less hostile intrusions" than typical searing police searches, and that inspection laws were essentially civil rather than criminal in nature had to yield to new realities.

Mr. Justice White, in *Camara,* stressed that even the most law-abiding citizen has a very tangible interest in limiting the circumstances under which the serenity of his home may be broken by official authorities. The possibility of warrantless governmental entry into our homes under the guise of official business is a serious threat to personal and family security.

Calling attention to the fact that most regulatory laws—fire, health, and housing codes—are enforced by criminal prosecution, the majority in *Camara* underscored that the entire area of government inspection is permeated with criminal sanctions.

Balancing the need for routine inspections to promote the general welfare against the nature of the governmental intrusion into privacy, the Supreme Court gave "full recognition to the competing public and private interests . . . at stake" and determined, in *Camara,* that the Fourth Amendment's concept of safeguarding the privacy and security of our citizens was paramount. Emphasizing that the right of officers to thrust themselves into a home is of grave concern not only to the individual but to a society which chooses to dwell in reasonable security and freedom from surveillance, the Court in *Camara* insisted on the constitutional protection of the warrant process in contested routine inspection cases. Essentially, the Court held:

> When the right to privacy must reasonably yield to the right to search (or inspection) has, as a rule, to be decided by a judicial officer, not by a policeman or government enforcement agent.

The Camara opinion, in reversing *Frank v. Maryland,* demonstrates once again the fact that the concept of due process under our system of laws is never inflexibly frozen or petrified into unyielding stone. Our law–particularly our constitutional law–is flexible, and it meets the demand of new realities, new attitudes, and new times.

CONSTITUTIONAL SAFEGUARDS FOR INSPECTIONS. The Supreme Court in *Camara* emphatically adhered to the "warrant machinery" contemplated by the Fourth Amendment. In cases of dispute the occupant–before the inspector can gain entrance –must know whether or not the inspection is actually required, and whether or not the inspector is exceeding the lawful limits of his authority. The protections provided by the warrant procedure provide for individualized review of the prior needs and justification for inspections.

Specifically, the Supreme Court held in *Camara:*

> . . . We hold that administrative searches of the kind at issue here are significant intrusions upon the interests protected by the Fourth Amendment; that such searches authorized and conducted without a warrant procedure lack the traditional safeguards which the Fourth Amendment guarantees to the individual, and that the reasons set forth in *Frank v. Maryland,* and in other cases, for upholding these warrantless searches are insufficient to justify so substantial a weakening of the Fourth Amendment's protections.

The really difficult question for the Supreme Court to face in this case was whether or not an undiluted standard of probable cause should be applied when the governmental intrusion was a mere inspection rather than an incriminating search.

Mr. Justice White, for the majority, began by examining the governmental interest requiring official intrusion:

> Unlike the search pursuant to a criminal investigation, the inspection programs at issue here are aimed at securing city-wide compliance with minimum physical standards for private property . . . because fire and disease may ravage large urban areas, and because unsightly conditions effect the economic values of neighboring structures . . . these inspections are necessary.

However, continued the Court, in determining whether a particular inspection is reasonable, "the need for the inspection must be weighed in terms of . . . reasonable goals of enforcement."

The Court determined that since inspections are "neither personal in nature, nor aimed at the discovery of evidence of a crime," and since "they involve a relatively smaller invasion of the urban citizen's privacy" *a lesser standard of probable cause would justify court authorization of inspections.*

The standard of probable cause for inspections, according to the Supreme Court, would vary with the municipal program being enforced. But the important aspects would be the passage of *time* since the last inspection, the *nature* of the building (a home or an apartment house), the *need* for the inspection, the *condition* of the entire area (for area inspections), and not necessarily on specific knowledge of the condition of a particular home.

Mr. Justice White argued that the majority was not "diluting the concept of probable cause" or authorizing "synthetic search warrants" or "lessening the overall protections of the Fourth Amendment." Underscoring the fact that the warrant procedure guarantees that the decision to search or inspect is justified in advance by a reasonable governmental interest, Mr. Justice White identified the rule here:

> If a valid public interest justifies the intrusion contemplated, then there is Probable Cause to issue a suitably restricted search warrant.

The majority opinion in *Camara* covers both individual inspections as well as general area inspections, when there is no particular compelling urgency to inspect immediately, Further, the majority stressed that in emergency situations, prompt, immediate – even if contested – inspections can be made lawfully without warrants.

Finally – on the practical side – the Supreme Court advised that *"warrants should normally be sought only if entry is refused."* Similarly, the requirement for warrant procedure does not suggest any change in what seems to be the prevailing local policy in most situations of authorizing entry, but not entry by force, to inspect.

CONCLUSION. The impact of the Camara decision on the practical methods of inspection will probably not be significant. It is only in unusually important or contested inspections that government officials must resort to the "warrant machinery" and get prior court approval for inspections. Undeniably, the warrant procedure must be invoked in all contested inspections. Emergency inspections are not affected in any way by this decision.

While the impact of the Camara decision will not be particularly great on law enforcement officers, the decision has far-reaching ramifications in constitutional law. This case demonstrates the Supreme Court's vigilance in protecting the citizen from even what appears to be mild, innocuous invasions of privacy.

In an era of changing, complexity and the computer – when government intrusions into privacy are becoming legion – it is undeniable that the Supreme Court has again struck a major blow for freedom.

Electronic Eavesdropping–Wiretapping

RALPH BERGER, *Petitioner v.* STATE OF NEW YORK

On Writ of Certiorari to the Court of Appeals of New York
(338 U.S. 41 – Decided June 12, 1967)

> Eaves-droppers, or such as listen under walls or windows or eaves of a house, to hearken after discourse, and thereupon to frame slanderous and mischievous tales, are a common nuisance, and are presentable at the court leet; or are indictable at the sessions, and punishable by finding sureties for their good behavior.
> *Blackstone's Commentaries, Vol. 4, Chap. XIII, Sec. 168.*

ISSUE. Ralph Berger was indicted and convicted in New York as the "go-between" in a conspiracy to bribe the Chairman of the New York State Liquor Authority. All of the evidence produced against Berger at his trial was in the form of electronic eavesdropping evidence that had been obtained by means of a minifon recording device – a bug. The bug had been installed in the office of a man named Harry Steinman by law enforcement officers under a court order authorized by New York's permissive eavesdropping statute.

Berger's lawyers objected at trial to the playing to the jury of relevant portions of the bugged recordings. Charging violations of the Fourth, Fifth, Ninth, and Fourteenth Amendments, the defense asserted that the New York statute permitting court-approved eavesdropping set up a system of electronic surveillance by trespassory intrusions into private, constitutionally protected premises, and was also an invasion of the guarantee against self-incrimination.

The trial court admitted the evidence and upheld the statute, and the highest court in New York, the Court of Appeals, affirmed the conviction. The Supreme Court of the United States granted certiorari to determine first whether or not electronic surveillance in itself was prohibited by the United States Constitution, and second, whether or not the New York statute authorizing court-supervised electronic eavesdropping was in itself constitutional.

EAVESDROPPING. Mr. Justice Clark, writing for the 6-3 majority of the Supreme Court in the Berger case, initially focused on the history and development of eavesdropping:

> Eavesdropping is an ancient practice which at common law was condemned as a nuisance. IV Blackstone, Commentaries, Sec. 168. In those days the eavesdropper listened by naked ear under the eaves of houses or their windows, or beyond their walls seeking after private discourse. The awkwardness and undignified manner of this method as well as its susceptibility to abuse was immediately recognized. Electricity, however, provided a better vehicle and with the advent of the telegraph surreptitious interception of messages began. As early as 1862 California found it necessary to prohibit the practice by statute. Statutes of California 1862, p. 288, CCLX 12. During the Civil War General J. E. B. Stuart is reputed to have had his own eavesdropper along with him in the field whose job it was to intercept military communications of the opposing forces. Subsequently newspapers reportedly raided one another's news gathering lines to save energy, time and money. Racing news was likewise intercepted and flashed to bettors before the official result arrived.
>
> The telephone brought on a new and more modern eavesdropper known as the 'wiretapper.' Interception was made by a connection with a telephone line. This activity has been with us for three-quarters of a century. Like its cousins, wiretapping proved to be a commercial as well as a police technique. Illinois outlawed it in 1895 and in 1905 California extended its telegraph interception prohibition

to the telephone. Some 50 years ago a New York legislative committee found that police, in cooperation with the telephone company, had been tapping telephone lines in New York despite an Act passed in 1895 prohibiting it. During prohibition days wiretaps were the principal source of information relied upon by the police as the basis for prosecutions. In 1934 the Congress outlawed the interception without authorization, and the divulging or publishing of the contents of wiretaps by passing Section 605 of the Communications Act of 1934. New York, in 1938, declared by constitutional amendment that "the right of the people to be secure against unreasonable interception of telephone and telegraph communications shall not be violated," but permitted by *ex parte* order of the Supreme Court of the State the interception of communications on a showing of "reasonable ground to believe that evidence of crime" might be obtained. McKinney Const. Art. I, Sec. 12.

Sophisticated electronic devices have now been developed (commonly known as "bugging") which are capable of eavesdropping on anyone in most any given situation. They are to be distinguished from "wiretapping" which is confined to the interception of telegraphic and telephonic communications. Miniature in size—no larger than a postage stamp (3/8″ x 3/8″ x 1/8″)—these gadgets pick up whispers within a room and broadcast them half a block away to a receiver. It is said that certain types of electronic rays beamed at walls or glass windows are capable of catching voice vibrations as they are bounced off the latter. Since 1940 eavesdropping has become a big business. Manufacturing concerns offer complete detection systems which automatically record voices under most any conditions by remote control. A microphone concealed in a book a lamp, or other unsuspecting place in a room, or made into a fountain pen, tie clasp, lapel button, or cuff link increases the range of these powerful wireless transmitters to a half mile. Receivers pick up the transmission with interference-free reception on a special wave frequency. And, of late, a combination mirror transmitter has been developed which permits not only sight but voice transmission up to 300 feet. Likewise, parabolic microphones, which can overhear conversations without being placed within the premises monitored, have been developed. . . .

Next the majority opinion discussed the law with regard to wiretapping and eavesdropping throughout the United States. In summary, Federal law unconditionally prohibits the interception and divulging of wiretaps, but it had no provision concerning other types of electronic eavesdropping. The laws of 36 states prohibit wiretapping, but 27 of these states permit "authorized interceptions" of some type. Seven states have laws prohibiting not only wiretapping but also surreptitious eavesdropping by mechanical or electronic devices. Six of these seven states, including New York, permit official court-ordered eavesdropping.

In June of 1968 the Congress of the United States enacted legislation outlawing not only wiretapping but also all electronic eavesdropping. A provision for closely supervised court-approved wiretapping or eavesdropping was also included. *Omnibus Crime and Safe Streets Act of 1968.*

FACTS. Two assistant district attorneys, working with the Rackets Bureau of the District Attorney's Office of New York County, signed affidavits requesting a court order under Section 813 of the New York Code of Criminal Procedure for the installation of an eavesdropping device in the office of a man named Harry Steinman. These affidavits recited that the District Attorney's Office had had a number of complaints indicating corruption in the State Liquor Authority, and that the Rackets Bureau had received information from a number of people who wanted to obtain or to retain liquor licenses that they were obliged to pay large sums of money to the Liquor Authority. The affidavits described in detail the methods by which bribe money was transmitted through certain lawyers to Authority officials. One of the affidavits asserted that a former employee of the Authority served as a "conduit" in these machinations and indicated that this evidence has been obtained by the installation of a prior court-approved electronic listening device in the former employee's office.

The affidavit continued that the initial eavesdropping order had enabled the District Attorney's Office to obtain evidence that secret criminal conferences setting up bribes had been held in Harry Steinman's office. The affidavit further recited that the evidence obtained from the first electronic eavesdropping order established that Steinman had agreed to pay $30,000 through the former employee of the State Liquor Authority in order to get a liquor license for the Palladium Ballroom in New York City. The Palladium had been the subject of hearings before the Liquor Authority because of narcotics arrests.

On this factual basis of information the District Attorney's office requested the court to permit them to install a recording device in Steinman's business office. On June 12, 1962, the court issued an order permitting "the recording of any and all conversations, communications and discussions" in Steinman's office for a period of 60 days.

After the listening device had been installed in Harry Steinman's office for 13 days, a definite criminal conspiracy was uncovered involving liquor licenses concerning the Playboy and the Tenement Clubs in New York City. The evidence obtained from the listening device installed in Steinman's office conclusively established Berger's role as the middleman for the principal conspirators in this large-scale, organised bribery ring.

All of the evidence admitted against Berger at his trial was in the form of recordings obtained from the court-approved electronic eavesdropping bug that had been placed in Steinman's office.

THE FEDERAL LAW CONCERNING EAVESDROPPING, REVISITED. Mr. Justice Clark, for the majority in *Berger*, presented a short history of the Supreme Court's treatment of electronic eavesdropping cases over the past forty years. His analysis—clear and concise—stated:

The Court was faced with its first wiretap case in 1928, *Olmstead v. United States,* 277 U.S. 438. There the interception of Olmstead's telephone line was accomplished without entry upon his premises and was, therefore, found not to be proscribed by the Fourth Amendment. The basis of the decision was that the Constitution did not forbid the obtaining of evidence by wiretapping unless it involved actual unlawful entry into the house. Statements in the opinion that "a conversation passing over a telephone wire" cannot be said to come within the Fourth Amendment's enumeration of "persons, houses, papers, and effects" have been negated by our subsequent cases as hereinafter noted. They found "conversation" was within the Fourth Amendment's protections, and that the use of electronic devices to capture it was a "search" within the meaning of the Amendment, and we so hold. In any event, Congress soon thereafter, and some say in answer to *Olmstead,* specifically prohibited the interception without authorization and the divulging or publishing of the contents of telephonic communications. And the *Nardone* cases, 302 U.S. 379 (1937) and 308 U.S. 338 (1939), extended the exclusionary rule to wiretap evidence offered in federal prosecutions.

The first "bugging" case reached the Court in 1942 in *Goldman v. United States,* 316 U.S. 129. There the Court found that the use of a detectaphone placed against an office wall in order to hear private conversations in the office next door did not violate the Fourth Amendment because there was no physical trespass in connection with the relevant interception. And in *On Lee v. United States,* 343 U.S. 747 (1952), we found that since "no trespass was committed" a conversation between Lee and a federal agent, occurring in the former's laundry and electronically recorded, was not condemned by the Fourth Amendment. Thereafter in *Silverman v. United States,* 365 U.S. 505 (1961), the Court found "that the eavesdropping was accomplished by means of an unauthorized physical penetration into the premises occupied by the petitioners." At 509. A spike a foot long with a microphone attached to it was inserted under a baseboard into a party wall until it made contact with the heating duct that ran through the entire house occupied by Silverman, making a perfect sounding board through which the conversations in question were overheard. Significantly, the Court held that its decision did "not turn upon the technicality of a trespass upon a party wall as a matter of local law. It is based upon the reality of an actual intrusion into a constitutionally protected area." At 512.

In *Wong Sun v. United States*, 371 U.S. 471 (1963), the Court for the first time specifically held that verbal evidence may be the fruit of official illegality under the Fourth Amendment along with the more common tangible fruits of unwarranted intrusion. It used these words:

> The exclusionary rule has traditionally barred from trial physical, tangible materials obtained either during or as a direct result of an unlawful invasion. It follows from our holding in *Silverman v. United States*, 365 U.S. 505, that the Fourth Amendment may protect against the overhearing of verbal statements as well as against the more traditional seizure of "papers and effects." At 485.

And in *Lopez v. United States*, 373 U.S. 427 (1963), the Court confirmed that it had "in the past sustained instances of 'electronic eavesdropping' against constitutional challenge, when devices have been used to enable government agents to overhear conversations which would have been beyond the reach of the human ear. . . . It has been insisted only that the electronic device not be planted by an unlawful physical invasion of a constitutionally protected area." At 438-439. In this case a recording of a conversation between a federal agent and the petitioner in which the latter offered the agent a bribe was admitted in evidence. Rather than "eavesdropping" the Court found that the recording "was used only to obtain the most reliable evidence possible of a conversation in which the Government's own agent was a participant and which that agent was fully entitled to disclose." At 439.

THE NEW YORK STATUTE. The New York statute authorized the issuance of "an *ex parte* order for eavesdropping" upon the oath or affirmation of the attorney general, a district attorney, or a police officer above the rank of sergeant of any police department in the state.

According to the statute, the oath or affirmation had to state that there were *reasonable grounds* to believe that evidence would be obtained. The statute demanded that the person or persons whose conversations were to be overheard and recorded had to be identified particularly, and that the reason for the eavesdropping order be presented. In the case of wiretapping, the particular telephone number had to be identified. The statute further provided that the judge could examine under oath any applicant or other witness to satisfy himself of the existence of *reasonable grounds* for the application. The statute required the order to state the length of time that the eavesdropping order would be in effect and specifically prohibited orders exceeding 60 days. Finally, the statute provided that the application and order were to be delivered to and kept by the applicant as authority for the eavesdropping authorized by the court.

THE SUPREME COURT'S VIEWS ON THE NEW YORK PERMISSIVE EAVESDROPPING STATUTE. The Supreme Court in *Berger* held that this New York eavesdropping statute was unconstitutional because it violated the Fourth and Fourteenth Amendments to the United States Constitution. In effect, the Supreme Court concluded that the statute permitted serious governmental intrusions into constitutionally protected areas of privacy without affording the citizen the traditional constitutional safeguards of the Fourth Amendment.

Emphasizing that electronic invasions of privacy to capture conversations are the most sweeping and the most penetrating of all searches, the Supreme Court declared the urgent need for the strictest judicial supervision of eavesdropping searches to assure absolute fairness of procedures.

The Supreme Court in *Berger* analyzed the New York statute by contrasting its procedural safeguards with those procedural safeguards which are absolutely required by the Fourth Amendment:

In declaring New York's eavesdropping statute unconstitutional, the Supreme Court, in *Berger*, repeatedly stressed that because of the sweeping nature of electronic searches for incriminating evidence the Fourth Amendment imposed a much heavier responsibility on the courts to assure fairness in the procedures. Judicial orders for court-approved eavesdropping searches must be authorized only "under the most precise and discriminate" procedures, affording "similar protections to those that are present in the use of conventional warrants authorizing the seizure of tangible evidence" under the Fourth Amendment. The Supreme Court emphasized that there was a necessity for courts to take strict precautions in the area of electronic searches to minimize the danger of unlawful searches and seizures.

THE SUPREME COURT'S RULING. The majority of the Court in the Berger case reemphasized that "conversations" are clearly within the protections of the Fourth Amendment, and that the use of electronic devices to capture conversations is a "search" that can be conducted only under the strictest procedural safeguards.

Since electronic searches cause the most devestating invasions of privacy, the Supreme Court directed that the Fourth Amendment imposes a severe responsibility on the courts to closely supervise the procedures authorizing such searches. Mr. Justice Clark indicated that electronic searches should be authorized only "under the most precise and discriminate circumstances" and that "the need for particularity and evidence of reliability . . . is especially great in the case of eavesdropping."

By far the most significant aspect of the Berger case is that the Supreme Court did *not* hold that electronic eavesdropping, as such, is in itself an unreasonable search and seizure. The Berger case, therefore, is authority for the proposition that under carefully drafted statutes that would assure all of the essential Fourth Amendment procedural safeguards, law enforcement officers – under close court supervision – may use electronic listening devices to catch and convict criminals.

Comparison of New York Law With the Fourth Amendment

	Fourth Amendment Procedural Safeguards
Application to Neutral Authority	The Fourth Amendment requires that applications for governmental searches should be made to a Judicial Officer.
Probable Cause	The Fourth Amendment specifically dictates that searches by government for incriminating evidence may be performed only where the government has prior knowledge of specific and reliable facts that would generate a reasonable *belief* that a crime has been or is being committed. Probable Cause is an absolute requirement for governmental searches.
Particularity	The Fourth Amendment requires that no warrants should be issued unless the application for the search *particularly* describes the place to be searched and the person or thing to be seized.

New York Eavesdropping Statute Procedural Safeguards	Supreme Court's Analysis of Procedural Safeguards
The New York statute provided that prior applications for searching for and capturing incriminating conversations by electronic surveillance should be made to the New York Courts.	"The New York statute satisfies the Fourth Amendment requirement that a neutral and detached authority be interposed between the police and the public."
Instead of requiring "Probable Cause" as the prior justification for an electronic eavesdropping search for incriminating conversations, the New York statute merely required the opinion of the governmental officer applying for the order that "there was reasonable grounds to believe evidence of crime may be . . . obtained."	The New York statute is "offensive" because eavesdropping is authorized without requiring *belief* that any offense has been or is being committed. . . . "The purpose of the probable cause requirement of the Fourth Amendment to keep the state out of constitutionally protected areas until it has reason to believe that a specific crime has been or is being committed is thereby wholly aborted."
The New York statute merely required the name of the "person or persons whose communications, conversations or discussions are to be overheard or recorded. . . ."	"New York's statute lacks . . . particularization. . . . It lays down no requirement for particularity in the warrant as to what specific crime has been or is being committed, nor 'the place to be searched,' or 'the persons or things to be seized' as specifically required by the Fourth Amendment. . . . Likewise, the statute's failure to describe the particular conversation sought gives an officer a roving commission to seize any and all conversations."

(Continued on pages 170 and 171.)

Comparison of New York Law With the Fourth Amendment (Continued)

	Fourth Amendment Procedural Safeguards
Reliability	The Fourth Amendment demands reliable evidence to justify a governmental search for incriminating evidence.
Time-Notice-Return	The Fourth Amendment requires that governmental searches for incriminating evidence be conducted "reasonably." The length of time it takes to conduct a search, the notice that is given to the person whose privacy is being invaded, and the reporting back to the Court concerning the search are all areas of grave procedural concern under the philosophy of the Fourth Amendment.

New York Eavesdropping Statute Procedural Safeguards	Supreme Court's Analysis of Procedural Safeguards
There were no specific standards concerning reliability of evidence to justify the issuance of an electronic eavesdropping order.	"The need for particularity and *evidence of reliability* in the showing required when judicial authority of a search is sought is especially great in the case of eavesdropping. By its very nature eavesdropping involves an intrusion in privacy that is broad in scope. . . . The 'indiscriminate' use of such devices in law enforcement raises grave constitutional questions under the Fourth and Fifth Amendments."
The New York statute authorized eavesdropping searches for a two-month period and permitted extensions on a mere showing that it would be in the "public interest." The New York statute had no provision requiring notification of the persons whose privacy was invaded, nor for a return on the warrant to the Court.	". . . authorization of eavesdropping for a two-month period is the equivalent of a series of intrusions, searches and seizures pursuant to a single showing of Probable Cause. . . . Moreover, the statute permits, as was done here, extensions of the original two-month period, presumably for two months each, on a mere showing that such extension is in the 'public interest.' Apparently the original grounds on which the eavesdropping order originally issued also form the basis of the renewal. This is, we believe, insufficient without a showing of present probable cause for the continuance of the eavesdropping." The Court further found the New York statute faulty in that it did not provide for notice or for a return on the order to the Court.

CONCLUSION. Electronic surveillance is "the single most valuable weapon in law enforcement against organized crime," according to New York District Attorney Frank S. Hogan. After 27 years of fighting against crime in New York City, Mr. Hogan's word is not to be taken lightly.

Mr. Justice Black does not discount Hogan's evaluation. In his dissent in *Berger,* he focused eloquently on the urgent need for the use of scientific eavesdropping in the fight against crime:

> Today this country is painfully realizing that evidence of crime is difficult for governments to secure. Criminals are shrewd and constantly seek, too often successfully, to conceal their tracks and their outlawry from law officers . . . It needs no empirical studies or statistics to establish that eavesdropping testimony plays an important role in exposing criminals and bands of criminals who but for such evidence would go along their criminal way with little possibility of exposure, prosecution, or punishment. Such, of course, is this particular case before us.
>
> The eavesdrop evidence here shows this petitioner to be a briber, a corrupter of trusted public officials, a poisoner of the honest administration of government upon which good people must depend to obtain the blessings of a decent orderly society. No man's privacy, property, liberty, or life is secure, if organized or even unorganized criminals can go their way unmolested, ever and ever further in their unabandoned lawlessness. However obnoxious eavesdroppers may be they are assuredly not engaged in a more "ignoble" or "dirty business" than are bribers, theives, burglars, robbers, rapists, kidnapers, and murderers, not to speak of others. And it cannot be denied that to deal with such specimens of our society, eavesdroppers are not merely useful, they are frequently a necessity.

Electronic Surveillance

Charles Katz, *Petitioner v.* United States

On Writ of Certiorari to the United States Court of Appeals for the Ninth Circuit
(389 U.S. 347 – Decided December 16, 1967)

> What a person knowingly exposes to the public, even in his own home or office, is not a subject of Fourth Amendment protection .... But what he seeks to preserve as private, even in an area accessible to the public, may be constitutionally protected .... Wherever a man may be, he is entitled to know that he will remain free from unreasonable searches and seizures .... For the Fourth Amendment protects people not places ....
>
> Mr. Justice Stewart
> *Katz v. United States*

FACTS. "Give me Duquesne minus 7 for a nickel," Katz said as he sat securely in a telephone booth in Los Angeles. It was February of 1965, and Katz was using the "nickel system." A $500 bet was a "nickel," a $1,000 bet was a "dime," and a $100 bet was called a "dollar." Miami was on the other end of the line, and – unknown to Katz – the FBI was on the ceiling!

From February 19 to February 25, 1965, at just the right moments, special agents of the Federal Bureau of Investigation activated microphones that had been taped on the tops of two public telephone booths. Prior surveillance had shown that Katz habitually used a bank of three phones at certain hours on a daily basis. The third phone was conveniently placed out of order by the telephone company, so Katz was lured into one of the booths under FBI surveillance. A wire recorder also located on top of one of the phone booths made six three-minute recordings of Katz's interstate gambling conversations. These recordings, clear and irrefutable evidence of Katz's guilt, were admitted into evidence by the trial court after a suppression hearing. Katz was convicted on eight counts of using telephone facilities to transmit bets interstate in violation of Title 18, U.S.C., Section 1084.

The Court of Appeals for the Ninth Circuit affirmed Katz's conviction and the Supreme Court of the United States granted review.

Mr. Justice Stewart, speaking for the majority of eight justices in *Katz,* reversed the conviction, holding that the interceptions and recordings of Katz's telephone conversations represented "unreasonable" searches and seizures of those conversations in violation of the Fourth Amendment.

> The government agents here ignored *"the procedure of antecedent justification* . . . that is central to the Fourth Amendment," a procedure that we hold to be a *constitutional precondition of the kind of electronic surveillance* involved in this case. Because the surveillance here failed to meet that condition, and because it led to the petitioner's conviction, the judgment must be reversed.
>
> (Emphasis added.)

But ironically, out of the ashes of the Katz reversal rises the phoenix of specific Supreme Court approval for closely supervised, court-approved electronic surveillance as a police technique to combat crime. In clear, unequivocal language, Mr. Justice Stewart stated in *Katz* that electronic surveillance by police, under strict protective limitations, is constitutional:

> . . . It is clear that this surveillance (in *Katz*) was so narrowly circumscribed that a duly authorized magistrate, properly notified of the need for such investigation, specifically informed of the basis on which it was to proceed, and clearly apprised of the precise intrusion it would entail, *could constitutionally have authorized, with appropriate safeguards,* the very limited search and seizure that the Government asserts in fact took place . . . . Here . . . a . . . *judicial order could have accommodated "the legitimate needs of law enforcement" by authorizing the carefully limited use of electronic surveillance.*
>
> (Emphasis added.)

CONSTITUTIONAL SAFEGUARDS FOR ELECTRONIC SURVEILLANCE. The cardinal rule for electronic surveillance – and all searches – is that society's need for the search must be carefully balanced against the individual's need for privacy. No greater invasion of privacy will be permitted by the courts other than is actually necessary.

Since electronic surveillance involves the most devastating and penetrating invasions of privacy now known to man, the need and justification for the surveillance must be clear, detailed, and persuasive. The "precise and discriminate" circumstances justifying the use of electronic surveillance must be carefully reviewed by the judicial branch of government before the electronic surveillance is authorized "for the narrow and particularized purpose of ascertaining the truth..."

In *Berger v. New York*, 388 U.S. 41, the Supreme Court emphasized with approval the safeguards for the electronic surveillance that had been followed in *Osborn v. United States*, 385 U.S. 323. The safeguards in *Osborn* "afforded similar protections to those ... of conventional warrants authorizing the seizures of tangible evidence." The virtue of the Osborn approach to electronic surveillance was that the closely supervised court protections assured "no greater invasion of privacy ... than was necessary under the circumstances."

Probable Cause. In *Katz*, the investigation was well along before the FBI agents employed their electronic surveillance techniques. The record indisputably establishes that prior to the electronic surveillance, the FBI had uncovered persuasive guilt-laden probable cause facts that Katz was engaged in interstate gambling racketeering. The facts were *reliable* because they were direct observations by highly skilled, professional Federal Bureau of Investigation agents.

The facts had *particularized* the place where the electronic surveillance should be used (the phone booth); the person against whom the electronic surveillance would be directed (Katz); and the type of anticipated criminal conversation (interstate gambling conversation.)

The Supreme Court indicated that the search and seizure by electronic surveillance of Katz's conversations would have been lawful if the agents had gone to a judge with this *probable cause, reliable evidence, and particularization.*

Limited Surveillance. Because of the pervasive nature of electronic surveillance, the Supreme Court has indicated that every effort must be made to limit the scope and duration of the electronic search. In *Katz,* the electronic surveillance was restricted in scope to the telephone booth, and only Katz's conversations were intercepted and recorded. In Katz, the duration of the electronic surveillance was only about 18 carefully controlled minutes.

Focusing on the objective – the need to capture criminal conversations – courts are required to narrowly circumscribe the scope and duration of electronic surveillance so as to severely limit the deadly potential of such sweeping invasions of privacy. The Supreme Court in *Katz* underscored the fact that the FBI agents had, by their own restraint, narrowly circumscribed the magnitude of the electronic penetration of Katz's privacy. But, the Court continued, the agents did not have a court order or court supervision so that the electronic surveillance, of necessity, had to be held "unreasonable."

Notice. Mr. Justice Stewart, writing for the majority in *Katz,* focused in a footnote on the vital fact that no self-defeating prior notice of electronic surveillance is required by the Fourth Amendment:

> Although the protections afforded the Petitioner in *Osborn* were "similar . . . to those . . . of conventional warrants," they were not identical. A conventional warrant ordinarily serves to notify the suspect of an intended search. But if *Osborn* had been told in advance that federal officers intended to record his conversations, the point of making such recordings would obviously have been lost; the evidence in question could not have been obtained. In omitting any requirement of advance notice, the Federal Court that authorized electronic surveillance in *Osborn* simply recognized, as has this Court, that *officers need not announce their purpose before conducting an otherwise authorized search if such an*

announcement would provoke the escape of the suspect or the destruction of critical evidence. See *Ker v. California*, 374 U.S. 23, 37-41.
(Emphasis added.)

CITIZENS' PROTECTIONS AGAINST GOVERNMENTAL INVASIONS. Lawyers for both the defense and the prosecution in *Katz* chose to fight on the battleground of "constitutionally protected areas." The defense maintained in argument before the Supreme Court that a telephone booth was a "constitutionally protected area" that could not be invaded by government without probable cause warrants. The prosecution argued that a telephone booth in effect was a semi-public area – open, visible, and not entitled to the privacy that attaches to the home under the philosophy of the Fourth Amendment.

In *Katz*, Mr. Justice Stewart, writing for the majority, rejected this analysis of the issues by both the defense and the prosecution:

> We decline to adopt this formulation of the issues. In the first place, the correct solution of Fourth Amendment problems is not necessarily promoted by incantation of the phrase, "constitutionally protected area."

Declaring that the Fourth Amendment could not be subjected to the restrictive concept of protected places of privacy, the Supreme Court emphasized heavily that the protections of privacy relate to people.

The Court went further and enumerated the broad pattern of constitutional protections under the Fourth Amendment that are designed to protect the individual citizen from a varied range of governmental intrusions. A footnote quoted the Douglas dissent in *Griswold v. Connecticut*, 381 U.S. 479, 509, to develop the theme that the Fourth Amendment's protections "go further, and often have nothing to do with privacy at all:"

> The average man would very likely not have his feelings soothed any more by having his property seized openly than by having it seized privately and by stealth . . . and a person can be just as much, if not more, irritated, annoyed and injured by an unceremonious public arrest

> by a policeman as he is by a seizure in the privacy of his office or home.
>
> (Footnote 4, *Katz v. United States.*)

But, continued Mr. Justice Stewart in *Katz,* the full constitutional protections for our citizens go even further beyond the outer limits of the right to privacy to prevent virtually every kind of arbitrary governmental intrusion:

> The first Amendment, for example, imposes limitations upon governmental abridgment of "freedom to associate and privacy in one's associations." . . . The Third Amendment's prohibition against the unconsented peacetime quartering of soldiers protects another aspect of privacy from governmental intrusion. To some extent, the Fifth Amendment too reflects the Constitution's concern for . . . the right of each individual "to a private enclave where he may lead a private life." . . . *Virtually every governmental action interferes with personal privacy to some degree. The question in each case is whether that interference violates a command of the United States Constitution.*
>
> (Footnote 5, *Katz v. United States,* emphasis added.)

The government's contention that, because Katz was calling from a glass telephone booth where he was fully visible he had no right to privacy, was succinctly dispatched by Mr. Justice Stewart in two memorable sentences:

> But what he sought to exclude when he entered the booth was not the intruding eye—it was the uninvited ear. He did not shed his right to do so simply because he made his calls from a place where he might be seen.

People in offices, in apartments, in rooms, in taxicabs and in telephone booths, continued the Court, should be able to rely upon the protections of the Fourth Amendment.

The right to privacy, then, envelops the person, rather than settling only in certain places. In the future, no one need fear seeking out zones of "constitutionally protected areas" to speak or to act without the chilling restraint of an overview by some arbitrary governmental official.

THE "OLMSTEAD TRESPASS RULE"—REJECTED. In 1928, the Supreme Court, in *Olmstead v. United States*, 277 U.S. 438, was faced with its first governmental electronic surveillance case. Evidence against Olmstead, a large-scale gambling racketeer, had been obtained by wiretapping from locations outside of Olmstead's gambling operation. As it later turned out, a critical factor in the case was that the government agents did not physically trespass on Olmstead's property in any way when they intercepted his telephone conversations.

In *Olmstead*, the supreme Court held first that "conversations" were not the type of "physical, tangible property" that was protected by the Fourth Amendment. Second, because the officers did not trespass, a divided Court reasoned that there was no physical intrusion into Olmstead's privacy and therefore the wiretapping evidence was admissible. The primary reason for the admissibility of the conversations, according to the Court, was that the officers had not trespassed onto Olmstead's property.

In the past decade the Supreme Court specifically rejected the first Olmstead doctrine—that the Fourth Amendment protects only "physical, tangible property." Oral statements and conversations, in addition to tangible property, have been declared in several cases to be fully protected by the Fourth Amendment.

But the Olmstead Trespass Rule had lingered on, becoming more and more anachronistic in an advanced electronic age. The government contended in *Katz* that there had been no physical penetration of the telephone booth by their electronic equipment and that, therefore, they had not in any way physically trespassed upon Katz's privacy in the telephone booth.

Mr. Justice Stewart, for himself and seven other justices, emphatically rejected the 40-year-old Olmstead Trespass Rule:

> . . . The reach of that Amendment [the Fourth] cannot turn upon the presence or absence of a physical intrusion into any given enclosure. We conclude that the underpinnings of *Olmstead* . . . have been so eroded by our

subsequent decisions that the "trespass" doctrine there enunciated can no longer be regarded as controlling. The government's activities in electronic listening to and recording of the petitioner's words violated the privacy upon which he justifiably relied while using the telephone booth and thus constituted a "search and seizure" within the meaning of the Fourth Amendment. The fact that the electronic device employed to achieve that end did not happen to penetrate the wall of the booth can have no constitutional significance.

THE JUDICIAL OFFICER IS ESSENTIAL. The Supreme Court, zeroing in on the fatal defect of the Katz investigation, stated:

> It is apparent that the agents in this case acted with restraint. Yet the inescapable fact is that this restraint was imposed by the agents themselves and not by a judicial officer. They were not compelled during the course of the search itself to observe precise limitations established, *in advance by a specific court order. Nor were they directed, after the search had been completed, to notify the authorizing magistrate in detail of all that have been seized.*
>
> (Emphasis added.)

From *Osborn, Berger,* and *Katz,* it is clear that the judicial officer is the essential, irreplacable constitutional safeguard against governmental abuses by electronic surveillance techniques. To assess the need for a searching electronic surveillance and to assure that the invasion of privacy is no greater than necessary under the circumstances, the court emerges from these three cases as the single most important constitutional protection for the citizen.

The Supreme Court has emphasized that searches outside the judicial process are all "unreasonable" unless they come under the specific exceptions of emergency arrests, the doctrine of hot pursuit, or some other limited exception to the warrant rule.

Failure to go to the courts with prior justification for the search bypasses this most essential constitutional safeguard of a fully objective, impartial prior determination of probable cause and leaves the citizen's fate "only in the discretion of the police." The grave responsibility of the police is to catch and prosecute criminals and to prevent crime. Under our unique system of law they are adversaries and advocates against criminals. The police are not "neutral and detached" men in the battle against crime. This is the principal reason why the Supreme Court insists that the magistrate be placed between the citizen and the police – to assure absolute impartiality and absolute fairness in the critical determination of whether or not society should strike out at the citizen.

Mr. Justice Douglas in a concurring opinion in *Katz* emphasized this aspect:

> Under the separation of powers created by the Constitution, the Executive Branch is not supposed to be neutral and disinterested. Rather, it should vigorously investigate . . . and prosecute those who violate . . . laws. The President and the Attorney General (the police) are properly interested parties, cast in the role of adversary . . . to the citizen.

In all fairness, law enforcement officers are vitally interested parties in criminal investigations and prosecutions. They are unquestionably cast in the role of adversaries to their quarry. This is why the police cannot assume, if our citizens are to be secure under the Constitution, the dual, inconsistent roles of adversary-prosecutor and disinterested magistrate. Our citizens would certainly suffer the inevitably harmful effect of blending these two disparate roles. Only a dangerous, pathological police schizophrenia – harmful to individual rights – could result. The absolute necessity of prior justification from the courts for sweeping invasions of privacy assures all of us, citizens and police alike, the safest course to maintain freedom and dignity in an unprecedented and frightening era of electronics.

Objects in Plain View

JAMES H. HARRIS, *Petitioner v.* UNITED STATES

(390 U.S. 234—Decided March 5, 1968)

FACTS. The defendant's automobile had been spotted in the District of Columbia leaving the place of a robbery. The car was traced and the defendant was arrested near his home as he was getting into his car. At the time the officer arrested Harris, he made a quick inspection of the car and then took the defendant to the police station.

There the decision was made to hold the car as evidence. Harris' car was towed to the police station about an hour and a half after he had been arrested. When the car arrived at the precinct, its windows were open and the door was unlocked. It began to rain.

The arresting officer was required by police regulations to search all impounded vehicles carefully, remove any valuable property from it and prepare a written inventory and report concerning the impounding.

The officer entered the car on the driver's side, tied a property tag on the steering wheel and searched the car. The officer stepped out of the car, rolled up an open window of one of the back doors and then started to close a front door window. Then he saw for the first time a registration card which lay face up on the metal stripping over which the door closes. This registration card belonged to the victim of the robbery.

The defendant moved to suppress the registration card on the grounds that its seizure by the police officer was not contemporaneous with his arrest. The defense relied heavily on the case of *Preston v. U.S.*, 376 U.S. 364, in which the Supreme Court of the United States ordered the suppression of evidence that had been seized from Preston's car approximately two hours after he and his companions had been arrested and placed in cells. The Preston rule is based on the fact that police officers have the right to search incident to arrest only to protect themselves or to prevent the destruction of evidence. When a prisoner is in custody, he can no longer harm the arresting officer, nor can he destroy evidence.

SUPREME COURT RULING. In a *per curiam* opinion, the Supreme Court initially stated that "the 'sole' question for our consideration is whether the officer discovered the registration card by means of an illegal search."

Emphasizing that the detailed findings of the trial court were that the discovery of the card was not the result of a search of the car, but a measure taken to protect the car while it was in police custody, the High Court held that the officer had a right to open the door to protect the car. The officer's purpose in opening the door was not to search but to secure the windows of the car. In contrast, a search implies the prying into hidden places for the purpose of finding incriminating evidence.

The Supreme Court stated:

> It has long been settled that objects falling in the plain view of an officer who has a right to be in the position to have that view are subject to seizure and may be introduced in evidence. *Ker v. California,* 374 U.S. 23 . . . (1963); *the U.S. v. Lee,* 274 U.S. 559 . . . (1927); *Hester v. U.S.,* 265 U.S. 57 . . . (1924).

Therefore, anything that an officer sees in plain view when he has a right to be where he is, is not the product of a search and is subject to seizure without the necessity for the police to obtain a warrant. In effect, the strictures of the Fourth Amendment do not apply to incriminating evidence lying out in the open.

Defendant's Testimony at a Suppression Hearing

THOMAS EARL SIMMONS, ET AL., *Petitioners v.* UNITED STATES

(390 U.S. 377—Decided March 18, 1968)

FACTS. Two armed robbers invaded a Chicago savings and loan bank in the early afternoon of February 27, 1964. It took the two gunman about five minutes to stuff the money in a sack and clear out of the bank.

Luckily, a bank employee rushed out into the street after they left and saw one of the robbers in a 1960 Thunderbird that was pulling away from the bank. The bank employee noticed that there was a large scrape on the right door of the Thunderbird. This information was promptly given to the Chicago police and, amazingly enough, it only took an hour for them to locate the car. The police discovered that the car belonged to Simmons' sister-in-law. She told the police that she had loaned her car that afternoon to her brother.

About 5:15 P.M. on the same day as the robbery, two FBI agents went to the house of Simmons' mother-in-law and asked for permission to search the house. The mother-in-law agreed, and the agents found two suitcases in the basement that the mother-in-law claimed she knew nothing about. In one of the suitcases the agents found a gun holster, a sack similar to the one used in the robbery, and several coin cards and bill wrappers from the bank that had been robbed.

The next day, the FBI obtained some snapshots from Simmons' in-laws and showed the pictures to the five bank employees who had witnessed the robbery. Each of the bank employees identified Simmons' picture as one of the robbers.

A week or two later three of these bank employees identified the second gunman. Simmons, his brother-in-law, and the second gunman were indicted for robbery. The defendants moved to suppress the evidence. The second gunman, Garrett, testified at the suppression hearing that although he could not absolutely identify the suitcase as his, he said that he had a similar one and that he owned the clothing that was found inside the suitcase.

Garrett testified at the suppression hearing because he had to establish "standing" in order to move to suppress the evidence. The Fourth Amendment rule relating to "standing" is that constitutional rights are personal rights that may be protected only on behalf of the person whose privacy was invaded by the search and seizure. In other words, in order to suppress seized evidence, the person who moves to suppress must have a right to privacy in the area that was searched. However, the Supreme Court of the United States ruled in *Jones v. U.S.*, 362 U.S. 267, that where the crime charged is possession of the seized evidence and where possession is an essential element of the offense, the defendant has, in effect, automatic "standing" to suppress regardless of whether or not his right to privacy was actually invaded. *Jones* was a prosecution for the illegal possession of narcotics, and the Supreme Court ruled that he had the right to move to suppress even though he was not the owner or tenant of the room that he was in when the police seized him and found narcotics.

The district court refused to suppress the evidence, and at the trial, Garrett's testimony that the suitcase containing the incriminating evidence was his was admitted in evidence against him. All three defendants were convicted, and the convictions of Simmons and Garrett were affirmed by the United States Court of Appeals for the Seventh Circuit. The Supreme Court of the United States granted review to decide the narrow question as to whether or not Garrett's constitutional rights were violated because his suppression hearing testimony was used against him at the trial.

THE SUPREME COURT DECISION. Defense counsel argued that the prosecution made an error in using testimony drawn from

Garrett's unsuccessful motion to suppress evidence. Mr. Justice Harlan, who delivered the opinion of the Court, considered the contention in detail.

The Court first emphasized the fact that Garrett had no possessory interest in the house where the suitcase was found, nor was he even in the house at the time the suitcase was seized. The Supreme Court developed the thesis that the only way Garrett could have "standing" to move to suppress the suitcase with the incriminating evidence was to testify that he was the owner. In effect, therefore, Garrett was forced to the witness stand at the suppression hearing. In other words if Garrett hadn't taken the witness stand at the suppression hearing, he could not have moved to suppress the evidence.

Mr. Justice Harlan asserted that a defendant who knows that his suppression testimony may be used against him at the trial will be hard pressed in determining the critical decision as to whether or not he should testify to prove "standing."

The Court felt that it is unfair to deter a defendant from asserting Fourth Amendment objections by requiring him to run "the risk that the words which he utters may later be used to incriminate him." This, said the Court, puts the defendant in the uneviable position of having to waive his Fifth Amendment privilege against self-incrimination in order to invoke his Fourth Amendment claim to suppress the evidence. "In these circumstances," said the Court, "we find it intolerable that one constitutional right should have to be surrendered in order to assert another."

Reversing Garrett's conviction, the Court held that "When a defendant testifies in support of a motion to suppress evidence on Fourth Amendment grounds, his testimony may not thereafter be admitted against him at trial on the issue of guilt unless he makes no objection."

EPILOGUE. Mr. Justice Black filed a blistering dissent to this new rule which bars the defendant's testimony at a suppression hearing from being used against him at trial. This dissent, which was joined by Mr. Justice White, demonstrates the recurrent fact that there are generally two good sides to every legal argument. Men charged with the difficult responsibility of determining constitutional issues can reasonably disagree. In the Fourth Amendment area however, not everything is Black and White, although some people wish it were. The heart of the powerful dissent says:

> The consequence of the Court's holding, it seems to me, is that defendants are encouraged to come into court, either in person or through other witnesses, and swear falsely that they do not own property, knowing at the very moment they do so that they have already sworn precisely the opposite in a prior court proceeding. This is but to permit lawless people to play ducks and drakes with the basic principles of the administration of criminal law.
>
> There is certainly no language in the Fourth Amendment which gives support to any such device to hobble law enforcement in this country. While our Constitution does provide procedural safeguards to protect defendants from arbitrary convictions, that governmental charter holds out no promises to stultify justice by erecting barriers to the admissibility of relevant evidence voluntarily given in a court of justice. Under the first principles of ethics and morality a defendant who secures a court order by telling the truth should not be allowed to seek a court advantage later based on a premise directly opposite to his prior solemn judicial oath. This Court should not lend the prestige of its high name to such a justice-defeating strategem.

Seizure of Incriminating Evidence by Private Citizens

BURDEAU, *Petitioner v.* MCDOWELL

(256 U.S. 465—Decided June 1, 1921)

FACTS. J. C. McDowell was a director in the Cities Service Company and one of its subsidiary companies, and he had offices in Pittsburgh, Pennsylvania. Like Caesar, he should have feared the Ides of March. The executives of the Cities Service Company had reason to suspect McDowell's loyalty to the company, apparently because they had substantial information that he was double-dealing in real estate which the company was buying or selling. Becoming alarmed, Cities Service executives decided to take action.

On March 23, 1920, a representative of the company and some private detectives went to McDowell's private office in Pittsburgh and with the detectives in charge, blew open two safes. In one safe, the larger one, some papers belonging to McDowell were found and taken. McDowell's desk was also forced open and papers were taken from it.

In June, 1920, the executives of the Cities Service Company were contacted by the U.S. Department of Justice and turned over a letter that had been seized from McDowell's desk by the private detectives. The man in the Justice Department who received the letter was Joseph V. Burdeau, a special assistant to the Attorney General of the United States.

With this evidence, Burdeau and his assistants intended to present to a Federal Grand Jury sitting in the Western District in Pennsylvania an indictment charging J. C. McDowell with mail fraud.

The attorneys for McDowell, upon learning of the imminent Grand Jury proceeding, filed a petition in the Western District of Pennsylvania, asking for the return of all

McDowell's papers and letters on the grounds that presentation of this evidence before the Grand Jury would violate his Fourth Amendment rights.

The District Court judge, after hearing, ordered the federal prosecutors to return McDowell's papers and correspondence to him. The judge also ordered the Department of Justice not to present any evidence of "any nature whatsoever secured by or coming into their possession as a result of the knowledge obtained from the inspection of such books, papers, memoranda, etc." The District Court judge found that neither Burdeau nor any other official or agent of the United States "had anything to do with the search" of McDowell's offices. The judge felt that there had been a gross violation of McDowell's Fourth and Fifth Amendment rights even though the government had not been a party to the illegal seizure. The government appealed the District Court judge's decision to the Supreme Court of the United States.

THE COURT RULING. Mr. Justice Day delivered a short opinion reversing the District Court judge's decision. "The exact question to be decided here," said Justice Day, "is whether the Fourth Amendment prevents the Federal Government from retaining incriminating papers coming to it after they had been stolen by private detectives, with a view to using the incriminating evidence against the accused." The Court, stressing the fact that the amendments to the United States Constitution protect a citizen only against the wrongful acts of government officials, wrote:

> The Fourth Amendment gives protection against unlawful searches and seizures, and as shown in the previous cases, its protection applies *to governmental action.* Its origin and history clearly show that it was intended as a restraint upon the activities of *sovereign authority,* and was not intended to be a limitation upon other than *governmental agencies;* as against such authority it was the purpose of the Fourth Amendment to secure the citizen in the right of unmolested occupation of his dwelling and the possession of his property, subject to the right of seizure by process duly issued.

> In the present case the record clearly shows that no official of the Federal Government had anything to do with the wrongful seizure of the petitioner's property, or any knowledge thereof until several months after the property had been taken from him and was in the possession of the Cities Service Company. *It is manifest that there was no invasion of the security afforded by the Fourth Amendment against unreasonable search and seizure, as whatever wrong was done was the act of individuals in taking the property of another.* A portion of the property so taken and held was turned over to the prosecuting officers of the Federal Government. We assume that petitioner has an unquestionable right of redress against those who illegally and wrongfully took his private property under the circumstances herein disclosed, but with such remedies we are not now concerned.
>
> (Emphasis added.)

Mr. Justice Day further buttressed the Supreme Court's decision by two concise paragraphs which concluded the Court's opinion:

> We know of no constitutional principle which requires the Government to surrender the papers under such circumstances. Had it learned that such incriminatory papers, tending to show a violation of federal law, were in the hands of a person other than the accused, it having had no part in wrongfully obtaining them, we know of no reason why a subpoena might not issue for the production of the papers in evidence. Such production would require no unreasonable search or seizure, nor would it amount to compelling the accused to testify against himself.
>
> The papers having come into the possession of the Government without a violation of petitioner's rights by governmental authority, we see no reason why the fact that individuals, unconnected with the Government, may have wrongfully taken them, should prevent them from being held for use in prosecuting an offense where the documents are of an incriminatory character.

SEIZURES BY PRIVATE PARTIES. The case of *Burdeau v. McDowell* was decided by the Supreme Court of the United States on June 1, 1921. Since that date, the Supreme Court of the United States has never re-examined its position with regard to the seizure of incriminating evidence by private parties. It seems rather incredible, but it is true that in nearly fifty years of federal decisions since the Burdeau case the Supreme Court has never revisited this vital area.

Some legal commentators are somewhat dubious about the firmness of the Burdeau doctrine, particularly when projected against the relatively recent Supreme Court Fourth Amendment explosion. Added concern is the fact that two legal giants, Mr. Justice Brandeis and Mr. Justice Holmes, filed a scathing dissenting opinion in the Burdeau case. This dissent minced no words:

> Plaintiff's private papers were stolen. The thief, to further his own ends, delivered them to the law officer of the United States. He, knowing them to have been stolen, retains them for use against the plantiff . . .

Their dissent was based persuasively on the argument that, particularly for the government, the ends should never justify the means.

> At the foundation of our civil liberty lies the principle which denies to government officials an exceptional position before the law and which subjects them to the same rules of conduct that are commands to the citizen. And in the development of our liberty insistence upon procedural regularity has been a large factor. Respect for law will not be advanced by resort, in its enforcement, to means which shock the common man's sense of decency and fair play.

In the years since the Burdeau case, there have been a number of federal, lower court decisions, as well as state court decisions that wholeheartedly endorse the Burdeau doctrine. The Burdeau rule permits the use of stolen incriminating evidence or illegally seized incriminating evidence so long as the evidence was stolen or seized by private parties and government officials had no part in it.

The decisions relating to the seizure of incriminating evidence by private security officers, by store detectives, by private detectives, by airline security guards, by employees and by private citizens, uniformly hold that so long as government officials did not in any way take part in the seizing of the evidence, it would not be suppressed.

As an example, in *State v. Scrotsky,* 189 A. 2d 23 (1963), the Supreme Court of New Jersey re-stated the Burdeau ruling with added clarity:

> Constitutionally, where a private person steals or unlawfully takes possession of property from the premises of the owner and turns it over to the Government, which did not participate in the taking, it may be used as incriminating evidence against the owner in a subsequent criminal prosecution.

OTHER CASES. A national airlines security investigator forced a passenger off an airplane, took him to a room, searched him and seized some papers from him. The evidence was later turned over to District Attorney Hogan's office in New York City and resulted in a prosecution for forging airplane tickets and attempted grand larceny against the passenger, Anthony Trimarco. Emphasizing that the security officer was not a governmental officer but a private employee of the airlines, the New York Court refused Trimarco's motion to suppress the evidence on the basis that the seizure of the incriminating evidence was done by a private person and the Fourth Amendment did not apply. *People v. Trimarco,* 245 N.Y. S. 2d 795 (Sup. Ct. 1963).

A store detective in California discovered a shoplifter at work in one of the dressing rooms by investigative tactics that would have been clearly illegal for police. The California Supreme Court refused to suppress the incriminating evidence once again on the basis of the Burdeau doctrine that the store detective was not a "governmental officer." *People v. Randazzo,* 220 Cal. App. 2d 768, Cert. denied 377 U.S. 1000 (1964).

In *Wright v. U.S.*, 224 A. 2d, 475, a District of Columbia court held that the Fourth Amendment was not violated where a security officer of the Macke Company discovered a sawed-off shotgun in the defendant's locker and took it to the company manager, who later turned the gun over to the police. It is clear that if a police officer had searched for and seized the sawed-off shotgun in this case, it would clearly have been in violation of the Fourth Amendment.

In Essex County, New Jersey, a resourceful private detective searched for stolen silver ingots in the locker and in the car of an employee at the Englehard Industries plant in Newark. The private detective found eight pieces of silver in the defendant's locker and eleven pieces of silver in his car. This incriminating evidence was the basis for an indictment charging the man for larceny of over $50,000 worth of silver. Once again, it is clear that if a law enforcement officer had obtained incriminating evidence in this manner, it would clearly have been in violation of the defendant's Fourth Amendment rights. As it was, the Superior Court of New Jersey ruled that the silver thief's Fourth Amendment rights were not violated because the private detective was not a state or governmental official. *State of New Jersey v. Monroe Robinson,* 206 A. 2d 779.

Other cases supporting this position that the unlawful conduct of private citizens is not regulated by the Fourth Amendment are: *U.S. v. Goldberg,* 330 F. 2d 30 (3d. Cir.) Cert. denied 377 U.S. 953 (1964), and *People of California v. Crabtree,* 239 A.C.A. 874.

PARTICIPATION BY GOVERNMENT OFFICERS IN A SEARCH AND SEIZURE BY PRIVATE PARTIES. The Burdeau case clearly indicates that wherever there is participation—constructive or direct—by government officers in the seizure of incriminating evidence illegally by private citizens, the evidence must be suppressed. *People v. Tarantino,* 290 P. 2d 505 (1955). *Moody v. U.S.,* 163 A. 2d, 337 (1960). *State v. Scrotsky,* 189 A. 2d 23 (1960). *People v. Fierro,* 236 Cal. App. 2d, 334 (1965).

CONCLUSION. If a person becomes a victim of illegal search and seizure by a citizen or by a private security officer not connected with any official law enforcement agency, his redress is not the Fourth Amendment but rather a civil suit for damages. Individuals or companies who are sued under these circumstances win or lose the case on the issue of probable cause. This is equally true in the area of interrogation by private citizens or by private security officers. Any potential suits for false imprisonment are resolved by the issue of probable cause.

The best legal advice in this area is to advise private citizens and private security officers not to take the law in their own hands. Wherever possible, the citizen should rely on police for enforcement. From a viewpoint of potential civil liability, it is much wiser for private security officers to call in the police when they have probable cause to believe that someone is committing a crime. Only in an extreme emergency should private citizens or private security police respond themselves.

From the viewpoint of individual rights, every search into someone's privacy is a very serious matter—regardless of who makes the search. That is why it is best to have the police go to the courts for orders to search. This method assures the fairest treatment of the accused, but at the same time, it will guarantee the greatest likelihood of using the incriminating evidence to convict. This method assures the maximum protection for the constitutional rights of the individual and the maximum guarantee that if incriminating evidence is found, it will be used to convict the accused.

The Frisk

JOHN W. TERRY, *Petitioner v.* STATE OF OHIO

On Writ of Certiorari to the Supreme Court of Ohio
(88 S. Ct. 1968 – Decided June 10, 1968)

A police officer's right to make an on-the-street "stop" and an accompanying "frisk" for weapons is of course bounded by the protections afforded by the Fourth and Fourteenth Amendments. The Court holds, and I agree, that while the right does not depend upon possession by the officer of a valid warrant, nor upon the existence of probable cause, such activities must be reasonable under the circumstances as the officer credibly relates them in Court . . .

. . . The right to frisk . . . depends upon the reasonableness of a forcible stop to investigate a suspected crime.

Where such a stop is reasonable, however, the right to frisk must be immediate and automatic if the reason for the stop is, as here, an articulable suspicion of a crime of violence. Just as a full search incident to a lawful arrest requires no additional justification, a limited frisk incident to a lawful stop must often be rapid and routine. There is no reason why an officer, rightfully but forcibly confronting a person suspected of a serious crime, should have to ask one question and take the risk that the answer might be a bullet . . .

Mr. Justice Harlan, concurring in *Terry v. Ohio.*

ISSUE. For the first time in more than 50 years of decisions concerning constitutional limitations on police, the Supreme Court squarely faced and decided the delicate issue of a police officer's right to confront a citizen acting suspiciously on the street.

The Supreme Court had to balance the right of privacy of the citizen to be free from unreasonable government intrusions against the need for police to investigate suspicious street activity. Because street encounters frequently unfold rapidly and because the police often find themselves in hazardous situations, they must have a series of escalating, constitutionally sound responses to meet the very real dangers that can occur in investigatory encounters.

In *Terry v. Ohio,* the Supreme Court set forth detailed guidelines concerning why, when, and how police may act when confronted with a combination of suspicious circumstances.

FACTS. On the last day of October, 1963, in the early afternoon, a Cleveland plainclothes officer with nearly forty years of police experience became curious about two men who were standing on the corner of Huron Road and Euclid Avenue in downtown Cleveland.

What had attracted the officer had been the fact that one of the men left the other, strolled casually past a store, paused for a moment, looked in the store window, then casually doubled back around to where the other man was standing. The second man then did exactly what the first man had just done – looking in the same store window, and then doubling back to join the first man.

The officer, standing off at a distance, watched the two men as they repeated this same ritual. Each man made six trips past the store window and each man doubled back to his waiting partner six times. At this time they were joined by a third man.

Now the officer was thoroughly suspicious. It looked to him as if the immediate purpose of the men was to case the store and that their ultimate objective was armed robbery.

After observing these elaborate maneuvers for ten or twelve minutes, the officer decided to move in. As the plainclothes officer approached the three men, they were now in front of Zucker's Store. He immediately identified himself as a police officer and asked them for their names. The men "mumbled something" unintelligible as the officer swung into action. He grabbed one of the men – Terry – spun him around quickly while facing the other two and patted down the outside of Terry's clothing. In the left breast pocket of Terry's overcoat the officer felt a pistol. He reached inside the coat but could not get the gun out. Keeping Terry between himself and the two other men, the officer ordered all of them into Zucker's Store. He then took Terry's coat from him, removed a .38 caliber revolver from it, and ordered all three men to face the wall with their hands up. He then checked the other two men for weapons and discovered a second revolver in an outside coat pocket of one of the other men. The officer yelled to the store owner to call the police, and a short time later a police wagon arrived and took all three men to the police station. Terry and the other man with the gun were charged with carrying concealed deadly weapons.

The defense promptly filed a motion to suppress, arguing that the officer had no probable cause to arrest and then search the two men for weapons and, therefore, the guns had to be suppressed. The defense contended that the only thing that the officer observed was a few suspicious circumstances that could not, under any circumstances, generate a reasonable belief that the men were about to commit a crime.

In contrast, the prosecution argued that the guns had been seized in a search incident to a lawful arrest for attempted armed robbery.

The trial court categorically rejected the prosecution's theory, stating that it "would be stretching the facts beyond reasonable comprehension" to find that the officer had probable cause to arrest the three men for attempted robbery before he patted them down for weapons.

Nonetheless, the trial court did uphold the officer's method of obtaining the guns on the basis that the officer had a duty to investigate the suspicious activity that he saw and that he had an absolute right to protect himself by frisking for weapons even though he did not have enough probable cause facts to make a lawful arrest for attempted armed robbery.

Terry and the other men were later tried and convicted,

and Terry was sentenced to a term of one-to-three years in the state Penitentiary.

Two appellate courts in Ohio upheld Terry's conviction, and the Supreme Court of the United States granted review in 1967. Showing rare solidarity, the Court decided by an 8 to 1 margin to uphold the officer's right to frisk and seize weapons under these circumstances.

THE SUPREME COURT VIEW OF STREET ENCOUNTERS. Chief Justice Warren, writing for the majority in *Terry*, focused initially on the fact that the Fourth Amendment protects people whether they are in their homes or on the streets. No matter where a citizen may happen to be, he has a "reasonable expectation of privacy." He has a right coming from Common Law to be free from restraint or interference. This right to be let alone yields only to clear, justifiable authority of law.

The authority of law for police to arrest, search, or seize citizens is based on two cardinal rules of the Fourth Amendment. The first rule is that whenever possible, officers should obtain advanced judicial approval for arrests, searches, and seizures. The second rule is that failure to obtain arrest and search warrants can generally be excused only by the need for immediate police action because of emergency situations.

Chief Justice Warren, for the majority of the Court in *Terry*, recognized the need to keep the lawful authority of the police in street encounters in harmony with these two main principles of the Fourth Amendment. In order to blend specific law relating to street encounters with the general law embodied in the Fourth Amendment, the Court had to probe with great intensity the nature of street encounters.

> . . . Street encounters between citizens and police officers are incredibly rich in diversity. They range from wholly friendly exchanges of pleasantries or mutually useful information to hostile confrontations of armed men involving arrests, or injuries, or loss of life. Moreover, hostile confrontations are not all of a piece. Some of them begin in a friendly enough manner, only to take a different turn upon the injection of some unexpected element into the conversation. Encounters are initiated by

> the police for a wide variety of purposes, some of which are wholly unrelated to a desire to prosecute for crime.

Later in the opinion, Chief Justice Warren indicated that the law concerning police conduct in street investigations stems from the second cardinal rule of the Fourth Amendment—that relating to emergency situations.

> . . . But we deal here with an entire rubric of police conduct—necessarily swift action predicated upon the on-the-spot observations of the officer on the beat—which historically has not been and as a practical matter could not be, subject to the warrant procedure . . .

Thus, said the Court, all police investigative conduct is regulated by the Fourth Amendment, and the penalty for violating the Fourth Amendment's requirements is the suppression of evidence. The Supreme Court has long emphasized that the major purpose of the suppression rule is a deterrent one. Chief Justice Warren underlined this theme:

> Ever since its inception, the rule excluding evidence seized in violation of the Fourth Amendment has been recognized as a principal mode of discouraging lawless police conduct. See *Weeks v. United States*, 232 U.S. 383, 391-393 (1914). Thus its major thrust is a deterrent one, see *Linkletter v. Walker*, 381 U.S. 618, 629-635 (1965), and experience has taught that it is the only effective deterrent to police misconduct in the criminal context, and that without it the constitutional guarantee against unreasonable searches and seizures would be a mere "form of words." *Mapp v. Ohio*, 367 U.S. 643, 655 (1961).

The second major reason for the suppression rule was declared by the Court in the case of *Elkins v. United States*, 364 U.S. 206, 222 (1960). In that decision the Court announced the doctrine of "the imperative of judicial integrity."

The Court, in *Terry*, crystalized this second vital function of the suppression rule:

> Courts sitting under our Constitution cannot and will not be made a party to lawless invasions of the constitutional rights of citizens by permitting unhindered governmental use of the fruits of such invasions.

Surging forward, the Court emphatically announced its full intention to supervise all police conduct as it affects citizens, and that whenever police investigative techniques were unfair or unreasonable the suppression rule would be invoked.

> . . . Nothing we say today is to be taken as indicating approval of police conduct outside the legitimate investigative sphere. Under our decision, courts still retain their tradiditional responsibility to guard against police conduct which is overbearing or harassing, or which trenches upon personal security without the objective evidentiary justification which the Constitution requires. When such conduct is identified, it must be condemned by the judiciary and its fruits must be excluded from evidence in criminal trials.

THE SUPREME COURT VIEW OF A STOP AND FRISK. Central to the Supreme Court's decision in *Terry* was the Court's view of a police stop and a police frisk. Chief Justice Warren underscored the Court's concern with the street encounter:

> Our first task is to establish at what point in this encounter the Fourth Amendment becomes relevant. That is, we must decide whether and when Officer McFadden "seized" Terry and whether and when he conducted a "search." There is some suggestion in the use of such terms as "stop" and "frisk" that such police conduct is outside the purview of the Fourth Amendment because neither action rises to the level of a "search" or "seizure" within the meaning of the Constitution. We emphatically reject this notion. It is quite plain that the Fourth Amendment governs "seizures" of the person which do not eventuate in a trip to the station house and prosecution for crime—"arrests" in traditional terminology. It must be recognized that whenever a police officer accosts an individual and restrains his freedom to walk away, he has "seized" that person. And it is nothing less than sheer torture of the English language to suggest that a careful exploration of the outer surfaces of a person's clothing all over his or her body in an attempt

> to find weapons is not a "search." Moreover, it is simply fantastic to urge that such a procedure performed in public by a policeman while the citizen stands helpless, perhaps facing a wall with his hands raised, is a "petty indignity." It is a serious intrusion upon the sanctity of the person, which may inflict great indignity and arouse strong resentment, and it is not to be undertaken lightly.

While recognizing the full dimensions of the impact of a stop and a frisk on a citizen, the Court contrasted the significant differences between a "stop-and-frisk" and an "arrest":

> . . . An arrest is a wholly different kind of intrusion upon individual freedom from a limited search for weapons, and the interests each is designed to serve are likewise quite different. An arrest is the initial stage of a criminal prosecution. It is intended to vindicate society's interest in having its laws obeyed, and it is inevitably accompanied by future interference with the individual's freedom of movement, whether or not trial or conviction ultimately follows. The protective search for weapons, on the other hand, constitutes a brief, though far from inconsiderable, intrusion upon the sanctity of the person . . .

THE SUPREME COURT STANDARD FOR STREET ENCOUNTERS. The Court, in *Terry*, announced a formula to test the reasonableness of police conduct when they are engaged in street encounters. First, the Court stated, it is necessary "to focus upon the governmental interest" that would justify the police officer's contact with the citizen, and, secondly, to explore the intensity and scope of the police contact. The reasonableness test is then a direct one. In reviewing police encounters with citizens, the Courts must balance "the need to search [or seize] against the invasion which the search [or seizure] entails."

Justification for the Street Encounter. The general justification for a street encounter, according to the Court, is the need for effective crime prevention and crime detection by police.

In each case of a police encounter with a citizen, however, there must, in addition to this general justification, be a specific, factual justification based on what the officer sees and experiences when drawn into an inquiry. The Court was explicit in demanding specific, factual justification for police encounters:

> . . . And in justifying the particular intrusion the police officer must be able to point to specific and articulable facts which, taken together with logical inferences from those facts, reasonably warrant that intrusion. . . .

Facts, said the Court, would be judged on a strict objective standard. All the facts confronting the officer at the moment that he stops someone or the moment that he frisks someone have to be evaluated by the reviewing courts to assure that the officer's actions were reasonable in light of the rapidly developing facts. This means that whenever a police officer stops a citizen he must be prepared to justify the stopping of the citizen by specific facts. These facts do not have to rise to the level of probable cause—the arrest standard—or a reasonable belief that someone has committed a crime. These facts have to be suspicious facts—sufficient enough to arouse the police officer's curiosity and specific enough that he can testify about them.

Intensity and Scope of the Search. The only justification for a frisk is to protect the officer who is drawn into an inquiry. The Court recognized that police officers are frequently in vulnerable positions when they stop people for on-the-spot investigations. Once the officer's initial action in stopping a citizen is justified at its inception by the suspicious circumstances that drew the officer into an inquiry, the officer may frisk the person he has stopped if he reasonably fears for his safety. The Court has indicated that the frisk or search must be reasonably limited in scope to the circumstances which justified the interference (with the citizen) in the first place. The scope of a search, whether it be a full search based on probable cause, or a frisk based on a combination of suspicious circumstances and a reasonable fear for safety are "strictly tied to and justified by" the circumstances in each case.

The Court emphasized traditional limitations upon the scope of searches by underscoring that it recognized a major distinction in purpose, character, and extent between a search incident to an arrest and a limited search for weapons. Police may make intrusions on a citizen short of arrest so long as they act reasonably under the facts unfolding before them.

Finally, the Court emphasized that the right to frisk

> . . . must be a narrowly drawn authority to permit a reasonable search for weapons for the protection of the police officer, where he has reason to believe that he is dealing with an armed and dangerous individual, regardless of whether he has probable cause to arrest the individual for a crime.

RULING IN TERRY. Applying these Fourth Amendment rules to the facts of the Terry case, the Court declared that the Cleveland police officer's conduct was reasonable at its inception and was reasonable at the time he found the guns.

The Court found significance in the facts that the police officer had more than 40 years' experience and that his judgment that the men were casing the store for an armed robbery was extremely persuasive under the circumstances. The Court found the officer's conduct completely reasonable here since he identified himself as a police officer, requested their names, and then immediately patted Terry down for a weapon.

Under all these circumstances, the Court refused to suppress the evidence and the convictions of the men for carrying concealed deadly weapons were sustained.

TWO VARIATIONS ON THE THEME

In two related cases decided the same day, the Supreme Court applied the facts of two additional police-citizen encounters to the rule of law affecting street encounters that it had announced in *Terry*.

Nelson Sibron, Appellant v. State of New York

FACTS. New York has a "Stop-and-Frisk" Law (N.Y. Code Crim. Proc. §180-a). This statute provides:

1. A police officer may stop any person in a public place whom he reasonably suspects is committing, has committed or is about to commit a felony or any of the crimes specified in section five hundred fifty-two of this chapter, and may demand of him his name, address and an explanation of his actions.

2. When a police officer has stopped a person for questioning pursuant to this section and reasonably suspects that he is in danger of life or limb, he may search such person for a dangerous weapon. If the police officer finds such a weapon or any other thing the possession of which may constitute a crime, he may take and keep it until the completion of the questioning, at which time he shall either return it, if lawfully possessed, or arrest such person.

The defense, in these two companion cases, argued that this New York statute was unconstitutional "on its face" but the Supreme Court refused to rule on the constitutionality of the New York statute and decided to determine the lawfulness of the frisks in these cases by the specific, concrete, factual circumstances involved in the police encounters in each case.

A New York City police officer was patroling his beat on March 9, 1965 and saw the defendant, Sibron, "continually from the hours of 4:00 P.M. to 12 Midnight . . . in the vicinity of 742 Broadway." The officer saw Sibron talking with six or eight people that he knew to be narcotics addicts. Admittedly, the officer did not overhear any of the conversations between Sibron and the addicts nor did he ever seen anything pass between Sibron and the others. Late in the afternoon, the officer saw Sibron enter a restaurant and begin speaking with three more addicts. Sibron sat down and began to eat when the patrolman approached him and told him to come outside. As soon as they got outside the restaurant the officer said, "You know what I'm after." Sibron mumbled something and reached hurriedly into his pocket. At the same time, the officer thrust his hand into the same pocket and discovered glassine envelopes which were later found to contain heroin.

The officer arrested Sibron, who was later convicted for

the unlawful possession of heroin. The New York Courts refused to suppress the incriminating evidence that the officer took from Sibron.

THE SUPREME COURT OPINION. The Supreme Court of the United States re-emphasized the rule it had announced in the Terry case:

> The police officer is not entitled to seize and search every person whom he sees on the street or of whom he makes inquiries. Before he places a hand on the person of a citizen in search of anything, he must have constitutionally adequate reasonable grounds for doing so. *In the case of the self-protective search for weapons, he must be able to point to particular facts from which he reasonably inferred that the individual was armed and dangerous.*
> (Emphasis added.)

Chief Justice Warren, again writing for the majority of the Court, held that on the record in the Sibron case there were no adequate facts that would constitutionally permit the officer to frisk Sibron. The Court found both that there was not sufficient specific justification for the frisk and that the frisk of Sibron exceeded reasonableness in intensity and scope.

In analyzing the facts, the Court found that:

> The suspect's mere act of talking with a number of known narcotics addicts over an eight-hour period no more gives rise to reasonable fear of life or limb on the part of the police officer than it justifies an arrest for committing a crime.

The Court further interpreted the police officer's intention was to search for narcotics and not to protect himself. According to the officer's own testimony at the suppression hearing, he thought that there was narcotics, not a weapon, in Sibron's pocket.

The Court contrasted the intensity and scope of the search for weapons in *Terry* with the search-frisk in *Sibron*. In *Terry*, there was a patting down of the outer clothing of the suspect for weapons and only after the weapon was discovered did the officer place his hand *inside* Terry's pocket. In Sibron –*"with no attempt at an initial limited exploration for arms"*–the officer physically invaded Sibron's pocket and grabbed the heroin. The Court found that the officer in *Sibron* was looking for narcotics and was not attempting to protect himself.

According to this interpretation of the facts, the Supreme Court had no alternative but to declare the search-frisk of Sibron unreasonable and in violation of the Fourth Amendment.

John Francis Peters, Appellant v. State of New York

FACTS. In *Peters,* an off-duty New York City police officer was in his apartment in Mt. Vernon, New York, on the afternoon of July 10, 1964. He had just finished taking a shower and was drying himself when he heard muted noises at his door. Interrupted momentarily by a telephone call, the officer hung up, and looked through the peephole into the hall to see if anything was going on. The officer saw "two men tip-toeing out of the alcove down the stairway." Calling the police, the officer put on civilian clothes, armed himself with his service revolver and started to investigate. The officer had lived in the 120-unit apartment house for 12 years and did not recognize either man as tenants. The officer opened the door, stepped into the hallway, and slammed the door loudly behind him. The officer's sudden arrival caused the two men to start running down the stairs. The officer took after them in close pursuit. Catching up to them two floors down, the officer grabbed one of the men–Peters–by the collar and tried unsuccessfully to capture the other one.

The officer asked Peters what he was doing in the apartment house and Peters said that he was visiting a girlfriend. When the officer asked him who the girlfriend was, Peters refused to identify the girl, saying that she was a married woman. The officer immediately patted Peters down for weapons and discovered a hard object in his pocket. The officer testified at the suppression hearing that it did not feel like a gun but he thought it might have been a knife. Quickly the officer removed the hard object from Peter's pocket and discovered an opaque plastic envelope containing burglar tools. Peters was tried and convicted for the unlawful possession of burglar tools and the New York Courts upheld the officer's search-frisk of Peters on the basis of the New York Stop-Frisk statute.

THE SUPREME COURT DECISION. The Supreme Court held that the officer was fully justified in stopping Peters under the suspicious circumstances as they occurred and that the facts in the Peters case were so strong that they rose to the level of probable cause to arrest Peters for attempted burglary.

The Court analyzed the probable cause as follows:

FACT 1. "The officer heard strange noises at his door which apparently led him to believe that someone sought to force entry."

FACT 2. "When he investigated these noises, he saw two men, whom he had never seen before in his 12 years in the building, tiptoeing furtively about the hallway."

FACT 3. "They were still engaged in these maneuvers after he had called the police and dressed hurriedly."

FACT 4. When the officer "entered the hallway, the men fled down the stairs."

The combination of these four facts persuaded all nine members of the Supreme Court that there was here a strong factual basis for an arrest of Peters for attempted burglary. As the Court phrased it:

> . . . deliberately furtive actions and flight at the approach of strangers or law officers are strong indicia of *mens rea,* and when coupled with specific knowledge on the part of the officer relating the suspect to the evidence of crime, they are proper factors to be considered in the decision to make an arrest.

In conclusion, the Court found that Peters' arrest and search were fully within the commands of the Fourth Amendment since it was a search incident to a lawful arrest based on probable cause.

CONCLUSION

These three cases illustrate what the Supreme Court had stated in *Mapp v. Ohio.* There they indicated *"There is no war between the Constitution and common sense."*

The Court, fully recognizing the need for officers to conduct on-the-spot investigations, permits stopping and frisking of suspects only where there is specific justification based on the facts of each case. It is important to keep in mind that the power of the police to stop and frisk citizens who are acting suspiciously is narrowly limited by these decisions. Routine, quota, harassment, or mass stops and frisks by police are absolutely prohibited. If any incriminating evidence is uncovered by these types of illegal police activity it will be categorically suppressed by the Courts.

In contrast, when police are conducting legitimate investigations of suspicious circumstances, they may stop a citizen and frisk him whenever the officer reasonably fears for his safety. If incriminating evidence—taken in the belief it is a weapon—is uncovered in these circumstances, it will not be suppressed.

The street encounter is important. It is important both to the police and to the citizen. Standing guard to assure fairness in this critical area is the Fourth Amendment—guaranteeing to the citizen his full right to privacy—and guaranteeing to the officer his full right to live.

CHAPTER VII

CASES INVOLVING THE FIFTH AND SIXTH AMENDMENTS

THE FIFTH AMENDMENT

No person . . . shall be compelled in any criminal case to be a witness against himself . . .

Fifth Amendment to the United States Constitution

The privilege against self-incrimination appears not only in the Fifth Amendment to the United States Constitution, but also in the constitutions of 48 states, by statute in New Jersey, and by statutory construction in Iowa. Until 1965, the Fifth Amendment was interpreted by the Supreme Court of the United States to apply only to federal proceedings. But, in 1965, in the cases of *Molloy v, Hogan,* 378 U.S. 1, and *Murphy v. Waterfront Commission* 378 U.S. 52, the Supreme Court held that the Fifth Amendment may be invoked in both state and federal proceedings. The effect of these two cases has given the United States uniform national standards in the area of the Fifth Amendment.

"**. . . IN ANY CRIMINAL CASE** . . ." The courts have applied the broad Common Law privilege against self-incrimination liberally, so the Fifth Amendment has been held to apply not only in criminal matters but also in civil proceedings. Moreover, the privilege may be invoked at any stage of a proceeding, civil or criminal, or at any stage of legislative or administrative hearings. The privilege applies not only to a criminal defendant but also to any ordinary witness. Corporations generally may not invoke the privilege against self-incrimination.

". . . WITNESS AGAINST HIMSELF . . ." Basically, the courts have held that the privilege against self-incrimination protects an accused from *testimonial* compulsion. Obtaining fingerprints, blood samples, handwriting samples, and other physical evidence to use against an accused has not been interpreted as violating a suspect's Fifth Amendment rights since the Fifth Amendment applies solely to oral compulsion – making a man incriminate himself by talking. The Fifth Amendment prevents government from compelling an individual to talk in cases when he will subject himself to possible punishment by his talk.

THE POLICIES OF THE PRIVILEGE. It is rather ironic that the Fifth Amendment privilege against self-incrimination is held in such low esteem by the general public whom the privelege was designed to protect. In the legal community, the Fifth Amendment privilege against self-incrimination is held in the highest esteem because of its unique values as well as its incredible history. The reason that the general public frowns on the Fifth Amendment is because in the last two decades it has been used as a refuge for Communists and hoodlums. But the Fifth Amendment is more than twenty years old; it has its roots deep in the Common Law, and the Fifth Amendment can only be judged intelligently on the basis of its full development in history.

In early Common Law government, the sovereign had the absolute right to torture the citizens in order to determine whether or not the citizen had broken the King's law. During the same period of Common Law there were more than two hundred crimes where capital punishment was the penalty. Maiming, such as cutting off ears, arms, or hands, was naturally considered a much lesser punishment for crimes less serious than the ignoble "200." The English people began to be somewhat disenchanted with the concept of torture by the King's men, conviction by the King's Court, and punishment by the King's Justice, particularly when the only evidence that the King's men obtained against an individual was obtained from his own lips. In the later Common Law period the English sovereigns developed highly sophisticated techniques of compelling people to incriminate themselves so that they could later be blackmailed into paying large sums of money into the King's treasury. The origin of the privilege against self-incrimination is closely linked in English history with the abolition of government-inflicted torture. By 1650, the English-speaking people had done away with the infamous "Star Chamber" and established a strong policy that a man was not to be his first accuser. Following this, the use of torture by government was gradually abolished.

We have acquired our legal heritage from the five hundred years of the growth of the English law, as commonly referred to as the Common Law. The central theme of the Englishmen's battle for individual justice against the supreme power of the King was the emerging concept of a true "adversary" system. Mr. Justice Fortas has expressed this unique feature of the later common law:

> The Englishman himself was a sovereign. He had the sovereign right to refuse to co-operate. He could put the State to its proof.
>
> The State and he could meet as the law comtemplates, in adversary trial, as equals—strength against strength, resource against resource, argument against argument. The duty to co-operate came to an end at the threshhold of conflict between the State and the individual.
>
> The principle that a man is not obliged to furnish the State with ammunition to use against him is basic to this conception. Equals meeting in battle owe no such duty to one-another, regardless of the obligations that they may be under prior to battle. A sovereign state has no right to compel the sovereign individual to surrender or impair his right to self-defense.
>
> The Fifth Amendment, 25 Clev. B.A.J. 9 (1954).

THE ADVERSARY SYSTEM. Our system of criminal law is adversary rather than inquisitorial. The Fifth Amendment right against self-incrimination is the equalizer protecting the citizen from unfair governmental force. Historically, our "adversary" system developed gradually throughout our Common Law period.

In the earliest Common Law days the system of justice was known as Trial by Hue and Cry. Whenever the citizens in a local community felt that somebody had committed a crime, they would pick up clubs and search throughout the neighborhood for the culprit. If they found him they would beat him to death. This crude experiment in justice was soon abandoned by the early English-speaking people after they had made a few horrible mistakes.

The second type of justice developed in the Common Law was known as Trial by Ordeal. In this system of justice the accused person was, in effect, pitted against God. If a person were accused of a crime he would faceTrial by Ordeal, which would be either having his hands and feet tied behind him and dropping him into ten feet of freezing water, or placing a red-hot poker in his hand three steps outside a church and forcing him to race into the church and place the hot poker on the altar. The trial was decided, in the first instance, on the basis that if the man imersed in the cold water sank to the bottom, he was innocent. Unfortunately, he would also usually be dead. If, on the other hand, he floated on the surface, he was guilty, and he would immediately be fished out and drawn and quartered. In the case of the hot poker, the accused's hand would be bound up immediately and if, after 24 hours, the hand was infected, the accused was guilty. If the hand was healing, the accused was innocent. This system of justice was invoked for some time until fifty murderers and cut-throats were able to prove their innocence to King William Rufus under the healing hand technique.

Next there emerged the concept of justice of Trial by Battle. The accused person would meet in armed combat with the forces of government on an equal basis. It was here that the roots of our adversary system of justice were firmly planted. As highly skilled champions began to develop, the confidence of the English-speaking people in Trial by Battle gradually diminished. Trial by Jury finally emerged with the strong concept that the state and the individual meet as equals before the jury.

In *Murphy v. Waterfront Commission, supra,* Mr. Justice Goldberg outlined some of the values and purposes of the Fifth Amendment privilege against self-incrimination:

> The privilege against self-incrimination "registers an important advance in the development of our liberty—one of the great landmarks in man's struggle to make himself civilized." . . . It reflects many of our fundamental values and most noble aspirations: our unwillingness to subject those suspected of crime to the cruel dilemma of self-accusation; our preference for an accusatorial rather than an inquisitorial system of criminal justice; our fear that self-incriminating statements will be elicited by inhumane treatment and abuses; our sense of fair play which dictates "a fair state-individual balance by requiring the government to leave the individual alone until good cause is shown for disturbing him and by requiring the government in its contest with the individual to shoulder the entire load;" . . . our respect for the inviolability of the human personality and of the right of each individual "to a private enclave where he may lead a private life;" . . . our distrust of self-deprecatory statements; and our realization that the privilege, while sometimes "a shelter to the guilty," is often "a protection to the innocent . . ."

History, ancient and modern, is replete with examples of governments that established totalitarian rule by forcing citizens to incriminate themselves. One significant distinction of the Roman law was the right of a Roman citizen not be be tortured for incrimination purposes by Roman legions. The Bible contains an account of St. Paul being stretched out on the rack by Roman soldiers in Asia Minor and finally convincing them that he was a Roman citizen—requiring them to stop.

Today, the Chinese system of criminal justice is based almost exclusively on unlimited governmental right to interrogation. Today in China there are informal, secret inquisitions by the Chinese police with absolutely no right of a citizen to refuse to incriminate himself.

In-Custody Police Interrogation

ARTHUR CULOMBE, *Petitioner v.* STATE OF CONNECTICUT

(367 U.S. 568 – Decided June 19, 1961)

CULOMBE AND THE FIFTH AMENDMENT. The Culombe case was decided by the Supreme Court of the United States the same day that the Court rendered its opinion in *Mapp v. Ohio.* While *Mapp* had an immediate and direct legal impact on state law enforcement officers throughout the country, *Culombe v. Connecticut,* in contrast, made little or no immediate impression at the time the opinion was delivered. Actually, *Culombe* has had equally far-reaching effect on the criminal investigator. While *Mapp v. Ohio* was concerned with search and seizure and the Fourth Amendment, *Culombe v. Connecticut* was concerned with police in-custody interrogation and the Fifth Amendment. The seeds that Mr. Justice Frankfurter placed in 1961 in *Culombe* matured into the Supreme Court ruling on police interrogation in *Miranda v. Arizona,* 384 U.S. 436 (1966).

Many police officers fail to realize that the full impact of the Supreme Court decisions from *Mapp* to *Miranda* has brought the law enforcement officer within the ranks of the legal profession. These decisions have made it mandatory for all criminal investigators to have a far greater knowledge of the law. With increased demands for professional knowledge, the police have become an integral part of the legal profession. Since the law enforcement officer has become a member of the legal profession it is essential for him to know, evaluate, and understand the thoughts of the entire legal community so far as in-custody police interrogation is concerned. The Culombe case, in large measure, supplies the law enforcement officer with some of the legal community's concern with old, traditional police interrogation practices. One critic of traditional police interrogation – Hopkins – highlighted some of its more harmful side effects:

> In every city our police hold what can only be called Kangaroo Courts,—informal and secret inquisitions of people, usually indigents,—that are usually trials for crimes . . . Centering all upon the confession, proud of it, staking everything on it, the major canon of American police work is based upon the nullification of the Fifth Amendment . . . Trial by jury comes into operation only after the police are through; juries are reduced to the position of merely ratifying the plea of guilty which the police have obtained or else holding trials for the small percentage of people about whom the police could reach no conclusion . . . These inquisitions held by the police before trial—although no statute recognizes their existence—are the worst feature of American Criminal Justice.
>
> "The Lawless Arm of the Law," 148 *Atlantic Monthly* 279 (1931).

FACTS. Mr. Justice Frankfurter, in speaking for the majority of the Supreme Court in *Culombe v. Connecticut,* stressed the agonies confronting the Court when attempting to achieve a balance between the anxious task of the police to solve crimes and the right of an individual, however guilty, to be tried according to constitutional standards. The facts of the Culombe case were presented by Justice Frankfurter in one short paragraph:

> On December 15, 1956, the dead bodies of two men were found in Kurp's Gasoline Station in New Britain, Connecticut. Edward J. Kurpiewski, the proprietor, was found in the boiler room with a bullet in his head. Daniel J. Janowski, a customer, was found in the men's toilet room shot twice in the head. Parked at the pumps in front of the station was Janowski's car. In it was Janowski's daughter, physically unharmed. She was the only surviving eyewitness of what had happened at the station. She was eighteen months old.

The Kurp affair was one of a series of holdups and killings that had terrified operators of gasoline stations and small shops in the New Britain area. Toward the end of February,

1957, the focus of suspicion for some of these holdups and killings fell upon two men, Arthur Culombe and Joseph Taborsky. On the evening of February 23, 1957, teams of police officers approached the two men and asked them to come to Connecticut State Police Headquarters. The two suspects were never again to be out of police custody. Culombe was held in custody for four days in a carefully controlled police interrogation environment. Culombe was not told he had a right to remain silent. Although he stated he wanted a lawyer, the police made no attempt to get him one, and, instead of arraigning him before a magistrate promptly, as Connecticut law required, he was taken before a New Britain Police Court on the palpable ruse of a breach of the peace charge concocted to give the police time to pursue their interrogation. The purpose of bringing Culombe into the Police Court on a misdemeanor charge rather than the grave murder charge of which he was suspected was commented upon by Mr. Justice Frankfurter.

> First, it kept Culombe in police hands without any of the protections that a proper magistrate's hearing would have assured him. Certainly, had he been brought before it charged with murder instead of an insignificant misdemeanor, no court would have failed to warn Culombe of his rights and arrange for appointment of counsel. Second, every circumstance of the Police Court's procedure was potentially intimidating. Culombe had been told that morning that he would be presented in a court of law and would be able to consult counsel. Instead, he was led into a crowded room, penned in a corner, and, without ever being brought before the bench, or given a chance to participate in any way, his case was disposed of. Culombe had been convicted of crimes before and presumably was not ignorant of the way in which justice is regularly done. It would deny the impact of experience to believe that the impression which even his limited mind drew from this appearance before a court which did not even hear him, a court which may well have appeared a mere tool in the hands of the police, was not intimidating.

The Connecticut police officers frankly admitted that they had charged Culombe with breach of the peace specifically for the purpose of investigating the murder case. After four days of intermittent questioning for a total of about twelve and a half hours, Culombe confessed to the killings at Kurp's Gas Station. The defense established at the suppression hearing that Culombe was a 33-year-old mental defective of the moron class with an intelligence quotient of 64 and a mental age of nine to nine and a half years.

THE SUPREME COURT DECISION. Mr. Justice Frankfurter initially focused on the American police technique of in-custody interrogation:

> In the United States, "interrogation" has become a police technique, and detention for purposes of interrogation a common, although generally unlawful, practice. Crime detection officials, finding that if their suspects are kept under tight police control during questioning they are less likely to be distracted, less likely to be recalcitrant and, of course, less likely to make off and escape entirely, and not infrequently take such suspects into custody for "investigation."
>
> This practice has its manifest evils and dangers. Persons subjected to it are torn from the reliances of their daily existence and held at the mercy of those whose job it is if such persons have committed crimes, as it is supposed they have to prosecute them. They are deprived of freedom without a proper judicial tribunal having found them guilty, without a proper judicial tribunal having found even that there is probable cause to believe that they may be guilty. What actually happens to them behind the closed door to the interrogation room is difficult if not impossible to ascertain. . . . In any case, the risk is great that the police will accomplish behind their closed door precisely what the demands of our legal order forbid: make a suspect the unwilling collaborator in establishing his guilt. . . .
>
> In the police station a prisoner is surrounded by known hostile forces. He is disoriented from the world he knows

> and in which he finds support. He is subject to coercing impingements, undermining even if not obvious pressures of every variety. In such an atmosphere, questioning that is long continued—even if it is only repeated at intervals, never protracted to the point of physical exhaustion—inevitably suggests that the questioner has a right to, and expects, an answer. This is so, certainly, when the prisoner has never been told that he need not answer and when, because his commitment to custody seems to be at the will of his questioners, he has every reason to believe that he will be held and interrogated until he speaks.

While Mr. Justice Frankfurter outlined the need for reasonable interrogation so long as it is conducted fairly reasonably and within proper limits with regard to the rights of those being questioned, he stressed the counter-legal concept in this vital area:

> At the other pole is a cluster of convictions each expressive, in a different manifestation, of the basic notion that the terrible engine of the criminal law is not to be used to overreach individuals who stand helpless against it. Among these are the notions that men are not to be imprisoned at the unfettered will of their prosecutors, nor subjected to physical brutality by officials charged with the investigation of crime. Cardinal among them, also, is the conviction, basic to our legal order, that men are not to be exploited for the information necessary to condemn them before the law, that, in Hawkins' words, a prisoner is not "to be made the deluded instrument of his own conviction." 2 Hawkins, *Pleas of the Crown* (8th ed. 1824), 595. This principle, branded into the consciousness of our civilization by the memory of the secret inquisitions, sometimes practiced with torture, which were borrowed briefly from the continent during the era of the Star Chamber, was well known to those who established the American governments. Its essence is the requirement that the State which proposes to convict and punish an individual produce the evidence against

> him by the independent labor of its officers, not by the simple, cruel expedient of forcing it from his own lips.

On the facts in this case, the Supreme Court announced with regret that Culombe's confession was involuntary and, therefore, not admissible in evidence against him. The Court found that nearly all the circumstances of the interrogation were potentially intimidating and that the confession was not the product of Culombe's free will. In the final paragraph of the Supreme Court opinion, the Court emphasized that while they were aware of police investigative problems, they had to uphold the constitutional rights of a citizen, however guilty, against sustained police interrogation. In a free society, the ends cannot justify the means.

> Regardful as one must be of the problems of crime detection confronting the States, one does not reach the result here as an easy decision. In the case of such unwitnessed crimes as the Kurp's killings, the trails of detection challenge the most imaginative capacities of law enforcement officers. Often there is little else the police can do than interrogate suspects as an indispensable part of crime investigation. But when interrogation of a prisoner is so long continued, with such a purpose, and under such circumstances, as to make the whole proceeding an effective instrument for extorting an unwilling admission of guilt, due process precludes the use of the confession thus obtained. Under our accusatorial system, such an exploitation of interrogation, whatever its usefulness, is not a permissible substitute for judicial trial.

The Right to Counsel

ESCOBEDO, *Petitioner v.* STATE OF ILLINOIS

(378 U.S. 902 – Decided June 24, 1964)

ISSUE. On June 22, 1964, the Supreme Court of the United States breathed new life into what before had been a relatively little-used clause contained in the Sixth Amendment to the United States Constitution. It was on that day that the Supreme Court of the United States dramatically announced that all accused persons have the right to the assistance of counsel, not only at trial but at every "critical stage" of a criminal proceeding.

Specifically, the Escobedo case holds that the refusal by the police to allow an accused person to consult with his lawyer during a police interrogation constitutes a denial of the Sixth Amendment's protection of the Assistance of Counsel. Since there was a denial of Sixth Amendment rights, a confession that the Chicago police obtained during the interrogation of Escobedo was held to be inadmissible. The Escobedo case deals a deathblow to what was formally known as the protracted "third degree."

FACTS. On the night of January 19, 1960, Danny Escobedo's brother-in-law was fatally shot. At 2:30 A.M. that morning, Escobedo was arrested without a warrant and interrogated for approximately fifteen hours. During that time he made no statement and was released at 5 P.M., only after his attorney had obtained a writ of habeas corpus from the state courts.

On January 30, 1960, 11 days after the fatal shooting, Escobedo was arrested a second time at about 8:00 and taken into the police station for interrogation. Shortly after he arrived at police headquarters, his lawyer arrived but the police did not permit the attorney to see his client. The attorney repeatedly requested to see his client and at the same time it appears unequivocally from the record that Escobedo requested to see his lawyer. The police told Escobedo that his lawyer didn't want to see him and that they would not allow him to see his attorney until they were finished interrogating him. It was during this second interrogation that Escobedo made certain incriminating statements that were used against him when he was convicted for his involvement in his brother-in-law's murder in the state courts. The defense raised the issue at trial and before the Supreme Court of the United States that the interrogation stage was a "critical stage" in Escobedo's case and that he had been denied the right to counsel under the Sixth Amendment. The defense further argued that since he was denied his right to counsel under the Sixth Amendment, his incriminating statements should have been suppressed and should not have been used against him.

THE SUPREME COURT DECISION. The Supreme Court of the United States agreed that Escobedo's right to counsel under the Sixth Amendment was denied and consequently suppressed his incriminating statements. The Court based its opinion on five pivotal facts in the interrogation:

First. Escobedo's interrogations was not a general inquiry into an unsolved crime but rather the interrogation of an accused person with the purpose of getting him to confess his guilt.

Second. Escobedo was in "total police custody," not for the purpose of interrogation for investigation but rather for interrogation for incrimination.

Third. Escobedo had, according to the record in this case, unequivocally requested to see his attorney during his interrogation.

Fourth. The police unequivocally denied Escobedo the right to consult with his attorney despite the fact that the attorney was there at police headquarters attempting to see his client.

Fifth. No one had advised Escobedo of any of his constitutional rights; in other words, Escobedo was never warned of his right to remain silent or that anything he said could be used against him in a court of law.

The Supreme Court summed up its ruling in this case stressing these five facts:

> We hold, therefore, that where, as here, the investigation is no longer a general inquiry into an unsolved crime but has begun to focus on a particular suspect, the suspect has been taken into police custody, the police carry out a process of interrogations that lends itself to eliciting incriminating statements, the suspect has requested and been denied an opportunity to consult with his lawyer, and the police have not effectively warned him of his absolute constitutional right to remain silent, the accused has been denied 'the Assistance of Counsel' in violation of the Sixth Amendment to the Constitution as 'made obligatory upon the States by the Fourteenth Amendment,' *Gideon v. Wainwright,* 372 U.S., at 342, and that no statement elicited by the police during the interrogation may be used against him at a criminal trial.
>
> Nothing we have said today affects the powers of the police to investigate 'an unsolved crime,' *Spano v. New York,* 360 U.S. 315, 327, by gathering information from witnesses and by other 'proper investigative efforts.' *Haynes v. Washington,* 373 U.S. 503, 519. We hold only that when the process shifts from investigatory to accusatory – when its focus is on the accused and its purpose is to elicit a confession – our adversary system begins to operate, and, under the circumstances here, the accused must be permitted to consult with his lawyer.

The Supreme Court in the Escobedo decision stressed the doctrine that ours is an adversary system of justice, pitting the state against the accused as "equals." In *Escobedo,* the state called in an experienced and skilled assistant district attorney who obtained the incriminating statements from Escobedo. The Supreme Court, in noting this fact, indicated:

> It would be highly incongruous if our system of justice permitted the district attorney, the lawyer representing the State, to extract a confession from the accused while his own lawyer, seeking to speak with him, was kept from him by the police.

The Supreme Court then indicated that Escobedo's interrogation was probably the most "critical stage" of his criminal proceedings; that, in effect, as soon as the skilled assistant district attorney was finished, the trial was no more than a mere appeal from the interrogation, and that the most illustrious defense counsel could no nothing for Escobedo at trial.

Finally, the Supreme Court indicated that:

> We have learned the lesson of history, ancient and modern, that a system of criminal law enforcement which comes to depend on the "confession" will, in the long run, be less reliable and more subject to abuses than a system which depends on extrinsic evidence independently secured through skillful investigation.

CONCLUSION. *Escobedo* legally and historically represents a strong judicial attempt to destroy the "third degree" as a police technique in this country. This constitutional concept is aimed 'primarily at preventing prolonged incommunicado interrogation such as a case involving George Whitmore. Whitmore, after 26 hours of grueling interrogation by the New York City police, confessed in a 60-page confession to the brutal murders of Janice Wylie and Emily Hoffert on August 28, 1963. It was Manhattan's District Attorney Frank Hogan who investigated in depth some of the inconsistencies in Whitmore's confession and who cleared Whitmore of these murders. Shortly after Whitmore was cleared by Hogan, another man, Richard Robels, was indicted and convicted for the twin murders that Whitmore had been charged with. District Attorney Hogan's final statement in the Whitmore case demonstrates the Supreme Court's motivating purpose in *Escobedo:*

> If this had not been a celebrated case, if this case hadn't got the tremendous publicity, if this was what we so-called professionals call a run-of-the-mill murder, Whitmore might well have been slipped into the electric chair and been killed for something he didn't do.

The Escobedo decision stands resolutely against protracted incommunicado interrogations by the police. The clear thrust of the Escobedo case then is the destruction of what has been heretofore known as the invincible "third degree."

Custodial Police Interrogation

ERNESTO A. MIRANDA, *Petitioner v.* STATE OF ARIZONA
(384 U.S. 436—Decided June 13, 1966)

FACTS. According to the record in this case, on the evening of March 3, 1963, an 18-year-old girl was forcibly abducted and forcibly raped in Phoenix, Arizona. Ten days later, Ernesto A. Miranda was arrested at his home by Phoenix police and taken to police headquarters where he was put into a police line-up. There he was immediately identified by the victim and within a two-hour period signed a confession, admitting that he had seized the girl and raped her.

When the prosecution attempted to introduce Miranda's confession into evidence at the trial, defense counsel questioned the officer who obtained the statement from Miranda:

[Defense Attorney]: May I ask some questions on voir dire?

The court: Yes, you may.

[Defense Attorney]: Officer Cooley, in the taking of this statement, what did you say to the defendant to get him to make this statement?

A. I asked the defendant if he would tell us, write the same story that he had just told me, and he said that he would.

Q. Did you warn him of his rights?

A. Yes, sir, at the heading of the statement is a paragraph typed out, and I read this paragraph to him out loud.

Q. Did you read that to him outloud?

A. Yes, sir.

Q. But did you ever, before or during your conversation or before taking this statement, did you ever advise the defendant he was entitled to the services of an attorney?

A. When I read –

Q. Before he made any statement?

A. When I read the statement right there.

Q. I don't see in the statement that it says where he is entitled to the advice of an attorney before he made it.

A. No, sir.

Q. It is not in that statement?

A. It doesn't say anything about an attorney. Would you like for me to read it?

Q. No, it will be an exhibit if it is admitted and the jury can read it, but you didn't tell him he could have an attorney?

The signed statement admitted in evidence is as follows:

I, Ernesto A. Miranda, do hereby swear that I make this statement voluntarily and of my own free will, with no threats, coercion, or promises of immunity, and with full knowledge of my legal rights, understanding that any statement I make may be used against me.

The Trial Court admitted the confession and Miranda was convicted of one count of kidnapping and one count of rape, and was sentenced to serve from 20 to 30 years on each count, the sentences to run concurrently. Miranda appealed to the Supreme Court of Arizona and that court, on April 22, 1965, affirmed the trial court's conviction of Miranda and ruled that, particularly since Miranda had been arrested in California on suspicion of armed robbery and had been convicted in Tennessee for violations of the Dyer Act, he knowingly waived his rights under the Fifth and Sixth Amendments at the time he gave his confession to the Phoenix Police.

Justice McFarland, in speaking for the Supreme Court of Arizona, emphasized the fact that Miranda, from his previous arrests, was familiar with legal proceedings and individual rights and had made an intelligent waiver. Miranda appealed the Supreme Court of Arizona's decision to the Supreme Court of the United States. On June 13, 1966, Mr. Chief Justice Warren delivered the 5-4 decision of the

Supreme Court of the United States, which reversed the Supreme Court of Arizona and set up precedent-shattering new rules with regard to custodial police interrogation.

Mr. Chief Justice Warren reversed the Supreme Court of Arizona in one paragraph:

> We reverse. From the testimony of the officers and by the admission of respondent, it is clear that Miranda was not in any way apprised of his right to consult with an attorney and to have one present during the interrogation, nor was his right not to be compelled to incriminate himself effectively protected in any other manner. Without these warnings, the statements were inadmissible. The mere fact that he signed a statement which contained a typed-in clause stating that he had "full knowledge" of his "legal rights" does not approach the knowing and intelligent waiver required to relinquish constitutional rights.

THE SUPREME COURT'S VIEW OF CUSTODIAL POLICE INTERROGATION. In the majority opinion the history and development of the privilege against self-incrimination was developed in great detail. After tracing the Fifth Amendment's heritage, Mr. Chief Justice Warren emphasized its meaning and purpose:

> Thus we may view the historical development of the privilege as one which groped for the proper scope of governmental power over the citizen. As a "noble principle often transcends its origins," the privilege has come rightfully to be recognized in part as an individual's substantive right, a "right to a private enclave where he may lead a private life. That right is the hallmark of our democracy." . . . We have recently noted that the privilege against self-incrimination – the essential mainstay of our adversary system – is founded on a complex of values . . . All these policies point to one overriding thought: the constitutional foundation underlying the privilege is the respect a government – state or federal – must accord to the dignity and integrity of its citizens. To maintain a "fair state-individual balance," to require the government

> "to shoulder the entire load," . . . to respect the inviolability of the human personality, our accusatory system of criminal justice demands that the government seeking to punish an individual produce the evidence against him by its own independent labors, rather than by the cruel, simple expedient of compelling it from his own mouth. . . . In sum, the privilege is fulfilled only when the person is guaranteed the right "to remain silent unless he chooses to speak in the unfettered exercise of his own will."

The Court then considered whether the privilege against self-incrimination would be fully applicable during a period of custodial police interrogation. Here the Supreme Court projected in detail the majority's undocumented abhorrence of traditional interrogation practices in the United States:

> It is obvious that an interrogation environment is created for no purpose other than to subjugate the individual to the will of his examiner. This atmosphere carries its own badge of intimidation. To be sure, this is not physical intimidation, but is equally destructive of human dignity. The current practice of incommunicado interrogation is at odds with one of our Nation's most cherished principles—that the individual may not be compelled to incriminate himself. Unless adequate protective devices are employed to dispel the compulsion inherent in custodial surroundings, no statement obtained from the defendant can truly be the product of his free choice.
>
> * * *
>
> An individual swept from familiar surroundings into police custody, surrounded by antagonistic forces, and subjected to the techniques of persuasion described above cannot be otherwise than under compulsion to speak. As a practical matter, the compulsion to speak in the isolated setting of the police station may well be greater than in courts or other official investigations where there are often impartial observers to guard against intimidation or trickery.
>
> * * *

The entire thrust of police interrogation there, as in all the cases today, was to put the defendant in such an emotional state as to impair his capacity for rational judgment. The abdication of the constitutional privilege —the choice on his part to speak to the police—was not made knowingly or competently because of the failure to apprise him of his rights; the compelling atmosphere of the in-custody interrogation, and not an independent decision on his part, caused the defendant to speak.

Emphasizing that contemporary interrogation practices throughout the United States by the police brutalizes the police, hardens the accused against society and lowers the esteem of justice in the eyes of the public, the Supreme Court set up two specific safeguards to assure that the constitutional rights of persons being interrogated by the police would be protected.

The first safeguard provided by the Supreme Court in the Miranda opinion guarantees to a person being interrogated a full and unrestricted right to counsel. The Court indicated that counsel was necessary at interrogation to protect the Fifth Amendment privilege against self-incrimination, to reduce the untrustworthiness of confessions, and to prevent coercion.

The second safeguard for persons being interrogated by the police is that they must be adequately and effectively apprised of all of their constitutional rights. In other words, people being interrogated, according to the Supreme Court, must be warned of their constitutional rights in order to combat the coercive pressures of police interrogation. Any confessions obtained by the police after June 13, 1966, have to comply with the directives of the Supreme Court of the United States in its Miranda opinion. The accused person has to be fully and effectively advised of his constitutional rights and have a full and unrestricted right to the effective aid of counsel.

CONSTITUTIONAL PROTECTIVE DEVICES FOR THE ACCUSED AT INTERROGATION.

RIGHT TO COUNSEL. After describing the pressures of police interrogation in detail, the Supreme Court declared that the coercive tendencies of interrogation demanded that certain counter-protective devices are necessary to protect the Fifth Amendment privilege in the anxiety-ridden interrogation setting. The Court indicated that the presence of an attorney at interrogation would assure that the statements made in a government-dominated atmosphere are not the product of compulsion. The lawyer's role at interrogation is, therefore, to protect his client's privilege against self-incrimination under the Fifth Amendment. The right to counsel to protect the Fifth Amendment privilege encompasses not only the right to consult with counsel prior to questioning but also to have counsel present during any questioning of the accused, if he so desires. The Supreme Court further indicated that an accused person does not have to make a request for a lawyer when he is being interrogated and that his failure to ask for a lawyer at interrogation could not constitute a waiver, for the Court has asserted that no effective waiver of the right to counsel during interrogation can be recognized unless specifically made *after* the proper warnings have been given.

WARNINGS. The second Fifth Amendment protective device guaranteed by the Supreme Court to accused persons at the interrogation level requires the police, regardless of the background of the person being interrogated, to adequately and effectively tell the person being interrogated of his rights under the Fifth Amendment.

There must be a warning of the right to remain silent, accompanied by an explanation that anything said by the accused can and will be used against him in court. This warning is needed, according to the Supreme Court, in order to make an accused person aware of his Fifth Amendment privilege and also the consequences to him of foregoing his rights under the privilege. The accused person should also be advised that he is free to exercise his Fifth Amendment privilege at any point in time during the interrogation.

The police must also clearly inform the person being interrogated that he has the right to consult with a lawyer and to have a lawyer with him during his interrogation. As is the warning of the right to remain silent, this warning is an absolute prerequisite to interrogation. The police have the burden under the Miranda decision not only to advise the accused person that he has the right to counsel while he is being interrogated, but also to advise the accused person being interrogated that if he is unable to get a lawyer himself, one will be obtained for him. In other words, if an accused person is indigent, a lawyer will be appointed to represent him, and the accused must be so advised.

The warnings concerning constitutional rights must be given by the police prior to any questioning of the accused. If the individual indicates in any manner, at any time prior to or during questioning, that he wishes to remain silent the interrogation must cease. If he indicates he wants an attorney, the interrogation must cease until an attorney arrives.

According to the Supreme Court, the purpose of placing heavy requirements on the police to warn accused persons of their constitutional rights before interrogating them is to overcome the coercive pressures of police interrogation so that intelligent waivers of constitutional rights may be obtained. In order for an accused person to waive his rights at interrogation under the Fifth and Sixth Amendments, a heavy burden is placed on the government to show that the defendant knowingly and intelligently waived his privilege against self-incrimination and his right to retained or appointed counsel. Lengthy interrogation, incommunicado interrogation, or confessions obtained by threats or trickery would invalidate any potential waivers.

The Court held:

> The warnings required and the waiver necessary in accordance with our opinion today are, in the absence of a fully effective equivalent, prerequisites to the admissibility of any statement made by a defendant. No distinction can be drawn between statements which are direct confessions and statements which amount to "admis-

sions" of part or all of an offense. The privilege against self-incrimination protects the individual from being compelled to incriminate himself in any manner; it does not distinguish degrees of incrimination.

CONCLUSION. According to the Supreme Court of the United States, the adversary system of criminal proceedings commences at the time an individual is first subjected to police interrogation while in custody at the station house or otherwise deprived of his freedom of action in any way. General on-the-scene questioning as to facts surrounding a crime or general questioning of citizens is not affected by the Miranda decision, nor are volunteered statements. In conclusion, Mr. Chief Justice Warren summarized the Miranda opinion:

> . . . We hold that when an individual is taken into custody or otherwise deprived of his freedom by the authorities and is subjected to questioning, the privilege against self-incrimination is jeopardized. Procedural safeguards must be employed to protect the privilege, and unless other fully effective means are adopted to notify the person of his right of silence and to assure that the exercise of the right will be scrupulously honored, the following measures are required. He must be warned prior to any questioning that he has the right to remain silent, that anything he says can be used against him in a court of law, that he has the right to the presence of an attorney, and that if he cannot afford an attorney one will be appointed for him prior to any questioning if he so desires. Opportunity to exercise these rights must be afforded to him throughout the interrogation. After such warnings have been given, and such opportunity afforded him, the individual may knowingly and intelligently waive these rights and agree to answer questions or make a statement. But unless and until such warnings and waiver are demonstrated by the prosecution at trial, no evidence obtained as a result of interrogation can be used against him.

SUGGESTED WARNINGS ABOUT CONSTITUTIONAL RIGHTS

The paragraphs below give a suggested format for police to use before they interrogate a suspect. Those statements, coupled with the suggested consent form that follows, should assure that police are complying with the terms of the Miranda *decision.*

Before we ask you any questions you must understand your legal rights.

You have the right to remain silent.

Anything you say can and will be used against you in court.

Before we ask you any questions you have the right to talk to a lawyer and get his advice, and you have the right to have a lawyer here with you while we are questioning you.

You have the same right to the advice and presence of a lawyer while you are being questioned even if you cannot afford to hire one.

If you cannot afford a lawyer and you want one, a lawyer will be appointed for you before we ask you any questions.

If you decide to answer our questions now without a lawyer, you still have the right to stop answering our questions at any time and you still have the right to stop answering our questions at any time until you talk with a lawyer.

It is particularly desirable when persons are interrogated without counsel to obtain a written consent of the person being interrogated which states that he knows his constitutional rights and nonetheless he is willing to answer questions.

SUGGESTED CONSENT TO ANSWER QUESTIONS

I have been advised of my right to remain silent; that anything that I say can be used against me in court, and that I have the right to a lawyer to be present with me while I am being questioned. I understand these rights and

I am willing to make a statement and answer questions. I do not want a lawyer and I understand and know what I am doing. No promises or threats have been made to me and no pressures of any kind have been used against me.

/s/ ______________________

Finally, it is advisable for interrogating officers to file certifications that the accused person consented to answer questions, which recite the fact that the police officer read the warnings to the accused person and witnessed his signature.

Self-Incrimination of Police

EDWARD J. GARRITY, *et al., Petitioners v.* STATE OF NEW JERSEY

(385 U.S. 493—Decided January 16, 1967)

ISSUE. Law enforcement officers have for a long time felt that they were second-class citizens in the area of the Fifth Amendment. Throughout the country, officers have been compelled to testify at inter-departmental hearings or be subject to firing. In other words, if a police officer were to invoke his Fifth Amendment privilege on the basis that something he is compelled to testify to might possibly incriminate him, then that officer would be subject to removal from office. Any statement that the law enforcement officer gave to his department could later be used against him.

FACTS. Recently, in the Garrity case, the Supreme Court of the United States was faced with just such a situation. Edward J. Garrity was the Chief of Police in Bellmawr, New

Jersey and had been charged in a prosecution by the Attorney General's Office in that state with alleged irregularities in the handling of traffic tickets in the local municipal courts. Subsequently, Garrity and other defendants were investigated by the State Attorney General's Office for allegedly fixing traffic tickets. At the beginning of the investigation, Garrity and each of his fellow officers was warned that anything he said might be used against him in state criminal proceedings, and that each had the right under the Fifth Amendment to refuse to answer any questions. Finally, all of the officers were advised that if they refused to answer the questions by the Attorney General's Office they would be subjected to removal from office under a New Jersey state statute.

Chief Garrity and the other officers answered all of the questions, and all of the officers were later convicted. At their trial the statements that they had made to the Attorney General's Office were admitted in evidence against them. As Mr. Justice Douglas stated in the majority opinion, at the time the investigation began the officers were faced with the choice of self-incrimination or job forfeiture. In other words, if the police officers invoked their constitutional right against self-incrimination they would be severely penalized because they would lose their means of livelihood. That practice, said Mr. Justice Douglas, like interrogation practices, was likely to exert pressure on the individual and prevent him from making a free and voluntary choice not to incriminate himself. Just as confessions are infected by the coercion of the police inherent in in-custody interrogation, so compelling the police officers to testify or to be fired cannot be sustained as voluntary.

CONCLUSION. The Court held that in circumstances in which a police officer is compelled to incriminate himself or else lose his job that the statement can never be used against him in a criminal proceeding. The interesting aspect of the Supreme Court's majority opinion is the fact that they see a strong analogy to decisions concerning involuntary confessions. The Court held:

> We now hold the protection of the individual under the Fourteenth Amendment against coerced confessions

prohibits use in subsequent criminal proceedings of confessions obtained under threat of removal from office, and that it extends to all, whether they are policemen or other members of our body politic.

The Court stated unequivocally that government cannot use the threat of discharge to secure incriminating evidence against a person because the privilege against self-incrimination would be reduced to a "hollow mockery."

Finally, Mr. Justice Douglas, with a stroke of the pen, reinforced the concept that a police officer is a full-fledged, first-class citizen of the United States:

> We conclude that policemen, like teachers and lawyers, are not relegated to a watered-down version of constitutional rights.

THE SIXTH AMENDMENT

> *In all criminal prosecutions, the accused shall enjoy the right to a speedy and public trial . . . and to be informed of the nature and cause of the accusation; to be confronted with the witnesses against him; to have compulsory process for obtaining witnesses in his favor, and to have the assistance of counsel for his defense.*
>
> Sixth Amendment to the United States Constitution

Right to Counsel

GIDEON *v.* WAINWRIGHT, *Corrections Director*

(372 U.S. 335—Decided March 18, 1963)

> Lawyers to prosecute are everywhere deemed essential to protect the public's interest in an orderly society. . . . That government hires lawyers to prosecute and defendants who have the money hire lawyers to defend are the strongest indications of the widespread belief that *lawyers in criminal courts are necessities, not luxuries* . . .
>
> Mr. Justice Black in *Gideon v. Wainwright.* (Emphasis added.)

FACTS. Mr. Justice Black, for the majority of the Court in *Gideon v. Wainwright,* initially addressed himself to a concise, straightforward presentation of the facts.

> Petitioner was charged in a Florida state court with having broken and entered a poolroom with intent to commit a misdemeanor. This offense is a felony under Florida Law. Appearing in court, without funds and without a lawyer, petitioner asked the court to appoint counsel for him. . . .

The trial court refused Gideon's request, and, continued Justice Black:

> Put to trial before a jury, Gideon conducted his defense about as well as could be expected from a layman. He made an opening statement to the jury, cross-examined the State's witnesses, presented witnesses in his own defense, declined to testify himself, and made a short argument "emphasizing his innocence . . ." The jury returned a verdict of guilty, and petitioner was sentenced to serve five years in state prison . . .

Gideon appealed on the ground that the trial court's refusal to appoint counsel for him violated his constitutional rights.

Gideon's appeal to the United States Supreme Court was in *forma pauperis*—again he had no lawyer. This time the Supreme Court appointed a lawyer to represent Gideon before the High Court. That lawyer was later to make an important rendezvous with history. The lawyer was Abe Fortas, who was to become an associate justice of the United States Supreme Court and President Johnson's choice for Chief Justice.

THE RIGHT TO COUNSEL. In 1942, the Supreme Court of the United States had decided that indigent defendants in state felony cases did not have the constitutional right to have lawyers appointed to represent them. *Betts v. Brady,* 316 U.S. 455 (1942). In *Gideon* in 1963, a majority of the Court unequivocally rejected the Betts doctrine and repudiated the rule denying lawyers to defendants who were too poor to get a lawyer to defend them in state felony cases. Declaring that the appointment of counsel is a fundamental right essential to a fair trial, the Court persuasively developed the reasons why the Betts doctrine had to be overruled:

> . . . Reason and reflection require us to recognize that in our adversary system of criminal justice, any person hauled into court, who is too poor to hire a lawyer, cannot be assured a fair trial unless counsel is provided for him. This seems to us to be an obvious truth. Governments, both state and federal, quite properly spend vast sums of money to establish machinery to try defendants accused of crime . . . Similarly, there are few defendants charged with crime, few indeed, who fail to hire the best lawyers they can get to prepare and present their defenses . . . *The right of one charged with crime to counsel may not be deemed fundamental and essential to fair trials in some countries, but it is in ours . . .*
>
> (Emphasis added.)

The Sixth Amendment provision that, "In all criminal prosecutions, the accused shall enjoy the right . . . to have the assistance of counsel for his defense," suddenly acquired new and dazzling dimensions when the Supreme Court reversed Gideon's conviction because he was not given a lawyer. Holding expressly that this Sixth Amendment right was obligatory on the states under the Fourteenth Amendment, the Court in the next six years was to push this hitherto obscure constitutional guarantee into center stage.

President John F. Kennedy once said that everytime he read the Declaration of Independence, he heard a trumpet blast. Everytime a lawyer reads the Gideon decision, he too hears a trumpet blast. The arbitrary, invisible walls of injustice that encircled the poor in this country when they became involved in our criminal justice system were to come tumbling down at the sound of Gideon's trumpet.

WHEN DOES AN ACCUSED HAVE THE RIGHT TO COUNSEL?

POLICE INVESTIGATION

INTERROGATION. In the six short years since the Gideon decision, the Supreme Court has held that a defendant under the Sixth Amendment has the right to counsel at *every critical stage of a criminal proceeding. Gideon* established that trial was a critical stage. In 1964, in *Escobedo,* and in 1966 in *Miranda,* the Supreme Court determined that police in-custody interrogation is also a critical stage of a criminal proceeding, and that the guiding hand of counsel was essential to protect a suspect's right against self-incrimination. The required Miranda warnings – the prerequisite to a valid waiver of the Fifth Amendment rights – are heavily laden with reminders about the right to counsel. If police do not give the Miranda warnings or attempt to give the accused the full benefit of consulting with his attorney or an appointed one, the confession violates both the Fifth and Sixth Amendments and is inadmissible.

LINEUPS. An out-of-court identification of an accused in a police-controlled lineup is also a *critical stage* of a criminal prosecution where the accused has the undiluted right to counsel. *United States v. Wade,* 388 U.S. 218 (1967), and *Gilbert v. California,* 388 U.S. 263 (1967). The Supreme Court emphasized that there is a grave likelihood of preconditioning identification witnesses – whether intentionally or not – that requires the safeguard of an attorney for the accused at the lineup. Police must notify an accused person's lawyer of the time and place of the lineup and must do everything possible to preserve fairness of procedures at the lineup.

INFORMANTS. In *Hoffa v. United States,* 385 U.S. 293 (1966), the Supreme Court explored the problem of a government informer's impact on Hoffa's right to counsel. While Hoffa was on trial in his first indictment in Nashville, Tennessee, he made several attempts to fix the Nashville jury. A government informer – a guest in Hoffa's hotel suite – heard and reported Hoffa's attempts to fix the jury to federal authorities. At no time did the informer listen, intervene, or report any conversations between Hoffa and his lawyers. The defense argued strongly in *Hoffa* that the government, by its informer, had illegally and surreptitiously invaded the legal camp of the defendant and violated Hoffa's Sixth Amendment rights. The Supreme Court turned aside this defense argument on the ground that the government had neither insinuated itself by the informer into the councils of the defense not received any information about the attorneys-client manipulations and strategies.

A second remarkable argument was projected by Hoffa's defense lawyers. They argued that the government, early in the Nashville trial, had more than sufficient evidence to arrest Hoffa for jury tampering and that the focus was on Hoffa as an accused for jury tampering, so that he had the right to counsel while the informer was at work. Mr. Justice Stewart utterly demolished this defense thrust:

> Nothing in *Massiah,* in *Escobedo,* or any other case that has come to our attention, even remotely suggests this novel and paradoxical constitutional doctrine, and we

decline to adopt it now. *There is no constitutional right to be arrested. The police are not required to guess at their peril the precise moment at which they have probable cause to arrest a suspect, risking a violation of the Fourth Amendment if they act too soon, and a violation of the Sixth Amendment if they wait too long. Law enforcement officers are under no constitutional duty to call a halt to a criminal investigation the moment they have the minimum evidence to establish probable cause, a quantum of evidence which may fall far short of the amount necessary to support a criminal conviction.*

(Emphasis added.)

Informants, then, should be carefully controlled to assure that they in no way impinge on the consultations between the man under informant scrutiny and his lawyer.

Note: There is no right to counsel for a defendant when he is being fingerprinted, having his blood or breath checked, and giving handwriting specimens. None of these activities is a *critical stage* of a criminal proceeding according to the Supreme Court. *Schmerber v. California,* 384 U.S. 757 (1966): *Gilbert v. California,* 388 U.S. 263 (1967); *United States v. Wade,* 388 U.S. 218 (1966).

TRIAL. *Gideon* assures the right to counsel at felony trials for adults while *In re Gault* assures the right to counsel for juveniles at critical court stages. *In re Gault,* 387 U.S. 1 (1967); *Kent v. United States,* 383 U.S. 541 (1966).

OTHER CRITICAL STAGES

APPEAL. A defendant has an absolute right to counsel when he appeals his case to higher courts. *Hardy v. United States,* 375 U.S. 277 (1964); *Swensen v. Bosler,* 386 U.S. 258 (1967); and *Anders v. California,* 386 U.S. 738 (1967).

SENTENCING AND PROBATION VIOLATIONS. In *Memphis v. Rhay,* 19 L.ed.2d 336 (1967), Mr. Justice Marshall attached the right to counsel to hearings for violations of probation and traced the escalating history of this vitalized constitutional right:

In 1948 this Court held in *Townsend v. Burke*, 334 U.S. 736 (1948), that the absence of counsel during sentencing after a plea of guilty coupled with "assumptions concerning his criminal record which were materially untrue" deprived the defendant in that case of due process. Mr. Justice Jackson there stated in conclusion, "In this case, counsel might not have changed the sentence, but he could have taken steps to see that the conviction and sentence were not predicated on misinformation or misreading of court records, a requirement of fair play which absence of counsel withheld from his prisoner." . . . Then in *Moore v. Michigan*, 355 U.S. 155 (1957) . . . (the Court ruled), "The right to counsel is not a right confined to representation during the trial on the merits.

* * *

In *Hamilton v. Alabama*, 368 U.S. 52 (1961) it was held that failure to appoint counsel at arraignment deprived the petitioner of due process . . . See also *Reece v. Georgia*, 350 U.S. 85 (1955), and *White v. Maryland*, 373 U.S. 59 (1963) . . .

* * *

There was no occasion in *Gideon* to enumerate the various stages in a criminal proceeding at which counsel was required, but *Townsend, Moore*, and *Hamilton* . . . clearly stand for the proposition that appointment of counsel for an indigent is required at every stage of a criminal proceeding where substantial rights of a criminal accused may be affected . . .

CONCLUSION

Since *Gideon*, we have experienced a meaningful legal breakthrough so that men confronted with the criminal machinery of the state no longer have tailor-made defenses commensurate with the size of their pocket-books. After *Gideon*, rich and poor alike stand as equals with attorneys before the accusations of the law.

Juvenile Court Proceedings

In the matter of the application of Paul L. Gault and Marjorie Gault, father and mother of Gerald Francis Gault, a Minor, Appellants

On Appeal from the Supreme Court of Arizona
(387 U.S. 1 – Decided May 15, 1967)

JUVENILE COURT SYSTEMS. At the turn of the century a system of specialized criminal justice began to evolve throughout the country for juvenile offenders. Mr. Justice Fortas in the Gault decision initially traced the history and underlying theory of the juvenile court system in this country:

> The early reformers were appalled by adult procedures and penalties, and by the fact that children could be given long prison sentences and mixed in jails with hardened criminals. They were profoundly convinced that society's duty to the child could not be confined by the concept of justice alone. They believed that society's role was not to ascertain whether the child was "guilty" or "innocent" but "What is he, how has he become what he is, and what had best be done in his interest and in the interest of the state to save him from a downward career." The child – essentially good, as they saw it – was to be made "to feel that he is the object of (the State's) care and solicitude," not that he was under arrest or on trial. The rules of criminal procedure were therefore altogether inapplicable. The apparent rigidities, technicalities, and harshness which they observed in both substantive and procedural criminal law were therefore to be discarded. The idea of crime and punishment was to be abandoned. The child was to be "treated" and "rehabilitated" and the procedures, from apprehension through institutionalization, were to be "clinical" rather than punitive.

> These results were to be achieved, without coming to conceptual and constitutional grief, by insisting that the proceedings were not adversary . . .

Mr. Justice Black, in a concurring opinion in the Gault case, emphasized:

> The juvenile court planners envisaged a system that would practically immunize juveniles from "punishment" for "crimes" in an effort to save them from youthful indiscretions and stigmas due to criminal charges or convictions . . .

The special system of justice for juveniles in this country was designed, then to lighten or avoid punishing children for crimes with the hope that encouragement, treatment, and rehabilitation would benefit the child more than four prison walls.

Since the juvenile system of justice was a special system of criminal justice, it differed substantially – particularly in the area of constitutional rights – from the adult system of criminal justice. Throughout the country, constitutional rights were guaranteed to adults, particularly at trial, but withheld from juveniles. As an example, the juvenile court system throughout the country did not provide for bail for juveniles, nor for notice of the charges, nor for right to trial, nor for right to counsel, nor for right to confrontation and cross-examination of witnesses, nor for the privilege against self-incrimination.

Therefore, under our main system of criminal justice, adults charged with crimes were entitled to public formal hearings with a definite guarantee of all the procedural rights guaranteed by the Constitution. In contrast, the juvenile system of justice provided for secret, informal tribunals where the constitutional rights of the accused would be held in abeyance.

The planners of our juvenile system of criminal justice hoped, by the establishment of special courts, procedures, and sanctions, to create a system of justice that would be less harsh and more flexible for children than the adult system of criminal justice.

DISCONTENT WITH THE JUVENILE COURT SYSTEM. While the people who set up the special system of justice for juveniles in this country were highly motivated and genuinely attempted to create a special system of justice to help juveniles, the practical operations of the system soon fell far short of the ideal.

Wide discretion exercised by juvenile court judges throughout the country, even when benevolently invoked, was a poor substitute for constitutional rights. Mr. Justice Fortas indicated in the Gault majority opinion that as early as 1937, Dean Pound indicated, "The powers of the Star Chamber were a trifle in comparison with those of our juvenile courts..."

The late Arthur T. Vanderbilt, Chief Justice of the Supreme Court of New Jersey, continued to sound the alarm in 1953:

> In their zeal to care for children neither juvenile judges nor welfare workers can be permitted to violate the Constitution, especially the constitutional provisions as to due process that are involved in moving a child from its home. The indispensable elements of due process are: first, a tribunal with jurisdiction; second, notice of a hearing to the proper parties; and finally, a fair hearing. All three must be present if we are to treat the child as an individual human being and not to revert, in spite of good intentions, to the more primitive days when he was treated as a chattel.

By 1966, the inequities and dangers of the special system of justice for juveniles erupted forcefully. As Mr. Justice Fortas indicated, the Chairman of the Pennsylvania Council of Juvenile Court Judges observed in 1966:

> Unfortunately, loose procedures, high-handed methods and crowded court calendars, either singly or in combination, all too often, have resulted in depriving some juveniles of fundamental rights that have resulted in a denial of due process.

While the summary procedures of juvenile courts were designed "to hide youthful errors from the full gaze of the public and bury them in the graveyard of the forgotten past . . ." sometimes it was the juvenile himself that got buried—in prison.

Finally, in 1967, the National Crime Commission's Report indicated grave concern with our system of criminal justice for juveniles and strongly recommended that substantial constitutional rights be afforded juveniles, particularly when their liberty was at stake.

FACTS. Gerald Gault, a 15-year-old boy, was committed as a juvenile delinquent to the Arizona State Industrial School for a term of six years by a judge of the Juvenile Court of Gila County, Arizona. The Gault boy's crime was allegedly calling a woman neighbor and making indecent remarks to her on the telephone. Under Arizona law, if the Gault boy had been an adult, the maximum penalty for this offense would have been not more than two months in jail.

According to the record in the case, the Sheriff of Gila County took the Gault boy into custody at about 10 A.M. on Monday, June 4, 1964. The Sheriff had taken action on the basis of an oral complaint by a Mrs. Cook, a neighbor of the Gaults, charging that she had received an obscene telephone call from the boy. The police did not notify the boy's parents that they were taking him into custody, but the Gaults found out later that evening that their son was in custody and that he would have a hearing in juvenile court the next day. No notice was given to Mr. and Mrs. Gault concerning the nature of the charges against their son.

The complainant, Mrs. Cook, was not present at the hearing. No one was sworn. No transcript of the proceedings was made, and the boy was questioned by the juvenile court judge about the telephone call. The record was confused as to whether or not the boy admitted making one of the allegedly lewd statements. After the hearing the boy was kept in custody and sometime around June 15, 1964, the juvenile judge adjudged the boy delinquent and sentenced him to confinement in the Arizona State Industrial School until he reached 21 years of age.

The family filed a Petition for Writ of Habeas Corpus which the Superior Court of Arizona dismissed, and then they sought review in the Arizona Supreme Court. The family alleged that the Arizona Juvenile Code was unconstitutional because it did not require that parents and children be notified of the specific charges. The appeal also challenged the failure to advise the family and the boy of certain constitutional rights, including the rights to counsel and confrontation, and the privilege against self-incrimination. The Supreme Court of Arizona dismissed the Writ of Habeas Corpus and upheld the Arizona Juvenile Code. The case was appealed to the Supreme Court of the United States.

DUE PROCESS

> *". . . nor shall any State deprive any person of life, liberty, or property, without due process of law . . ."*
> Fourteenth Amendment to the United State Constitution

Mr. Justice Black, in his concurring opinion in the Gault decision, briefly sketched the history of this clause of the Fourteenth Amendment:

> The phrase "due process of law" has through the years evolved as the successor in purpose and meaning to the words "law of the land" in Magna Charta which more plainly intended to call for a *trial* according to the existing law of the land in effect at the time an alleged offense had been committed. That provision in Magna Charta was designed to prevent defendants from being tried according to criminal laws or proclamations specifically promulgated to fit particular cases or to attach new consequences to old conduct.
> (Emphasis added.)

The Due Process Clause of the Fourteenth Amendment has been interpreted in recent years by the Supreme Court of the United States to embrace all of the constitutional rights guaranteed by the first ten amendments to the United States Constitution. The constitutional limitations on police powers contained in the first ten amendments were traditionally applied only to federal law enforcement authorities. The Supreme Court of the United States, particularly in the last six years, has "incorporated" the constitutional limitations on police powers into the Fourteenth Amendment, thus making these constitutional limitations binding on state law enforcement officers.

THE SUPREME COURT'S DECISION. Mr. Justice Fortas in the majority opinion *emphasized the fact the the Supreme Court's decision in Gault concerned only trial or hearing procedures or constitutional rights applicable to the prejudicial stages of the juvenile process.* The Court narrowed the effect of its decision in the Gault case to juvenile proceedings where the determination is whether or not the minor is a "delinquent" or where the child may be committed to prison.

The basic determination announced by the Court in the Gault decision was that the Due Process Clause of the Fourteenth Amendment requires, in respect to proceedings to determine delinquency which may result in commitment to prison, that certain basic constitutional rights be afforded to the child. To paraphrase Professor Monrad G. Paulsen,"A Children's Hour has at long last come to the Supreme Court of the United States."

The Court held that in juvenile proceedings where the child may be imprisoned the child has certain indestructible rights. They are:

(a) Notice of the charges.
(b) Right to counsel.
(c) Right to confrontation and cross-examination.
(d) Privilege against self-incrimination.
(e) Right to a transcript of the proceedings.
(f) Right to appellate review.

NOTICE OF THE CHARGES. Mr. Justice Fortas indicated in the majority opinion that Due Process requires advance notice of the specific charges that are the basis for taking the juvenile into custody.

> Notice, to comply with due process requirements, must be given sufficiently in advance of scheduled court

> proceedings so that reasonable opportunity to prepare will be afforded, and it must "set forth the alleged misconduct with particularity."

When a youth's freedom is at stake, the Fourteenth Amendment requires notice and the opportunity to defend.

RIGHT TO COUNSEL. In *Kent v. United States,* the Supreme Court announced unequivocally, "The right of representation by counsel is not a formality. It is not a grudging gesture to a ritualistic requirement. It is the essence of justice."

The juvenile, prior to the Gault decision, had the worst of both systems. Although the juvenile could lose his liberty for a number of years, prior to the Gault decision he did not have the constitutional right to counsel. Mr. Justic Fortas in the Gault decision indicated:

> The juvenile needs the assistance of counsel to cope with problems of law, to make skilled inquiry into the facts, to insist upon regularity of the proceedings, and to ascertain whether he has a defense and to prepare and submit it. The child "requires the guiding hand of counsel at every step in the proceedings against him."

Professor Paulsen, in a 1966 *Law Review* article (54 Calif. L. Rev. 694), stated the pressing necessity for lawyers in the juvenile court system:

> A court without lawyers leaves only the judge to perform the triple role of prosecutor, defense lawyer, and impartial arbiter. These functions, necessary to a full hearing of both sides to a dispute, ought not to be joined. To Americans arguments about the facts forming a basis for a judicial decision ought to be submitted to a tribunal which tests evidence through cross-examination. In fact, in lawyerless juvenile court proceedings the judge cross-examines the witness; the very skill and energy which he brings to the task of pushing witnesses to tell the truth may present a frightening picture to a child looking to the judge for help in one of life's difficult moments.

Both at the point of intake and at a dispositional hearing an attorney may present arguments for the point of view which parents might assert, were they gifted with communication skills. Every juvenile court act requires that parents be notified of hearings, requirements which are thought so central that the court is without power to proceed if they are not satisfied. Why is so much importance attached to the notice requirement? Surely, the reason must be that the parents are expected to participate in some meaningful way. Yet any observer of a big city court knows how few parents come forward with argument and how ineptly those few go about it. A lawyer experienced in speaking up and making points clearly can be of enormous help to a vulnerable, poorly educated parent and to the youngster. Further the judge may find lawyers useful because, through them, they may be able better to explain to the parents the aims of the court and the purposes underlying a particular decision.

The majority opinion holds, therefore, that "whenever the awesome prospect of incarceration" is facing a juvenile, the Due Process Clause of the Fourteenth Amendment requires that the juvenile have the right to the assistance of counsel.

CONFRONTATION, SELF-INCRIMINATION, AND CROSS-EXAMINATION. The majority opinion emphasized the need for caution concerning confessions of juveniles. The Court referred to its language in *Haley v. Ohio*, where the problem was projected with particular clarity:

> What transpired would make us pause for careful inquiry if a mature man were involved. And when, as here, a mere child—an easy victim of the law—is before us, special care in scrutinizing the record must be used. Age 15 is a tender and difficult age for a boy of any race. He cannot be judged by the more exacting standards of maturity. That which would leave a man cold and unimpressed can overawe and overwhelm a lad in his early teens. This is the period of great instability which

> the crisis of adolescence produces. A 15-year-old lad, questioned through the dead of night by relays of police, is a ready victim of the inquisition. Mature men possibly might stand the ordeal from midnight to 5 A.M. But we cannot believe that a lad of tender years is a match for the police in such a contest. He needs counsel and support if he is not to become the victim first of fear, then of panic. He needs someone on whom to lean lest the overpowering presence of the law, as he knows it, crush him. No friend stood at the side of this 15-year-old boy as the police, working in relays, questioned him hour after hour, from midnight until dawn. No lawyer stood guard to make sure that the police went so far and no farther, to see to it that they stopped short of the point where he became the victim of coercion. No counsel or friend was called during the critical hours of questioning.

The Court concluded that the constitutional privilege against self-incrimination applies in the case of juveniles as it does with respect to adults. The Court further held that in juvenile proceedings where possible imprisonment could result, that the defense had the rights to confrontation of witnesses and cross-examination.

In the Gault case, the chief witness, Mrs. Cook, was never called and never cross-examined, and after the informal proceedings the Gault boy received a six-year sentence of imprisonment. The privilege against self-incrimination and the rights to confrontation and cross-examination are essential safeguards contained in our Constitution, and are designed to protect the basic liberties of our citizens. It is somewhat ironic that until this decision only adults had had these. The Supreme Court, in its 8-to-1 opinion in the Gault case, concluded by stating that the Due Process Clause requires states to notify citizens of the nature of any juvenile court proceedings and timely notice must be given so that counsel may appear in any such proceedings. The Court also stated that juvenile court judges have to show reasons for their conclusions so that an intelligent record can be presented on appeal. One of the greatest difficulties in the Gault case itself was the fact that none of the proceedings had been transcribed and the history of the case was presented in large measure from the recollections of the central figures – the judge, the parole officer, and the family.

Once again, to quote Professor Paulsen, "The Gault decision hurls constitutional thunderbolts at our nation's juvenile court systems and at police practices concerning juveniles."

At this time, it is impossible to calculate the impact of the Gault decision on our system of criminal justice for juveniles. All that can be stated is that we shall have – in addition to severe headaches and growing pains – a fairer system of criminal justice for juveniles because of this precedent-shattering decision.

The Line-Up

UNITED STATES, *Petitioner v.* BILLY JOE WADE

(388 U.S. 218 – Decided June 12, 1967)

ISSUE. In the Wade case, The Supreme Court of the United States for the first time was faced with the issue of whether or not trial identifications of an accused person should have been excluded from the evidence when the defendant was shown to witnesses before trial, at a post-indictment line-up, without notice of the line-up to the accused or his lawyer and without his lawyer being present at the line-up.

FACTS. On September 21, 1964, a federally insured bank in Eustace, Texas, was robbed by an armed bandit. The robber had small strips of tape on each side of his face as he held the cashier and vice president at gun point. After filling a pillow case with money, the bandit hurriedly left the bank.

On March 23, 1965, Billy Joe Wade was placed under a

federal indictment for this bank robbery. On April 2, 1965, Wade was arrested and on April 26, 1965, the Federal District Court appointed counsel to represent Wade in this prosecution.

Approximately fifteen days after Wade's lawyer had been appointed by the court, agents of the Federal Bureau of Investigation arranged a line-up for the purpose of having the bank personnel identify the defendant.

The line-up was conducted in a courtroom of the local county courthouse, and there were five or six people in addition to Wade in the line-up. Each person in the line-up wore strips of tape on each side of his face, and when ordered said, "Put the money in the bag."

At the actual trial, the two bank employees positively identified Wade as the robber. No mention was made about the line-up on direct examination by the prosecutor. Wade's lawyer cross-examined the identification witnesses and established that there had been a line-up as well as the facts surrounding the line-up. Wade's lawyer charged that the FBI line-up violated Wade's Fifth Amendment right against self-incrimination, as well as his Sixth Amendment right to counsel. The defense particularly emphasized the fact that Wade was already under indictment and had a lawyer at the time of the line-up, and that the failure to notify the lawyer of the line-up, as well as the absence of Wade's lawyer at the line-up, violated Wade's constitutional rights.

Wade was convicted in the District Court, but the United States Court of Appeals for the Fifth Circuit reversed Wade's conviction and held that the line-up did not violate Wade's Fifth Amendment right but that there was a violation of Wade's Sixth Amendment right to counsel. The United States appealed this decision of the Fifth Circuit to the Supreme Court of the United States.

THE FIFTH AMENDMENT AND THE LINE-UP. Mr. Justice Brennen, speaking for a majority of the Court, initially focused on the question as to whether or not Wade's line-up violated his Fifth Amendment right against self-incrimination. Emphasizing the history of the Fifth Amendment, particularly that aspect protecting an accused person from being forced by government to speak against himself, Mr. Justice Brennen emphatically stated:

> We have no doubt that compelling the accused merely to exhibit his person for observation by a prosecution witness prior to trial involves no compulsion of the accused to give evidence having testimonial significance.

Although the Court recognized that Wade was compelled to appear before the witnesses in a line-up, the compulsion was to show physical characteristics and not to force him to disclose any knowledge he had of the crime. Mr. Justice Brennen also indicated that even though Wade had been forced to say, "Put the money in the bag," this was not a violation of his Fifth Amendment right against self-incrimination since he was required to use his voice as an identifying physical characteristic, not to speak his guilt.

The Court considered that although there is police compulsion in fingerprinting, in photographing the accused, in obtaining handwriting specimens, and in line-ups, these practices do not violate an accused's Fifth Amendment right against self-incrimination because one of these practices involves testimonial compulsion.

THE SIXTH AMENDMENT AND THE LINE-UP. The government argued that the failure to notify Wade's lawyer of the line-up and the absence of Wade's lawyer from the line-up did not in any way violate Wade's Sixth Amendment right to counsel. The defense argued that Wade had been denied the assistance of counsel at the line-up and that Wade's basic right to a fair trial had been denied him since the identification witnesses could not be meaningfully cross-examined at trial. Wade's lawyer maintained that because he was not present at the line-up he could not effectively cross-examine the identifying witnesses as to the detailed manner in which the line-up was conducted.

Mr. Justice Brennen then discussed the meaning of the Sixth Amendment right to counsel:

> Although the Colonial provisions about counsel were in accord on few things . . . the colonists appreciated that

> if a defendant were forced to stand alone against the State, his case was fore-doomed . . .
>
> . . . When the Bill of Rights was adopted there were no organized police forces as we know them today. The accused confronted the prosecutor and the witnesses against him, and the evidence was marshalled largely at the trial itself. In contrast, today's law enforcement machinery involves *critical confrontations* of the accused by the prosecution at pre-trial proceedings where the results might well settle the accused's fate and reduce the trial itself to a mere formality. In recognition of these realities of modern criminal prosecution, cases have construed the Sixth Amendment's guarantee to apply to *"critical"* stages of the proceeding.
>
> (Emphasis added.)

The Court stressed that the period from arraignment to trial is "perhaps the most critical period of the proceeding" requiring the guiding hand of counsel if the Sixth Amendment guarantee is not to prove an empty right. Mr. Justice Brennen then announced:

> It is central to that principle (the right to counsel) that in addition to counsel's presence at trial, the accused is guaranteed that he need not stand alone against the State at any stage of the prosecution, formal or informal, in court or out, where counsel's absence might derrogate the accused's right to fair trial . . .
>
> The presence of counsel at . . . confrontations, as at the trial itself, operates to assure that the accused's interest will be protected consistently with our adversary theory of criminal prosecution.

The majority held that the Supreme Court has the duty under the Sixth Amendment to scrutinize any pre-trial confrontations of the accused to determine if the presence of counsel were necessary to assure the defendant a fair trial.

THE LINE-UP – A SUPREME COURT VIEW. The central issue in this case developed around the legal phrase "critical stage." In 1963 in the case of *Gideon v. Wainwright*, the Supreme Court indicated that the Sixth Amendment right to counsel applied not only to the trial stage but also to every "critical stage" of a criminal proceeding. In *Escobedo v. Illinois,* 378 U.S. 478 (1964), and in *Miranda v. Arizona,* 384 U.S. 436 (1966) the Supreme Court held that in-custody police interrogation was a "critical stage" of a criminal proceeding, and that the Sixth Amendment right to counsel applied in full strength at the police interrogation level.

The Government argued in *Wade* that the line-up was not "a critical stage" of a criminal proceeding but merely a preparatory step in the gathering of the prosecution's evidence. The defense argued that the line-up was "a critical stage" of a criminal proceeding because frequently evidence obtained at the line-up plays a dominant role in obtaining convictions.

Mr. Justice Brennen, in speaking for the majority in the Wade case, next presented the Supreme Court's evaluation of the line-up and existing police practices in that regard:

> . . . The confrontation compelled by the State between the accused and the victim for witnesses to a crime elicit identification evidence is peculiarly riddled with innumerable dangers and variable factors which might seriously, even crucially, derrogate from a fair trial.
>
> . . . A major factor contributing to the high incidence of miscarriage of justice from mistaken identity has been the degree of suggestion inherent in the manner in which the prosecution presents the suspect to witnesses for pretrial identification. A commentator has observed that "the influence of improper suggestion upon identifying witnesses probably accounts for more miscarriages of justice than any other single factor—perhaps it is responsible for more such errors than all other factors combined."—Wall, *Eyewitnesses Identification in Criminal Cases,* 26. Suggestions can be created intentionally in many subtle ways.

Emphasizing that normally, once an eyewitness has picked out an accused person at the line-up, he does not usually go back on his word, the Court indicated that the issue of identity was for all practical purposes decided before trial at the line-up. Stressing that there were great risks and dangers with regard to persuasive suggestion at the line-up, the Court focused on the practical difficulty of finding out at trial what actually happened at the line-up. Since traditionally no records are maintained as to the people who were in the line-up, the Court developed in some detail the fact that the defense lawyers were extremely disadvantaged in the area of effective cross-examination on the line-up issue.

The Court emphasized that since the manner and mode of the line-up was normally hard to reconstruct at trial and since the potential for improper influences and suggestions was particularly great, the accused, at a line-up without a lawyer, could be deprived of his only meaningful opportunity to attack the credibility of the witnesses' courtroom identifications.

Mr. Justice Brennen indicated that the line-up system in this country is a process attended with "hazards of serious unfairness." At the same time, the Court emphasized that it was the line-up system and not the police that left much to be desired:

> We do not assume that these risks are the result of police procedures intentionally designed to prejudice an accused. Rather, we assume they derive from the dangers inherent in eyewitness identification and the suggestibility inherent in the context of pre-trial identification.

THE SUPREME COURT'S RULING. The Supreme Court held in *Wade* that a line-up is a "critical stage" of a criminal proceeding, and that an accused person at a line-up has the right to counsel under the Sixth Amendment. The Court further indicated that the line-up is a "critical stage" because, in effect, the accused is denied his right to a fair trial if he does not have a lawyer representing him at the line-up. The lawyer's function at the line-up is to assure fairness in the viewing procedure and to obtain basic information by which the lawyer could meaningfully cross-examine identifying witnesses at trial.

Mr. Justic Brennen summed up the majority's decision by stressing the fact that the trial which may really determine the accused's fate may well be at the line-up rather than in the courtroom, and that since there was grave potential prejudice, Wade's post-indictment line-up was a critical stage of the prosecution where he was as much entitled to a lawyer as at trial.

The Court held that both Wade and his lawyer should have been notified of the impending line-up and lawyer's presence should have been a requisite to the conduct of the line-up unless there was an intelligent waiver by the accused.

The Supreme Court then directed that the case be sent back to the trial court in order to ascertain whether or not the government could establish by clear and convincing evidence that the in-court identifications of Wade were based on observations other than the line-up identification. If the prosecution could develop and show an independent source for the witnesses' trial identifications of Wade, the conviction would be sustained. In contrast, if the government's evidence were to demonstrate that the witnesses' identification of Wade were based solely on the illegal line-up, then the conviction would have to be reversed.

In a companion case, the Supreme Court ruled that the Sixth Amendment right to counsel at a line-up is not retroactive. In other words, in any criminal trials that begin after June 12, 1967, identification testimony based on a line-up will be inadmissible unless there was the notice to the accused and his lawyer, and unless the accused's lawyer was present at the line-up or the accused intelligently waived his right to have a lawyer at the line-up.

SUGGESTED LINE-UP SAFEGUARDS. The Supreme Court indicated in a footnote some suggested procedures that would assure fairness to the accused at a line-up. They include:

(a) The right to have a lawyer present during any line-up or confrontation of the accused should be observed.

(b) The witness or victim should give a written, signed description of the suspect before he views him.

(c) At least six persons in addition to the accused person —approximately the same height, weight, coloration of hair and skin, and bodily types as the suspect, should participate in the line-up.

(d) All of the people in the line-up should be dressed as nearly alike as possible.

(e) A complete written report should be made concerning the line-up containing the names and addresses of the people who participated in the line-up, as well as descriptive details of everything that happened including the reactions of the identifying witnesses.

On Thursday, June 27, 1967, the New York *Times* contained an article indicating that the New York Police Department and representatives of five District Attorney's offices met with regard to establishing line-up procedures in New York City. The proposed regulations that came from this meeting provide that when an attorney is present at a line-up, he may make suggestions to improve the fairness of the viewing procedure and that these suggestions should be followed if the officer thinks them reasonable and practical. The regulations also indicate that the suspect can voluntarily waive his right to counsel at a line-up, but two officers should witness his waiver and record it.

The proposed New York regulations also indicated that if the suspect refuses to waive his rights, and a lawyer cannot be obtained, a line-up may be held provided it contains safeguard protections. The recommendation of this group is that it is highly desirable to have safeguards even when a lawyer is present.

In view of the Supreme Court's decision in *Wade,* all law enforcement agencies should prepare and implement safeguard procedures immediately. Unless provisions are made by the police for notifying the accused and his lawyer of the proposed line-up and unless the accused's lawyer is given an opportunity to be present at the line-up (in the absence of a waiver), witnesses who can identify accused persons will be unable to testify at trial. This is the penalty every law enforcement agency suffers for failing to take affirmative action as required by the Wade case. Society cannot afford to pay that price.

Suppression of Evidence by the Prosecution

BRADY, *Petitioner v.* STATE OF MARYLAND

(373 U.S. 83—Decided May 13, 1963)

> *The State's obligation is not to convict, but to see that, so far as possible, truth emerges.* This is the ultimate statement of its responsibility to provide a fair trial under the Due Process Clause of the Fourteenth Amendment. *No respectable interest of the State is served by its concealment of information which is material . . . to the case; including all possible defenses.*
>
> Mr. Justice Fortas, concurring opinion, *Giles v. Maryland,* 386 U.S. 66. (Emphasis added.)

FACTS. In Maryland, Brady and a second defendant were convicted of first degree murder and were sentenced to death. The two men had been tried separately.

Brady had been tried first and while he admitted participating in the crime, he insisted that the second man, Bobbit, had actually done the killing. Brady's defense centered on this fact in the hope that the jury would not return a death penalty verdict.

Before the Brady trial, his lawyer requested to see all the statements that the prosecution had obtained from Bobbit. Several of Bobbit's statements were shown to Brady's lawyer; however, one very critical statement in which Bobbit had admitted the actual killing was intentionally withheld by the prosecution. The defense did not learn about this statement that had been suppressed by the prosecution until after Brady's conviction and sentence had been affirmed by the Maryland Court of Appeals.

In a post-conviction hearing, that same Maryland court ruled that this suppression of evidence by the prosecution required a new trial for Brady. The prosecution appealed this ruling and the Supreme Court of the United States affirmed the new trial order of the Maryland Court of Appeals.

Mr. Justice Douglas, speaking for a majority of the Court in *Brady,* stated that when the prosecution suppresses evidence favorable to an accused—particularly when it was requested by the accused—due process is denied. When, said Justice Douglas, the evidence is material, the good or bad faith of the prosecution is immaterial.

THE PROSECUTION ETHIC. About two hundred years ago Lord Camden postulated that the mere need to solve crime did not place law enforcement values above all other values. *Entick v. Carrington,* 19 Howell's State Trials 1029 (1765).

In 1928, the great dissenters Holmes and Brandeis echoed Lord Camden's emphasis that in combatting crime the ends do not justify the means. Government, they said, is a teacher and by its example sets the moral-legal tone of the nation. If government is a law-breaker or a deceiver, it sows by its conduct massive disrespect for the law. *Olmstead v. United States,* 277 U.S. 438 (1928).

In America, where voluntary compliance with the rule of law by the citizen guarantees order and freedom, the government should set an example and certainly not subvert the law by using unfair or unjust tactics that defeat the ends of justice.

There is, then, a strong fabric in the mosaic of Anglo-American law that requires a high standard of conduct on the part of prosecuting officials. The first ten amendments to the Constitution guarantee in part that government will not unfairly or unjustly overpower the citizen.

Central to this concept of absolute fair play by government is the underlying fact that ours is truly an "adversary" system of justice. While theoretically the individual and the government meet as equal adversaries in criminal confrontations in our courts, in reality the government has a tremendous edge. With legions of investigators, lawyers, and experts, and with almost unlimited resources, the government is truly a formidable adversary. In contrast, the individual defendant in most cases has extremely meager and limited resources, both in terms of money and of champions to defend him.

The trouble with the government's great powers of prosecution is that, as Senator Fullbright has said, power sometimes confuses itself with virtue. An exaggerated sense of power frequently leads to an exaggerated sense of virtue. This is why government officials must be particularly cautious in not overstepping the mark. When it comes to fairness and integrity—like Caesar's wife—the government must be above suspicion.

RULES FOR THE PROSECUTION

> The prosecution then must be both moral, and legal. *If the prosecution deliberately and intentionally misrepresents the truth—such as by knowingly using false evidence, due process is denied.*
>
> *Miller v. Pate, Warden,* 386 U.S. 1 (1967). (Emphasis added.)
>
> *Even if the prosecution, "although not soliciting false evidence allows it to go uncorrected when it appears," due process is denied.*
>
> *Napue v. Illinois,* 360 U.S. 269. (Emphasis added.)
>
> *When the prosecution has knowledge of additional evidence material to the defense of the accused, the prosecution has the duty to disclose that evidence or due process will be denied.*
>
> *Giles, et al v. Maryland,* 386 U.S. 66 (1967). (Emphasis added.)

Whenever due process is denied, the Supreme Court must reverse cases and order new trials.

For the prosecution there is no middle ground. Absolute fairness, honesty, and a quest for justice must be the dominant motives of all those charged with enforcing the law. Anything less is unworthy of those whose whole lives are dedicated to upholding the law.

Mr. Justice Sutherland, in *Berger v. United States*, 295 U.S. 78, declared the standard for the prosecution as adversary to the accused. It should be followed by every dedicated and professional law enforcement officer:

> [The prosecution] is the representative not of an ordinary party to a controversy but of a sovereignty whose obligation to govern impartially is as compelling as its obligation to govern at all; and whose interest therefore in a criminal prosecution is not that it shall win a case, but that justice shall be done. As such, the prosecution is in the peculiar and very definited sense the servant of the law, the two-fold aim of which is that guilt shall not escape or innocence suffer. They may prosecute with earnestness and vigor—indeed, they should do so. But while they may strike hard blows, they are not at liberty to strike foul ones. It is as much their duty to refrain from improper methods calculated to produce a wrongful conviction as it is to use every legitimate means to bring about a just one.

Glossary

ARREST. The apprehending of a person to answer to an alleged or suspected crime.

CONSENT. A free and voluntary waiver of constitutional rights under the Fourth Amendment.

EXCLUSIONARY RULE. A fifty-year-old Supreme Court rule—based on the Fourth, Fifth, and Sixth Amendments—that requires courts to exclude from the courtroom all illegally seized evidence. Also known as the **SUPPRESSION RULE.**

FRISK. A search or a limited patting of the outer surfaces of a person's clothing in an attempt to find weapons.

PROBABLE CAUSE. Facts or apparent facts viewed through the eyes of the officer that generate a reasonable belief that someone is about to commit or has committed a crime.

SEARCH. Looking into or prying into places for the purpose of finding incriminating evidence.

SUPPRESSION HEARING. A pretrial criminal evidentiary hearing, held before a judge sitting without a jury, to determine whether the incriminating evidence obtained by the prosecution was obtained lawfully.

Index